Uninformed

Uninformed

Why People Know so Little about Politics and What We Can do about It

ARTHUR LUPIA
University of Michigan

OXFORD

UNIVERSITY PRESS

Oxford University Press is a department of the University of
Oxford. It furthers the University's objective of excellence in research,
scholarship, and education by publishing worldwide.
Oxford is a registered trademark of Oxford University Press
in the UK and in certain other countries.

Published in the United States of America by
Oxford University Press
198 Madison Avenue, New York, NY 10016, United States of America

First issued as an Oxford University Press paperback, 2017

Library of Congress Cataloging-in-Publication Data
Lupia, Arthur, 1964–
Uninformed : why people know so little about politics and what we can do about it /
Arthur Lupia.
pages cm
Includes bibliographical references.
1. Political socialization.   2. Political participation   3. Civics—Study and
teaching.   4. Citizenship—Study and teaching.   5. Education—Political
aspects.   6. Education—Social aspects.   I. Title.
JA76.L865 2016
320—dc23
2015025315
ISBN 978-0-19-026372-0 (hardcover); 978-0-19-065993-6 (paperback)

1 3 5 7 9 8 6 4 2
Printed in Canada on acid-free paper

In memory of
William Henry Slack Jr.
Buffalo Fire Department, U.S. Army, Purple Heart, hero

and

Thomas John Mroz Jr.
Your zest for life, family, and politics continues to inspire.

Contents

List of Figures and Tables

FIGURES

TABLES

Acknowledgments

This book brings together two of my greatest passions: conducting research on how people learn and interacting with diverse audiences on the topics of communication and education. Many people and events inspired me to write this book. These inspirations run the gamut from my parents, to great high school and college teachers, to the many people with whom I work on improving public understanding of political processes and on making science communication more effective. The energy with which all of these people devote themselves to improving others' lives offers a constant reminder to me of the importance of effective education.

Many people helped me write this book. Some helped with research assistance. Others read drafts of chapters. Some asked difficult questions. Others helped by giving me opportunities to put my research into action. Over the last decade, I have had opportunities to work with some of the finest minds in political science, civic education, and science communication. I am grateful for the lessons that I have learned from all of these collaborations. I thank Rosario Aguilar, Logan S. Casey, Cassandra Grafstrom, Julia Kamin, Kristyn L. Karl, Thomas Bradley Kent, Kenyatha Vauthier Loftis, William MacMillan, Justin Magouirk, Erin McGovern, Jesse O. Menning, Spencer Piston, Timothy J. Ryan, Gisela Sin, Christopher Skovron, Elizabeth Suhay, and Alexander von Hagen-Jamar for research assistance and editorial suggestions. I thank James N. Druckman, Yanna Krupnikov, and

Adam Seth Levine for thorough readings of an early draft of the entire book. The ability to work with each of these scholars for an extended period of time was one of the most valuable experiences of my professional life. I thank Jesse Crosson, Dumitru Minzarari, and John Tryneski for their reviews of a more recent draft. I thank Jay Goodliffe, Christopher Karpowitz, David Magleby, Jeremy Pope, and their colleagues for a very helpful workshop at Brigham Young University that influenced my presentation of chapter 12. I thank Ashley Gearhardt, Ben Highton, Carl Palmer, Joshua Pasek, Gaurav Sood, and Kaare Strom for advice about other chapters. I thank Matthew Berent, Matthew DeBell, and Jon A. Krosnick for many interesting conversations about how the American National Election Studies (ANES) could more effectively measure what citizens know about politics. I thank Jon Krosnick and Gary Langer for their leadership in improving survey research—their tenacity and effectiveness on that topic influenced every page of the book's latter chapters. I thank Darrell Donakowski, David Howell, and the ANES staff for their dedication to the ANES during my term as principal investigator and for their assistance in the archival work described in part II. I thank Cheryl Boudreau, Matthew Levendusky, and Jasjeet Sekhon for helpful conversations about their work on measurement topics. I thank Baruch Fischhoff, Erika Franklin Fowler, Elisabeth R. Gerber, and Barbara Kline Pope for helpful editorial advice on the PNAS article that I wrote using material from early drafts of chapters 7 and 8. Their comments improved that offering and energized this one. The late Eugene Rosa provided helpful advice on how to interpret a range of scholarly claims about memory. I thank my literary agent Jill Marsal and Oxford University Press's David McBride for helping me bring this project to OUP. I thank the Department of Political Science, the Institute for Social Research, and the Center for Political Studies at the University of Michigan, the John Simon Guggenheim Foundation, and the National Science Foundation (grant SES-0535334) for supporting the research described in this book. I thank Daniel Abbasi, John H. Aldrich, the Honorable Brian Baird, John Bullock, Heidi Cullen, Doris Graber, Paul Hanle, Vincent L. Hutchings, Kathleen Hall Jamieson, Dan Kahan, James H. Kuklinski, Mathew D. McCubbins, Michael Neblo, Brendan J. Nyhan, Samuel L. Popkin, Wendy Schmidt, the late Lee Sigelman, Paul M. Sniderman, Ben Strauss, and the late Hanes Walton Jr. for advice, opportunity, and inspiration given to me through the course of writing this book.

In the time that I was working on this book, I drew from materials that I had recently published and I used some of the material that I was developing for this book in articles that I was asked to write for other outlets. The following sections of the book share wording and structure with existing publications.

- Sections 5A and 5B draw from Arthur Lupia, 2006, "How Elitism Undermines the Study of Voter Competence," *Critical Review* 18: 217–232.
- Section 5C draws from Arthur Lupia, 2001, "Dumber than Chimps? An Assessment of Direct Democracy Voters," in Larry J. Sabato, Bruce Larson, and Howard Ernst (eds.), *Dangerous Democracy: The Battle over Ballot Initiatives in America* (Lanham, MD: Rowman and Littlefield), 66–70.
- Chapters 7 and 8 and section 11B share structure and content with Arthur Lupia, 2013, "Communicating Science in Politicized Environments," *Proceedings of the National Academy of Sciences* 110: 14048–14054.
- Section 10D draws from Arthur Lupia, Adam Seth Levine, Jesse O. Menning, and Gisela Sin, 2007, "Were Bush Tax Cut Supporters 'Simply Ignorant'?, A Second Look at Conservatives and Liberals in 'Homer Gets a Tax Cut,'" *Perspectives on Politics* 5: 761–772.
- Sections 12A and 18A share structure and content with Arthur Lupia, 2011, "How Do Scholars Know What Voters Want? An Essay on Theory and Measurement," in Benjamin Highton and Paul M. Sniderman (eds.), *Facing the Challenge of Democracy: Explorations in the Analysis of Public Opinion and Political Participation* (Princeton, NJ: Princeton University Press), 23–46.
- Section 15C uses language from Cheryl Boudreau and Arthur Lupia, 2011, "Political Knowledge," in James N. Druckman, James H. Kuklinski, Donald P. Green, and Arthur Lupia (eds.), *The Cambridge Handbook of Experimental Political Science* (New York: Cambridge University Press), 171–183.

As substantial parts of this book focus on educators' activities, I close by thanking those who have taught me most of what I know. My family is filled with educators of many kinds. They have conveyed important insights on so many topics. Although a few have formal titles denoting this expertise, most do not—instead, they convey life-changing insights through their words and deeds. My children Francesca and William teach me new things every day, including unexpected and cherished corrections about what types of things are truly worth knowing. My spouse Elisabeth Gerber is my fundamental inspiration. Her light, strength, and compassion keep me connected to the things that matter.

1

From Infinite Ignorance
to Knowledge that Matters

When I wrote this paragraph, I lived in the city of Ann Arbor, Michigan, which is located in the United States of America. Here are some things that recently happened in these places. In the decade prior to the one in which I completed this book, members of Congress proposed over 40,000 bills.[1] In an average year, Congress passed and the president subsequently signed over 200 of these bills into law.[2] My state legislature was similarly active. In one of the years when I was writing this book, Michigan's House of Representatives produced 1,239 bills, 42 concurrent resolutions, 36 joint resolutions, and 174 resolutions.[3] During the same period, Michigan's Senate produced 884 bills, 25 continuing resolutions, 19 joint resolutions, and 106 resolutions. Michigan's governor signed 323 of these proposals into law.[4] In the same year, my city passed over 100 ordinances of its own.

In addition to these laws, federal agencies such as the United States Department of Commerce promulgated thousands of rules and regulations. These rules and regulations are not trivial matters. Laws intended to fight crime, educate children, care for the sick, or accomplish other social priorities often lack specific instructions for what to do in individual cases. Rules and regulations provide these instructions. They clarify how to interpret and implement these laws.

One other thing to know about these rules and regulations is that there are a lot of them. In one of the calendar years in which I was working on this book, federal agencies issued more than 3,500 rules spanning more than 82,000 pages of the *Federal Register*.[5] Every one of these 3,500 rules, and the comparable number of rules proffered in other years, carry "the full force of law."[6]

Beyond laws and rules, other participants in government activities make decisions that are legally binding on me. In law offices and court-rooms across the country, people challenge the meanings of the laws, rules, and regulations described above. Each case focuses on whether it is legal to interpret a law or rule in a particular way. As was the case with the laws, rules, and regulations described above, another thing to know about these cases is that there are a lot of them. In one of the years that I was working on this book, people filed over 289,000 federal civil cases, many of which produced new decisions about the legality of specific actions under the Constitution, laws, and treaties of the United States.[7]

Why is it worth drawing your attention to the numbers of laws, rules, and court decisions under which I live? *Because you are almost certainly in a similar situation.* Given these situations, an important question for both of us is this: "How much do we know about the politics and government that affect us?"

I'll begin by answering for myself. For many years, I have been referred to as an expert on political information and voter competence. At the same time, I know next to nothing about the content of most of the laws, rules, regulations, and court decisions that I just described—*and I am not alone.*

Over the past 25 years, I have met many, if not most, of the other experts on political information and voter competence. I would bet my house (and your house too) that when it comes to all of these laws, rules, and decisions, every one of these experts is approximately as ignorant as I am. Even world-renowned experts on specific legal or political topics are almost completely ignorant of almost all of the details of the many laws, rules, and regulations under which any of us live.

The number of facts that can be relevant to the operations of government is infinite. This number includes not just facts about laws but also facts about economics, history, and constitutions that can influence our decisions and expectations. This number also includes facts about how laws affect different types of people, facts about how these effects will change over time, facts about how people feel about these laws, and facts about whether these feelings might produce pressure to implement different laws in the future. Any of these facts can affect how government actually works.

With respect to these facts, there is no question that knowing some of them can change our decisions. There is no question that some of these changed decisions would improve our quality of life. There is also no question that the list of things that each of us does *not* know about politics and government is very, very long. I would argue that this particular fact is true for everyone. No one is immune.

From these facts, we can draw an important conclusion: *When it comes to political information, there are two groups of people.* One group understands that they are almost completely ignorant of almost every detail of almost every law and policy under which they live. The other group is delusional about how much they know. There is no third group.

Yet, as citizens, we recognize that certain types of ignorance can prevent us from achieving important aspirations. We know that learning can reduce the negative effects of certain kinds of ignorance. There is no question about this.

At the same time, every one of us usually has a limited willingness and ability to learn. At any moment, we pay attention to only a tiny fraction of what is in front of us. As Earl Miller and Timothy Buschman (2015: 113) describe, "Though we may feel that we are able to perceive most of the world around us, this sensation is, in fact, an illusion. . . . In reality, we sense a very small part of the world at any point in time; we 'sip' at the outside world through a straw."[8] So, getting us to pay attention to most anything can be a big challenge.

The challenge does not end there.

Even when we pay attention to information, we often do so in ways that make effective learning unlikely. We are easily distracted.[9] We almost always prefer quick and simple explanations over more detailed and accurate ones.[10] We also sometimes evaluate information based on whether it makes us feel good, rather than on whether it helps us make better decisions.[11] For example, when a political rival speaks, many partisans devote considerable mental energy to internally counter-argue what the rival is saying. They think to themselves, "[My rival] has no idea what she is talking about" and then works to conjure reasons to continue ignoring the rival). This defensive maneuver reduces the energy that a person can devote to actually hearing what the rival is saying.[12]

These attributes that make learning difficult come from strong and longstanding biological foundations. They are part of our nature. They are difficult and often impossible to change.

Nevertheless, there are people who seek to help us adapt to our ignorance. They want to give us information that we can use to align our beliefs and actions with certain facts and values. These people include teachers, scientists, faith leaders, issue advocates, journalists, reporters, and political campaigners. All of them act as *civic educators*—as teachers of various topics in politics or government.

Many people become civic educators because they want to inform us about important political decisions. These decisions include what votes to cast and what stands to take in certain policy debates. Some of these educators seek to help us make decisions that are consistent with a scientific knowledge base (e.g., making decisions about sums of numbers that are based on the logic of addition). Other educators seek to improve our skills at making decisions that are consistent with a partisan ideology or religious creed.

All of these civic educators face significant challenges. The challenges include limited time and energy, having to choose from all the different kinds of information that can be conveyed to others, and the fact that every person who attempts to learn has limited capacity to pay attention to new information. As a result, educators face important choices about what information to present.

This book is about how civic educators of all kinds can better achieve their communicative goals. To serve this mission, the book clarifies what kinds of information are (and are not) valuable to different audiences and what kinds of information can improve important kinds of knowledge and competence. It shows civic educators how to convey valuable information more effectively when resources are scarce, attention is limited, and ignorance is infinite.

In many instances, civic educators have the *potential* to help others make better decisions. Will that potential be realized? This book is dedicated to helping civic educators of all kinds achieve more of their potential.

2

Who Are the Educators and How Can We Help Them?

From this point of the book forward, I ask you to think about the challenges described in chapter 1 from a civic educator's perspective. That is, consider the perspective of a person who wants to increase other people's knowledge about politics or their competence at a politically relevant task. With that perspective in mind, I first convey a few important facts about civic educators and their aspirations. Next, I present a plan for helping many of them achieve these aspirations more effectively. The plan covers the book's main themes and offers a chapter-by-chapter description of what's ahead.

Let's start with a brief discussion of "ignorance"—a topic that motivates many people to become civic educators. According to numerous surveys and news reports, the mass public appears to know very little about politics, government, and policy. When pollsters ask even simple questions on any of these topics, many people fail to give correct answers. For example, while nearly every adult American can name the president of the United States, many cannot recall the names of their US senators. Millions cannot easily remember which political party holds a majority of seats in the US House of Representatives or the US Senate.[1] Many Americans give incorrect answers when asked to identify the chief justice of the United States by name.[2] They do the same when asked about basic aspects of the US Constitution.[3] Many provide incorrect answers to questions about who leads our nation's closest international allies, such as the United Kingdom and Israel.[4] Most seem not to know basic facts about our major trading partners, such as Canada and China.[5] People provide incorrect answers or no answers at all to survey questions about all kinds of policies and politics. In "The Star Spangled Banner," America is "the land of the free and the home of the brave," but when asked to answer fact-based questions about policy and politics, Americans appear to be, as filmmaker Michael Moore (2010) put it, "a society of ignorant and illiterate people."

In response to such evidence, the question becomes, "What can be done about it?" One response is to castigate the public. Critics who take this approach are frustrated by citizens' inabilities to answer the kinds of questions described above. They ask how we can expect ignorant citizens to choose qualified candidates for office or offer defensible views on social topics. Gary Ackerman, for example, served in the US Congress for over 29 years. When asked about the decline in congressional cooperation during his time in office, he blamed civic ignorance: "Society has changed. The public is to blame as well. I think the people have gotten dumber."[6]

Other critics suggest that some people should be kept from the polls because of how they respond to such surveys. Consider, for example, columnist LZ Granderson's (2011) advice:

> [W]e all know people who gleefully admit they know nothing about politics, don't have time to find out what the current issues are or even know how the government works, but go out and vote. . . . Want a solution? Weed out some of the ignorant by making people who want to vote first pass a test.

Political elites are not the only people who have these views. As *New York Times* columnist Tom Edsall wrote in the weeks leading up to the 2012 presidential election:

> When I met Kevin Balzer, a Romney supporter who is a Mack Truck supervisor, I asked him why his state looks likely to back Obama. "People are stupid," he said. Balzer continued by saying that "[t]he students don't know about civics, they don't know about our history, our government, our constitution. . . . That is what's happening in Pennsylvania, especially in Lehigh Valley."[7]

Others seek a more constructive response to evidence of civic ignorance. They seek to "educate" citizens. Former Supreme Court Justice Sandra Day O'Connor, for example, argues that "[t]he more I read and the more I listen, the more apparent it is that our society suffers from an alarming degree of public ignorance. . . . We have to ensure that our citizens are well informed and prepared to face tough challenges."[8]

Calls for education come from all over society. They come from the political right, center, and left. They come from people who are well informed about science. They come from people who are devoutly religious. They come from people who are both scientific and devout. They come from people who are neither of these things.

Many people answer these calls. To simplify the narrative of this book, I refer to all of these civic-minded individuals and groups by a simpler name: *educators*. They are people who believe that providing information to others is a path to greater civic competence and a better future. Educators are this book's protagonists and its potential heroes. My goal is to help these educators increase the value of the information they provide to others.

Educators develop and implement educational strategies (i.e., they design plans to provide certain kinds of information to certain people in certain ways). Educators' strategies produce a diverse set of actions. Some teach students. Others write books. Some write articles. Others give information to strangers through electronic mediums. Some do their work in neighborhood coffee houses. Some perform their educational craft at family dinner tables. Others seek to draw attention to important facts and causes while working for widely recognized and highly reputable media organizations. Some seek educational innovation through startups. Some seek to educate at places of work and places of worship. Others operate in more formal settings like high schools, colleges, and universities. Some educators do many of these things. In all cases, what makes a person an educator—as this book defines the term—is a motivation to mitigate the damage that various forms of civic ignorance can cause.

Educators differ not just in their strategies, but also in their ambitions. Some want to educate just a few neighbors, or a particular family member, about a single issue. Others want to educate a specific audience (e.g., young adults, farmers, inhabitants of particular neighborhoods, residents of a particular city) about a general topic. Some educators have grander plans; they want to alter the politics of entire nations.

Educators also have diverse perceptions of themselves. Some identify as advocates. These advocate-educators (e.g., the Sierra Club) are motivated by a desire to achieve a particular policy outcome (e.g., "a safe and healthy community in which to live"). Some advocate-educators seek policy change. Others seek to preserve policies that already exist.

Other educators identify themselves as experts on a topic rather than as policy-driven advocates. These expert-educators are motivated by ideas from fields such as science, medicine, or theology. They do not make explicit appeals for or against specific candidates or policies. These experts seek to educate audiences about how things work. Many academics, and a good number of journalists and reporters who write or speak about government and politics, think of themselves in this manner. I include most of my own work in this category.

Other educators identify themselves as advocates *and* experts. They not only want to teach audiences about how things work, but also want to enlighten others about how things could work if certain options were chosen.[9] These educators often provide information for the purpose of bringing policy outcomes in line with the lessons of their expertise and their own points of view.

Whether educators look in the mirror and see advocates, experts, neither, or both, they see themselves as knowing things *that can help others.* As opposed to a salesman whose objective is to get rich quickly without regard for those who would purchase his wares, my focus is on educators who believe that greater knowledge will benefit others. Highly visible national-level issues for which civic educators are active include world hunger, climate change, arms control, gun rights, maintenance of traditional values, the definition of marriage, and all manner of causes related to health. Other civic educators focus on more localized issues such as the policies of a given school district or whether specific pieces of land should be used for commerce or recreation, or whether land should be preserved.

Many people (including most people who make efforts to write or speak about government or politics) are civic educators of one kind or another. The fact that you are reading this book suggests that you may fit this description. After all, someone who chooses to read a book with this title is typically interested in understanding why people appear to know so little about politics and what can be done about that. You may even have firm ideas about the kinds of information that can help others make better decisions. If you fit into any of the categories described above, you may already be an educator or you may have a bright future as someone who can convey valuable information to others. In either case, you have my gratitude and admiration. Individuals and communities benefit from the fact that so many people like you dedicate themselves to educating others about important topics. It is for this reason that educators are this book's prospective heroes.

MEET THE EDUCATORS; THEY ARE US

With educators' identities established, the question becomes, "What kinds of information should an educator convey?" There are, after all, an infinite number of facts about politics and government that could be offered. Decision-makers from the smallest school boards to the largest democratic nations depend on educators like you to provide the right kinds of information to people who need it. This book is about how to do that.

In what follows, I seek to help educators develop more effective and efficient educational strategies. If you are seeking to increase others' knowledge of politics, policy, and government, this book explains how to provide information in ways that are more likely to benefit those people. If you are an expert or advocate, this book offers ways to differentiate between approaches that do—and do not—cause people to pay attention to new information and make better decisions as a result. If you are a scholar of topics such as political information or civic competence, the point of this book is to help improve the accuracy and value of your research. Indeed, this book uncovers common errors in scholarship on these topics and then explains how to fix them. These corrections can make subsequent scholarship more useful to educators of all kinds.

With the goal of helping educators in mind, it is also important to recognize that many educators channel their energies into ineffective strategies that do little to improve the knowledge, or increase the competences, that motivated them to develop educational strategies in the first place. Educational ineffectiveness occurs because many educators are mistaken about how people learn and make decisions.

Consider, for example, the belief that people who cannot correctly answer a few fact-based questions about politics on surveys *must* also be incompetent when formulating political opinions or casting important votes. We will discover that *this assumption is almost always incorrect.*

Mistaken beliefs like these lead many educators to offer information that others do not value or cannot use. We can do better.

In this book, you and I will examine relationships among the information to which people are exposed, the knowledge that such information produces, and knowledge's effect on important competences. The book's central proposition is that educators can be much more effective if they know a few things about how people think and learn about politics. In particular, the book offers a constructive way to differentiate between information to which prospective learners will pay attention and information that these same people will ignore. It also clarifies what kinds of information have the most power to broadly increase valuable kinds of knowledge and competence. Greater knowledge of these topics can empower educators to more effectively lead prospective learners to knowledge that matters.

PLAN OF THE BOOK

The book has two parts. Part I explains how to teach people about a subject in ways that make what is learned more likely to influence subsequent decisions. Part II shows that simple changes in how we measure knowledge can help educators better understand what others need to know. In both parts, I show that relatively simple principles can help educators deliver the kinds of information that make desired learning outcomes more likely.

Part I: The Value of Information

Part I shows how to distinguish information that has the power to increase valuable kinds of knowledge from information that appears to have this power but does not. In chapters 3 and 4, we begin by defining *competence, information, knowledge* and their relationships to one another. In these chapters we see that competence is always with respect to a task and an evaluative criterion. So, in this book, a competent choice is one that is consistent with a relevant set of facts (say, about climate change) and that is in sufficient alignment with a chosen criterion (e.g., how one feels about tradeoffs between environmental sustainability and economic growth). An example of a task for which competence concerns are common is a person's ability to choose a candidate for office that is most consistent with a relevant set of facts while also best aligning with a chosen set of values. Part

I clarifies the kinds of information and knowledge that help people cast competent votes.

Chapter 5 introduces a "logic of competence" that clarifies how different kinds of information affect knowledge and competence. The logic reveals that information is more valuable to an audience if it is necessary or sufficient to increase competence at highly valued tasks. While this statement may seem obvious on its face, many educators are mistaken about its implications for their endeavors. In particular, many educators misunderstand the role of cues. This book's "logic of competence" reveals how people can use simple cues (such as party identification or interest group endorsements) to make many competent decisions despite being ignorant about lots of seemingly relevant facts. In many other cases, of course, simple cues do not have this power. In chapter 5, we explain when cues do and do not have these effects.

In chapter 5, we also encounter critics who dismiss cue usage as an aberration or an undesirable practice to be avoided. Such critiques reflect a fundamental misunderstanding of how people use information. We will see that everyone uses cues in almost every decision they make. Educators who understand the logic of competence can make better choices about what information to provide to others and, as a result, can increase more competences with less effort.

Chapters 6 through 8 focus on how to convey information more effectively. These chapters' starting premise is that a person's ability to pay attention to information is extremely limited. Unchangeable aspects of human biology lead people to ignore almost all of the information to which they are, or could be, exposed. Since learning requires attention, educators who want to increase prospective learners' knowledge or competence must find ways to get their attention.

A common requirement for obtaining attention is prospective learners perceiving information as being highly relevant to their immediate needs. We will see that the ineffectiveness of many educational strategies can be linked to mistaken beliefs about how prospective learners perceive the value of different kinds of information. Consider, for example, the fact that some citizens perceive requests to learn about politics as burdensome and costly. Their "costs" can include money paid for instruction, time spent away from family, friends, and other activities, and the psychic difficulty of struggling to understand new things. At the same time, citizens often perceive as abstract or uncertain the benefits of learning about many of the things about which aspiring educators care. Educators who fail to recognize these perceptions tend to overwhelm prospective learners with information that they do not want and will not use. Chapter 7 describes how to tip attentional scales back in an educator's favor.

Chapters 7 and 8 focus particular attention on learning dynamics that are common to political environments. Many educators, for example, do not appreciate the extent to which political debates are waged over more than "just the facts." Political conflicts often reflect strong value differences in a society. An implication for educators is that when a prospective learner suspects that an educator's values are contrary to his or her own, the prospective learner can lose motivation to pay attention to the educator's information—even if the educator's information is factually correct and would be beneficial to the prospective learner if he or she paid attention. Chapter 8 focuses on how people choose whom to believe in a range of social circumstances. There I show how educators can build their credibility in ways that give otherwise doubtful audiences greater motivation to learn from them. Chapter 8 also shows how educators can maintain their credibility in politically difficult circumstances.

Chapters 9 through 13 offer ways for educators to increase the value and effectiveness of their educational strategies. Chapter 9 begins with the fact that people in political environments sometimes disagree about which actions are competent, what "competent" citizens should know, and what information is worth learning. To help educators manage such disagreements, I offer a simple framework called the "politics of competence." The politics of competence can help educators understand and articulate the value of different kinds of information in a wide range of political environments.

The politics of competence has four components: *value diversity, issue complexity, political roles,* and *learning costs.* Chapters 10 through 13 focus on one of the four components, describe the difficulties that the chapter's focal component can pose for educators, and offer constructive ways for educators to manage these difficulties so that they can offer information that truly makes a difference.

Chapter 10 begins this sequence by focusing on value diversity. When speaking of values, I follow Shalom Schwartz and Wolfgang Bilsky's (1987: 551) definition. They define values as "(a) concepts or beliefs, (b) about desirable end states or behaviors, (c) that transcend specific situations, (d) guide selection or evaluation of behavior and events, and (e) are ordered by relative importance." Value diversity leads people to make different claims about "what citizens *should* know." Poor people in America, for example, are often criticized by liberal elites for voting Republican. The claim is that if poor people knew the facts that critics hold dear, they would vote differently (and, not coincidentally, as the critics themselves voted). Problems with such claims include that they are often offered without evidence, and when evidence exists, it often shows that many poor voters have defensible reasons for voting as they did. Conservative elites make parallel errors. Similarly, while many broad "public ignorance" critiques are presented as objective and accurate statements about information that basic political competences require, I show that many of these claims are subjective and inaccurate. The causes of this problem are a misunderstanding of the logic of competence described in chapter 5 and the role that value diversity plays in competence assessments. Mistakes like these can cause educators to offer information that has no value to prospective learners. Chapter 10 shows educators how to avoid these mistakes and develop more effective ways of increasing useful kinds of knowledge in a wide range of political contexts.

Chapter 11 focuses on issue complexity. By complexity, I mean that an issue that has multiple parts. When an issue is complex, educators must choose how to frame it (i.e., they must choose what parts of the issue to emphasize). In chapter 11, I show how choices about how to frame an issue affect who pays attention to an educator's information and whether or not that information has any subsequent effect on others' knowledge and competence.

In chapter 12, the focus is on political roles. By political roles, I mean a person's opportunities to affect political outcomes. A president has different roles than do individual members of a legislature. Legislators, in turn have different roles than citizens who hold no elective offices. These role differences mean that information that increases a president's competence at his most important tasks may have little value to people with different roles (say, a member of a local school board)—and vice versa. In chapter 12, I show how understanding political roles can help educators direct information to more valuable ends.

In chapter 13, I focus on learning costs. Increasing knowledge or competence can take a lot of work. Educators must put effort into developing and implementing their strategies. Prospective learners must devote resources to learning. Everyone involved in educational efforts pays costs of one kind or another. For some, the costs are sacrificed time and effort. For others, money is the principal expense. Chapter 13 shows how these costs alter the net benefit of different types of information to different kinds of people. Understanding different types of learning costs reveals an important implication for educators: Even if people share important values and political roles, they may disagree about whether the costs of an educational effort are worth paying *because some people face greater costs than others.* Chapter 13 shows how educators can use this kind of knowledge to elicit broader participation in important educational endeavors and to accomplish important educational goals more efficiently.

In sum, part I describes how to provide more of the kind of information that is likely to increase knowledge and competence and less of the kind of information that will have no such effect. These insights matter because learning is more difficult than many educators believe. If human brains had unlimited processing capacities, remembering large amounts of new information would be possible. But human brains don't have these capacities. So, educators who want to increase knowledge and competence are forced to make critical decisions about what information to convey. Part I's main lesson offers a template for making these critical decisions in more effective ways. The main lesson is that, for information to increase knowledge or competence, it must have two attributes:

- The information's content must be necessary or sufficient to increase prospective learners' abilities to perform valuable tasks if they devote sufficient attention to it. These tasks can entail knowledge (remembering things) or competence (doing things).
- Prospective learners must perceive the information as a gift. They must see it as so beneficial that they devote sufficient attention to it.

Of course, the coming pages will explain why these attributes are critical and what kinds of information do (and do not) have these attributes.

One thing you may have noticed about this short list is that the educator's perception of the information's net benefits is not on it. This is an important point. If an educator perceives information as valuable (perhaps because it is factually correct), but a prospective learner does not share that perception (perhaps because they see the information as irrelevant to topics about which they care), learning will not occur. This is true even if

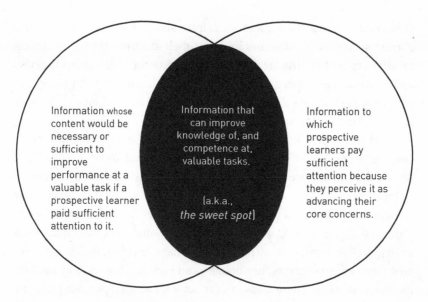

FIGURE 2.1. Information that Matters

the prospective learner would actually benefit from learning the educator's information. Perceptions are crucial.

Hence, understanding part I's main lesson (as depicted in figure 2.1) can be the difference between success and failure for many educators. Strategies whose information lacks one or both of the listed characteristics will not produce the outcomes that motivate people to become civic educators. To increase knowledge and competence, information must have both characteristics.[10]

Part II: How to Improve Political Knowledge

- How can I use data to accurately characterize the kinds of knowledge that people do and do not have?
- How do I know if I have increased a prospective learner's knowledge?

Educators ask questions like these for different reasons. Some educators ask these questions because they want to know if their services are needed. Evidence that prospective learners are ignorant of critical information signals to educators that their efforts can be valuable to prospective learners.

Other educators ask these questions to learn about the effectiveness of their current strategies. If educators find that their students are not obtaining valuable types of knowledge, the finding can give them the means to revise and improve their strategy. In other words, both current and prospective educators can use data about what citizens do and do not know to improve the effectiveness of their strategies.

Part II's purpose is to help scholars, journalists, and practitioners make more accurate claims about what others do and do not know about politics. To see the importance of such skills, suppose that an educator wants to claim that a particular competence needs improving, or that a particular strategy has improved a competence. What evidence would support these claims? Today, many educators try to support claims about an educational strategy's effectiveness by referencing how many email messages they sent, how many advertisements they bought, and how much work they put into their presentations. These measures can say a lot about input. But for many educators, output matters more.

To show that an educational strategy increases competence, evidence would need to demonstrate that a target audience was once incompetent, that the same audience was subsequently more competent, and that the educator's effort contributed to the change. Diagnosing incompetence and providing evidence of improved competence, in turn, require accurate measurements. Each chapter of part II focuses on a way to improve such accuracy. In chapter 15, I show what we can learn about knowledge and competence from questions that gauge individuals' abilities to recall specific facts. In chapter 16, I evaluate aggregate measures of what people know, often called "political knowledge" measures. In chapter 17, I assess the accuracy of "interviewer assessments," another means of attempting to measure what people know. In chapter 18, I explain how to produce better measurements of important concepts.

In all of these chapters, I show that *many current claims about civic ignorance do not accurately reflect what is in the data.* In some cases, I will show that writers appear not to have read the questions on which their "public ignorance" claims are based. In other cases, critics parlay a basic misunderstanding of statistics into erroneous claims about "political ignorance." We can do better.

To this end, every chapter in part II includes concrete and actionable advice about how to improve evidence-based claims about what other people know. In some cases, the improvement comes from interpreting existing data differently. In other cases, improvement comes from producing new data in new ways. In many cases, we will see that commonly made mistakes are relatively easy to fix. An implication of these findings is that there are many cases in which only a small amount of effort can produce big improvements in our understanding of what people know.

So, what you can expect to gain from reading parts I *and* II of this book is a foundation for greater effectiveness and efficiency in efforts to understand or increase knowledge and competence. A brief description of the foundation is as follows:

- Educators who wish to develop educational strategies that are of value to others must provide information that is necessary or sufficient to increase valuable types of knowledge and competence.
- Factual information is not enough. To increase knowledge or competence, information must induce prospective learners to pay attention. To get this attention, prospective learners must perceive the information as conferring sufficient net benefits. In many cases, these perceptions overrule reality in determining whether attention is paid.
- Perceived net benefits are influenced by a person's values, the complexity of the issues at hand, political roles, and learning costs.
- Educators can use data to better understand what people know. Unfortunately, existing data and interpretations of this data vary in quality. Many interpretations are incorrect. Simple changes can substantially improve what educators understand about what prospective learners know. Educators who have such an understanding can increase valuable knowledge and competence more effectively.

In addition to a stronger foundation, the book offers many analogies and examples of current attempts to increase knowledge and competence. In some cases, the highlighted practices are shown to be ineffective, inefficient, or in error. The good news is that many of these problems are correctable. Whenever possible, I offer corrections.

Although I have worked to make the text accessible, I have also committed to staying true to the research and examples on which my advice is based. To state this point in a different way, if we encounter questions about how to improve civic education that have easy answers, I give them. But some of the questions that we encounter do not have easy answers.

In chapter 4, for example, I describe requests for a "silver bullet"—a short and universally applicable set of facts that every citizen should know about politics. Many people, especially attention-seeking critics of the public's ignorance, claim to know what should be on such lists. However, when we ask for evidence of how knowing the content of these lists increases high value competences, we often receive speculation and wishful thinking instead of logic and evidence. Moreover, when we aggregate all of these claims about what people should know, the combined list is no longer short, and any seeming consensus about "what others should know" disappears. Indeed, the number of facts that are included on all such lists is *zero*. As a result, most claims about "what others should know" typically dodge, rather than advance, the cause of identifying information that increases important competences.

This book takes a different approach. It offers a framework for improving educational effectiveness. But since we are dealing with social issues and human brains of considerable complexity, some questions lack quick answers. In all cases, my method is to stay true to what researchers and leading practitioners know about these topics and to convey this knowledge in ways that readers can find accessible and actionable. So, while many existing books about civic ignorance advise citizens to improve their moral character and pay more attention to facts that the writer happens to hold dear, we can do better. My goal is to offer educators a set of insights and tools that they can use to more effectively help others. These insights and tools may not be a silver bullet, but they can be a silver lining.

HOW TO READ THIS BOOK

Now that you have a sense of what the book is about, I offer some advice about how to read it. If you are interested in learning about how to characterize civic competence, political knowledge, or if you want to more effectively increase knowledge and competence in a diverse set of environments, then part I is where that happens. Part II has a complementary, but different, focus. It focuses on how analysts, academics, and many others measure what people know. It seeks to improve the ways in which educators and others interpret data and evidence about knowledge, ignorance, and competence. Since part II is about measurement, it is a little more technical than part I. I have worked to make part II's material accessible to many different readers, but in the spirit of full disclosure, I will point out that its subject matter requires a slightly higher level of tolerance for social science research.

So, if you are interested in education or communication, but not measurement, read part I and then skip to chapter 18. There and in chapter 19, I summarize the relationship between parts I and II's main lessons.

If you are interested in measurement and not communication, part II will be of greater interest to you, but I recommend that you read part I to better understand why many current claims about "political knowledge" and ignorance are problematic—and to see how you can fix those problems. If you take this shortcut, chapters 3 to 5 will be the most important for you. If, however, you are interested in developing your own new knowledge or competence measures, or in developing more meaningful interpretations of existing data, then reading all of part I is the best way to do that.

I end this section by offering an argument for reading the whole book even if you think you are interested in improving education, but not interested in measurement. Many people with important expertise and great concern about others devote substantial energy to using education to try to improve others' lives. However, when we examine the actual consequences of many of these attempts, we observe educators providing information that prospective learners cannot or will not use. In these cases, the educator's expertise and generosity produce a missed opportunity to help others.

Part I gives educators a framework for understanding why good and smart people sometimes fail to achieve their goals in educating others. It then offers a foundation for doing better. Once educators have this knowledge, they may become more interested in measuring their efforts' effects. Here's the challenge for educators who want to pursue such measurements: part II of the book identifies widespread problems in how people interpret existing data about what people know. Hence, my belief is that if well-intentioned educators follow current practices in the measurement and interpretation of political knowledge data, they will be doing themselves a great disservice. It would be like finally deciding to live a healthier lifestyle and then using a toaster to measure your heart rate. Indeed, when I work with organizations that want to improve their educational effectiveness, a pivotal moment comes when they are able to articulate a valid measure of what they want to achieve. I want to help more educators make effective decisions at those moments and then show them how to obtain the data and tools that they need to complete an accurate evaluation. It is this type of reader, in addition to the intellectually curious, who can benefit from reading the entire book.

WHY IT MATTERS

I am often asked by researchers and communication practitioners to give presentations about how people make decisions when they don't know very much, or about how people learn about politics, policy, or science in politicized environments. So, I teach a lot and I travel a lot. Some of my presentations are highly technical and abstract. Other presentations use case studies and humorous examples to help these audiences improve communicative performance.

When I give these presentations, I meet many people. These people are diverse in many ways. I learn so much from them and the many different ways in which they view topics like politics and science.

While the people I meet are diverse, most of them share an important attribute. They care deeply about others. Some focus on the challenges facing the nations in which they live. Others focus on the quality of life in their communities. Others seek to make a difference in faraway places because they recognize salient fragments of their shared humanity.

Many of these people seek me out because they are concerned about qualities of public decisions. Instances of public ignorance are brought to my attention. In many cases, the circumstance motivates them to educate and they come to me for advice about how to do so more effectively. They often have great passion and innovative ideas about how to proceed. Some want to provide information that is rich in factual detail. Others want to provide information that packs an emotional punch. Some want to convey information that has both attributes. In nearly all cases that I have encountered, people want to offer this information because they believe that doing so can help others make better decisions. That's the good news.

The bad news is that these efforts often fail to have their desired effects. The increased competences that animate prospective educators never materialize. This happens even after these educators invest considerable time and effort. This book is for them. My motivation is to help more of them achieve their ambitions more effectively, more efficiently, and more often.

The reason that a book like this is potentially valuable is that many issues are so complex that collecting and conveying all available information would take more time and effort than anyone has. Even if an educator could collect such information, the people with whom they seek to share it have limited time, limited energy, limited attentional capacity and, quite often, little or no interest in politics. This is reality. Hence, an educator's success at educating others depends on understanding this reality and on building educational strategies that come from this understanding. This link between an educator's knowledge and their success is relevant whether educators offer information from doorsteps, dinner tables, podiums, or pulpits. The objective of this book is to clarify how people use information so that all kinds of educators can provide more information of more value to more people.

Part 1

The Value of Information

3

Three Definitions

This chapter defines three terms: *information, knowledge, competence*, and their relationships to one another. Here is a list of the chapter's main lessons:

- Information, knowledge, and competence are not one and the same. Understanding their differences is a key to increasing knowledge and competence.
- Information is what educators can convey to others directly. The same is not true for knowledge or competence.
- Knowledge is memories of how concepts and objects are related to one another. Knowledge requires information.
- Conveying information is the means by which educators can increase others' knowledge.
- Competence is the ability to perform a task in a particular way. Competence requires knowledge.
- An educator's information can increase an audience's competence only if the audience thinks about the information in ways that transform it into applicable types of knowledge.
- Educators can achieve their objectives more effectively and efficiently by understanding what kinds of information are most relevant to increasing specific competences.

Below, I begin with a brief discussion of the three terms: knowledge, information, and competence in that order. The reason for this ordering comes from my experience with educators and hearing their descriptions of what they are trying to accomplish. Of all the educators that I have met, many more describe themselves as seeking to increase others' knowledge, rather than increasing their information or competence. So, to convey the information in a manner that is most directly related to how many educators see their own challenges, I start where they start.

But there's a catch. By the end of this chapter, I hope to convince you that two things are true for most educators. First, offering information is their sole means for increasing knowledge. Second, increasing others' knowledge has limited value unless that knowledge can increase a valuable competence. In other words, for many educators, increasing others' knowledge is a means for achieving competence goals, rather than being the main goal itself. Hence, one of the most important things that educators can know about information and knowledge is how they relate to competence. Educators who understand these relationships will be better positioned to provide information of real value to others.

3A. KNOWLEDGE IS MEMORY

Knowledge is an attribute of memory. It is the ability to remember attributes of objects and concepts and relationships among them. The knowledge that each of us has comes from our memories of past experiences and how we connect these experiences to one another. When an educator seeks to increase a person's knowledge, they are actually seeking to cause a person to have new or different memories. Civic educators, for example, are trying to affect what comes to mind when people encounter certain politically relevant situations.

A second attribute of knowledge is that it is *factive*. Webster's Online Dictionary, for example, describes knowledge as "the fact or condition of knowing something with familiarity gained through experience or association," "acquaintance with or understanding of a science, art, or technique," "the fact or condition of being aware of something," "the range of one's information or understanding (answered to the best of my *knowledge*)," "the circumstance or condition of apprehending truth or fact through reasoning: COGNITION," and "the fact or condition of having information or of being learned (a person of unusual *knowledge*)."[1] Knowledge consists of justified or true attributes of memory.

In philosophy and related areas of study, long-running debates focus on whether or not a particular proposition is "true." For now, I focus on educators who seek to convey information and produce knowledge that they believe to be true. In chapters 9 and 10, we will examine the value of knowledge and the meaning of competence in settings where people view "truth" differently.

A third attribute of knowledge is that there are different kinds. When asked to recall a specific piece of information on a test, in a conversation, on a survey, or in a voting booth, people draw upon a kind of memory known as "declarative memory."[2] When you see your pet and remember its name, this memory constitutes knowledge of a specific attribute of an object or knowledge of a relationship between objects. This knowledge is the product of a declarative memory. When we say that a person "knows" the answer to a question in a trivia contest, we are recognizing specific contents of his declarative memory. Yet, such abilities do not constitute the whole of a person's knowledge.

A second type of memory called "non-declarative memory" is also relevant. Non-declarative memory includes memories of skills and procedures, as well as certain emotional and skeletal responses.[3] It often "accumulates slowly through repetition over many trials, is expressed primarily by improved performance, and cannot ordinarily be expressed in words."[4] Knowing where and how to find things is an important form of non-declarative memory. These procedural memories give us ways to access facts, such as locations of infrequently visited destinations or an old friend's contact information, that are difficult to store as declarative memories.[5]

Research on how people use Internet search engines like Google provides a vivid example of how we use both kinds of memory to accomplish common tasks. A relevant declarative memory in such circumstances is the memory that Google exists and is an Internet search engine that provides information on many topics. A relevant procedural memory is that if we type certain words into Google's search engine, useful information can emerge.

In a 2011 *Science* magazine article, psychologist Betsy Sparrow examined how the Internet changed not just what information people could find, but also the relationship between people's declarative and non-declarative memories. Her findings "support a growing belief that people are using the

Internet as a personal memory bank: the so-called Google effect."[6] Those of us who use search engines have experienced Sparrow's insight. Before search engines, there were a number of things (e.g., vote totals in previous US presidential elections) that we would have had to work hard to memorize if we wanted to recall the information quickly (e.g., if we wanted to use the information in conversations). If we were fortunate enough to have a book that printed the totals, or if we had written our own easily accessible notes, we could have relied on procedural memories to recall the information. That is, instead of memorizing the results, we could rely on the procedural memory that would lead us to look for the information in our notes or in a book. If we failed to take such actions, we were out of luck when it came to accessing the numbers quickly. Now, obtaining the information requires less effort.[7] Search engines have caused us to revise the content of our declarative memories. They have changed not just what questions we can answer on short notice, but what kinds of information we make an effort to memorize. As psychologist Roddy Rodriguez describes, "Why remember something if I know I can look it up again? In some sense, with Google and other search engines, we can offload some of our memory demands onto machines."[8]

When evaluating a candidate or a new policy proposal, people draw on declarative memories to remember a few facts about these matters and draw upon procedural memories to find additional information. Political scientist Doris Graber describes this process:

> Many political insights gained during election campaigns do not come from rote memorization of facts gleaned from news stories. Rather, they come from using past knowledge and powers of inference making to extract specific meanings from a tiny portion of the new factual data presented by the media.[9]

Declarative and non-declarative memories together constitute the knowledge that people have when thinking about politics[10]

3B. INFORMATION IS WHAT EDUCATORS CONVEY

An important distinction between information and knowledge is that educators have more direct control over the information they convey than they do over the knowledge that others might gain from that information. It is the combination of the information's content and a prospective learner's information processing that affects whether the educator's information becomes the learner's new knowledge. Educators have no direct control over prospective learners' information processing. Hence, educators have only indirect ability to influence others' knowledge. (Chapters 4 through 13 have more to say about how educators can increase their information's likely influence.)

I define information as a means of conveying attributes of observations, data, and ideas. Like other definitions, this book's definition casts information as "the knowledge or 'news' of some fact or occurrence; the action of telling or fact of being told something...."[11] For the purpose of increasing knowledge and competence, information's key attribute is that it can be communicated from one person to another.

Although this definition offers a starting point, it leaves out a property of information with which many educators need to grapple—*information need not be factual*. If, for example, a person believes that blue is the best color, this statement is information. This information can be stored in memory. It can be circulated to others. But it need not be true. Many observations, data, and ideas that manifest as information are actually erroneous, or potentially disagreeable, representations.

In some circumstances, giving a person information increases their knowledge and competence. In other circumstances, providing information has no such effect.[12] If, for example, people believe false information, giving them more of it can reduce their knowledge about its subject matter. In addition, certain types of information can reduce people's ability to perform a task. Consider, for example, the well-documented phenomenon of "stereotype threat."[13] Numerous researchers have found that when members of historically oppressed groups are told that other members of their group have scored badly on a particular test, they subsequently perform worse on the tests than similar subjects who are not given that information.[14] Similar outcomes were seen in 1980s drug education programs. As Dennis Rosenbaum and Gordon Hanson report, the DARE (Drug Abuse Resistance Education) program as a whole "had no long term effects on a wide range of drug use measures" and, in fact, corresponded to increased drug use for some participants.[15] Program reviews by the US Surgeon General and the National Academy of Sciences confirmed that "DARE's approach is ineffective."[16] While the intentions were good, the information that DARE presented did not have the effects that its organizers wanted or long claimed.

So information can be untrue and information need not be useful. Yet, knowledge increases require information. *How does information have this effect when it can be false or useless?*

We can answer this question, at least in part, by further distinguishing between information and knowledge. A first point of distinction is that conveying information from one person to another is required for the former to increase the latter's knowledge. But information transmission is only one step in a knowledge-building process.

To see the next step, suppose that an educator knows something that a prospective learner does not. To improve the learner's knowledge of the topic, the educator must convey information. Whether the educator's information becomes the person's knowledge depends on how the person processes the information. Information processing, a focal topic in chapters 7 and 8, depends not just on the content of information but on factors that have nothing to do with the content. These factors include a prospective learner's ability to pay attention to information, their beliefs about the educator's motives, and so on.

So, an educator can convey information to a person in an attempt to increase that person's knowledge—but information is all that the educator directly conveys. It is incorrect to say that an educator directly conveys knowledge. Increasing another person's knowledge is *one potential consequence* of conveying information to that person, but increased knowledge is not an automatic or even frequent consequence of information provision. Information can be incorrect, distracting, or simply ignored. Therefore, a lingering issue for educators is to determine what kinds of information can offer real value to the intended recipients. This is where the relationship between information and competence becomes relevant.

3C. COMPETENCE EXISTS WITH RESPECT
TO A TASK AND AN EVALUATIVE CRITERION

Webster's New Collegiate Dictionary defines a person as *competent* if she has "requisite or adequate ability or qualities."[17] As a synonym, it lists "able." Webster's definitions for able include "having sufficient power, skill, or resources to accomplish an object" and "marked by intelligence, knowledge, skill, or competence."[18] As examples, it offers phrases such as "a competent teacher" and "a competent piece of work."[19] So, to say that a person is competent is to say that they are competent *at* something. In other words, *competence is with respect to a task.*

My focus is on competence in political or policy domains. I refer to these skills as civic competences. A civic competence refers to a citizen's ability to accomplish well-defined tasks in roles such as voter, juror, bureaucrat, or legislator.

Many educators are motivated by the belief that increasing certain kinds of civic competence adds value to the societies in which they live. While educators may say that they want to "inform audiences" or "increase their knowledge", most educators are not motivated to change audience's thinking about random or undefined topics. Educators typically want audiences to apply certain kinds of knowledge to certain kinds of tasks. So, when I describe what educators do and how they can be more effective, I am referring to educators' efforts

- to provide information to prospective learners
- as a means of increasing their knowledge
- in ways that help the prospective learners align their beliefs or behaviors with a competence criterion—that is, a certain set of facts and values that are regarded as being "better" for prospective learners or a community to which they belong.

A common definition of competence in the context of a civil jury, for example, is that juries are competent if they convict defendants who are guilty and acquit defendants who are innocent of the crimes with which they are charged. An effort to increase competence in this setting is an effort to provide information that make such outcomes more likely. In cases like this, educators can claim that their endeavors are valuable to prospective learners if increased competence at these tasks is something that they or their communities value.

To get a broader sense of the tasks in which many civic educators are interested, consider the activities of the Spencer Foundation. Spencer offers grants to scholars and organizations to advance its vision of improved educational outcomes. Spencer's 2008 call for proposals for its Initiative on Civic Learning and Civic Action spells out a set of tasks at which it seeks improved competence:

> [W]e broadly frame the issues and outcomes that we recognize as civic action: voting; working together to solve a school or neighborhood

problem; participating in an organization aimed at a broader social goal; writing to a newspaper or on a blog about an issue; boycotting or buycotting; producing art with social themes, such as neighborhood murals, radio productions, or poetry readings; using the internet to rally people around various causes; choosing a career for its civic mission, or creating community gardens or green spaces.

I highlight the Spencer Foundation's call because it names measurable tasks. Each item on this list requires some knowledge to accomplish, and it is possible to measure whether individuals have sufficient knowledge to accomplish these goals. As a result, this list provides a foundation for building an educational endeavor with measurable outcomes. If Spencer can find audiences that are not accomplishing the listed tasks, and if they can obtain valid and accurate measures of what the audience knows, they can use the foundation they have set to identify information that would lead the audience to do so.

With such directions, Spencer lays a credible foundation for an educational program that can achieve their desired ends. They offer educators a criterion for evaluating an educational program's effectiveness. To provide value according to this criterion, educators must convey information that increases knowledge that, in turn, leads to greater effectiveness at one or more of the listed tasks. The chapters on "the politics of competence" (chapters 9 through 13) offer more details on how educators whose aims are different than Spencer's can develop their own effective criteria.

Clearly stated competence criteria can focus an educator's effort. Even then, however, a critical challenge remains—*What information should they offer?* It is to that topic that we now turn.

4

The Silver Bullet

People express different opinions about what types of information and knowledge others should have. They offer lists of names, institutional characteristics, or historical facts that are claimed to be essential for competent citizenship. One difficulty facing people who make such claims is that there are thousands of such lists in circulation—and these lists of "what others should know" tend not to look alike.

For example, some people make arguments about what others should know in an openly ideological manner—asserting that *certain facts and values with which they agree* are what everyone should know—and actively think about—when making particular decisions. In the debate over the legal status of abortion, for example, pro-life participants implore others to elevate information about the fetus over other available claims, while pro-choice participants seek to elevate information about the pregnant woman's well-being over other available claims. Participants in these debates regularly disagree about what kinds of information and knowledge are needed for people to make "competent" decisions about abortion's legal status.

At this point in the book's discussion of the relationship among information, knowledge, and competence, I want to tell you about a question that I am sometimes asked when giving presentations on these topics. The question is "What do people *really* need to know about politics (or government or science or climate or "Obamacare," etc.)?" Many people who ask this question believe it to be a simple one that is answerable in just a few words.

In these instances, I am being asked to produce a silver bullet. What is a silver bullet? In folklore, a silver bullet is a device that defeats many different types of monsters (such as werewolves and witches). Today, it refers to a simple solution to a complex problem. The silver bullet that people seek from me is a short set of "facts" that, if only everyone knew them, would guarantee a basic level of competence in tasks such as voting. My questioners are seeking a one-size-fits-all informational solution to a competence concern about which they care deeply.

In the search for a silver bullet, it is important to realize that what a citizen needs to know depends on what we are asking him or her to do. Competence is defined with respect to a task. Competence at some political tasks, such as writing a constitution or constructing a complex piece of legislation, can require considerable expertise in many highly technical areas. Competent performance at other tasks, such as voting for or against a simply worded ballot measure, does not require the same kind of expertise. A task's complexity affects what kind of knowledge affects competence.

When searching for a silver bullet, it is also important to realize that the effective functioning of modern societies requires competence at many different tasks. In my city, for example, we need people who know a lot about budgeting and accounting, people who know a lot about law enforcement, people who have expertise in educating young children, and so on. The communities in which you live have parallel requirements. No democracy can feasibly expect every person to be an expert at every valuable task. So, an initial answer to the question "What do people really need to know?" is that different people need to know different things.

Further complicating the search for a silver bullet is the fact that many political judgments are based on more than facts. In many cases, two people can be provided with identical information about an issue and come to different conclusions about what *should* be done. Some disagreements arise because people have different values, have different political roles, or are in different situations. Some people are young and some are old. Some are healthy, others are sick. Some are religious, others are not. Some serve in the military, others do not. Some are rich and some are poor. Some live on farms, others live in cities. These differences lead people to want different things and to have divergent preferences about societal priorities and the tradeoffs that governments should make.

In debates about the federal budget, for example, some people care most about a single issue, such as care for the elderly. Others care more about different issues, such as national security. Some care most about creating environments where industry flourishes. Others care about protecting the jobs that people currently have. Some want to protect the environments in which people currently live, even if that means constraining what industry can do. Others care most not about any one specific issue, but about organizing society according to a basic moral code.

These differences are unlikely to disappear. It is true, of course, that there exist societies in which an all-encompassing theology, natural law, or localized divination story provides a set of basic social facts upon which judgments of right and wrong and should and shouldn't are based. The foundations of most legal traditions of many modern nations can be traced to such origins. In recent centuries and decades, however, there has been a growing challenge to the validity of these foundations. Nationalisms that originated in contexts of dominant theologies now seek to have influence that transcends those theologies. Moreover, changes in global travel patterns and in the economies of scale of information transmission expose people to an increasing range of cultures and worldviews.[1] These changes in who-can-communicate-what-to-whom have helped to fuel skepticism toward traditional ways of thinking. In places where such skepticism is allowed to become part of the social discourse, questions are raised about whose notions of right and wrong should inform (or bind) collective decision-making.

As a result, the search for a short list of facts that can serve as a silver bullet is complicated by the fact that *ours is a world where facts and values tend not to exist in neatly separated piles.* Many political debates reflect more than simple disagreements about technical or scientific facts. Consider, for example, a case where participants disagree about whether one policy (say, one that reduces a fire department's average response time in a particular village by two minutes) is more deserving of taxpayer support than another policy (say, one that provides a dedicated teacher for 15 elementary school students with disabilities). Participants in this circumstance may agree on lots of facts about the effectiveness of both policies. At the same time, they may disagree on which policy is more deserving of funding. They may disagree because some prefer faster fire department responses more than they prefer the dedicated teacher, while others prefer the teacher more than the responses. Value differences can lead people to disagree about what tradeoffs societies should make.

Still, I meet many people who want a silver bullet—a list (preferably short) of facts or instructions that, if only all Americans knew them, would eliminate important social problems. For these people, I have good news—and I have "other" news.

The good news is that a silver bullet can be found for issues where there is no moral or ethical disagreement and there are no value differences. The silver bullet entails identifying a list of facts that are both necessary and sufficient for competent performance at the task (see the next chapter for more details on why "necessary and sufficient conditions" is the proper standard for evaluating information in this case). If the task is the ability to recall a specific fact, or to perform a simple task in the way that a very specific moral code proscribes, then competence may be very easy to evaluate and improve.

Here's the "other" news: Almost no educators are in this situation. I don't call this "bad news." I find it more constructive to call it "reality."

Most educators find themselves in circumstances where values are diverse, issues are complex, and individuals have different political roles. As I will show in subsequent chapters, each of these factors individually, as well as many combinations of these factors, can produce disagreements about who should know what. As the political scientist E. E. Schattschneider said (1960: 68, emphasis in original): "Political conflict is not like an intercollegiate debate in which the opponents agree in advance on a definition of the issues. As a matter of fact, *the definition of the alternatives is the supreme instrument of power*; the antagonists can rarely agree on what the issues are. . . ." Hence, for most educators most of the time, the main news about silver bullets is this: If we want a silver bullet that will produce a "good citizen" in some broad sense that everyone will accept—we are out of luck. *There are no silver bullets.*

But . . . if we want to help others by increasing a target audience's competence at a valuable task, we can be more effective by thinking about our situation in a more realistic way.

If you have chosen to read this book, it is very likely that you live in a circumstance in which it would be unwise to count on all persons agreeing that a particular set of facts is what a competent citizen needs to know. You and I also live in a world where educators can help people accomplish tasks that have high social value. To achieve these high-value outcomes, educators can gain support for their endeavors by making strong, clear, and evidence-based arguments about what is worth knowing.[2] If educators make these arguments in a compelling way, people who share their educational aspirations will have better reasons to support educators' efforts.

So, instead of a silver bullet, what educators can build is *a legitimate plan of action*. Developing such a plan requires taking the following steps:

- Identify a task that has demonstrable social value and demonstrate that an important audience does not perform the task competently (chapter 5).
- Determine what kinds of knowledge would increase the audience's competence at the task and what kinds of information produce that knowledge (chapter 5).
- When increasing competence requires attention to new information, offer information whose content not only enables competent choice (i.e., knowledge of necessary facts), but also elicits sufficient attention from needed audiences (chapters 6 to 8).
- Understand that people are motivated to pay attention to information if they perceive it as beneficial to their deepest needs (chapters 9 to 11).
- Understand that people may have different political roles (chapter 12) and costs of learning (chapter 13). As a result, a desired competence increase may come from different people knowing different things.
- Base an educational strategy on credible evidence for each of the previous bullet points.
- Commit to measurements of the extent to which the educational strategy is achieving the tasks listed above (chapters 14 to 18).
- Adjust the strategy if the evidence shows that it is not working.

Legitimate plans of action clarify for whom an educator's efforts are beneficial. For this reason, legitimate plans of action are as close to a silver bullet as many educators can get. When educators have to work hard to earn prospective learners' participation and attention, such plans can empower them to provide information of great value to others.

The rest of this book offers ways for educators to develop better plans. I start this part of the book by offering part of a plan right now. In circumstances where there is no universally accepted "silver bullet" that ties general notions of civic competence to specific pieces of information, we need a more credible foundation for making claims about what information is valuable to convey to others at any given moment. When attempting to develop such foundations myself, I have found the following advice from political scientists James Kuklinski and Paul Quirk (emphasis original) to be useful:

> [T]here are four principal conceptual components in any evaluation of performance.
>
> - First, one must identify the *task* that the actor is asked to undertake. . . .
> - Second, one must state a *criterion* by which the performance is to be evaluated—that is the property or attribute that is taken to constitute the quality of performance.
> - Third, one must recognize at least one empirical *indicator* of that criterion.
> - Finally, to categorize levels of performance, one must identify *standards* with respect to the indicator. Standards map levels of the indicator onto a set of evaluative categories: satisfactory or unsatisfactory; very good, good, fair, poor and the like.[3]

The context in which this advice was offered is instructive. Kuklinski and Quirk argue that many academic studies of topics such as "political knowledge," "political sophistication," or "civic competence" fail to articulate a clear standard and, as a result, offer little effective insight for most educators.

To help scholars (and educators) whose ambitions are to increase others' competence, Kuklinski and Quirk offer the following advice:

> It is important, therefore, that scholars spell out the elements of their evaluative approach and, where the rationale is not self-evident, provide the reasoning for their choices. In the absence of such discussion, the significance of any conclusion about citizen competence, positive or negative, is unclear. Even serious problems in the logic of an evaluation are likely to go undetected. And different studies or approaches will reach conflicting conclusions for reasons that are neither debated nor even recognized. In an important sense, such conclusions are essentially arbitrary.[4]

This advice provides a constructive foundation for more effective and efficient educational strategies. To say that a person or group has a civic competence is to say that the person or group is able to perform a particular task with respect to a particular standard. Without a task and without a standard, incompetence—and whether an educational strategy increased a competence—is difficult to assess in a constructive way.

In the chapters that follow, I offer educators a range of ways to develop legitimate action plans. These plans include defensible criteria, indicators, and standards. Educators who offer these plans can more effectively articulate and directly demonstrate the value of their efforts. In the next chapter, I begin by articulating a simple logic of the relationships among information, knowledge, and competence. Understanding such relationships can help educators more effectively and efficiently identify the kinds of information that can increase knowledge and competence and, in turn, improve people's lives.

5

The Logic of Competence

This chapter clarifies the logical relationship between the types of information an educator can convey and competence at the types of tasks that people perform. Here is a short summary of the chapter's main claims:

- Knowledge of many things does *not* require recalling "all the facts."
- Competence at many tasks does *not* require knowing "everything."
- Trying to give "all the facts" to an audience is usually a sign of inefficiency.
- Cues and non-declarative memories facilitate competence even when they leave people unable to answer certain fact-based questions about a task.
- The effectiveness of attempts to increase competence depends on what information is given to whom. For example, when the competence of a group is being measured, not all members of that group must have the same knowledge for the group as a whole to be competent.
- To improve efficiency, educators should understand what kinds of information are most relevant for increasing knowledge and competence.

To reach these conclusions, I rely heavily on two terms: *necessity* and *sufficiency*. These terms describe logical relationships between two or more items. Educators who understand these terms can better distinguish information that increases desired competences from information that has no such power.

X is a *necessary condition* for Y if Y can happen only after X happens. For example, suppose that earning at least a million votes is a necessary condition for a candidate to win an election. Two implications follow. First, any candidate who does not earn at least a million votes cannot win the election (which means that there may be no winner). Second, any candidate who earns at least a million votes has the potential to win the election.

X is a *sufficient condition* for Y if X happening means that Y must also happen. Suppose that earning a million votes is sufficient to win the election. Two implications follow. First, any candidate who earns at least a million votes wins the election (which implies that multiple candidates could win). Second, any candidate who does not earn at least a million votes retains the potential to win the election.

If it is the case that X happens *if and only if* Y happens, then X is a *necessary and sufficient condition* for Y. So, if earning at least a million votes is a necessary and sufficient condition for a candidate to win the election, then once the candidate has at least one million votes, she wins the election. Otherwise, she does not. End of story.

The concepts of necessity and sufficiency are simple to state. One implication of their definitions for the relationship between information and competence is as follows:

> If a person's ability to recall a specific fact is a necessary condition for competence at a particular task, then educators who want to enable competence must ensure that people recall this fact. If a person's ability to recall the fact is sufficient for competence, then information that enables the recall can also increase the competence. If the ability to recall a specific fact is neither necessary nor sufficient for competence, then offering this information will not produce the benefits just mentioned.

Table 5.1 summarizes the argument.

Many critics of the public, and some educators, are confused about necessity and sufficiency in the context of information, knowledge, and competence. This confusion manifests as claims that a person's ability to recall a particular fact is necessary for an important competence. Many critics make this claim when even basic logic or simple evidence shows

TABLE 5.1. **Logical Relations between Knowledge and Competence**

"If knowing fact F is [insert phrase here] for person P to have competence C and if . . .	. . . person P knows fact F, then *we* know	. . . person P does not know fact F, then *we* know
[necessary, but not sufficient]	that P **has the potential to be competent**	that P is *not* **competent**
[sufficient, but not necessary]	that P **is competent**	that P **has the potential to be competent**
[necessary and sufficient]	that P **is competent**	that P is *not* **competent**
[neither necessary nor sufficient]	nothing new about P's competence	nothing new about P's competence

otherwise. I will show that educators who base their strategies on such critiques are hindered, rather than helped, in their quests to help others.

In this chapter, I use the concepts of necessity and sufficiency to clarify what kinds of information are more (and less) able to increase knowledge and competence. In section 5A, I examine how a common, but widely ignored, fact about information processing affects the kinds of information that are necessary for a wide variety of competences. In section 5B, I clarify the type of information that is sufficient for many of these same competences. In section 5C, I examine informational requirements for *collective* competence—which matters when a group, rather than an individual, performs a task. In section 5D, I use the chapter's main insights to offer further advice about how to develop more effective and efficient educational strategies.

5A. CUES AFFECT WHAT INFORMATION IS NECESSARY FOR COMPETENCE

Many critics use peoples' inabilities to instantly recall the names of political figures, attributes of public policies, or select historical occurrences as the evidentiary basis for broad generalizations about civic incompetence. Consider, for example, law scholar Ilya Somin's claim:

> Overall, close to a third of Americans can be categorized as "know-nothings" who are almost completely ignorant of relevant political information (Bennett 1998)—which is not, by any means, to

suggest that the other two-thirds are well informed. . . . Three aspects of voter ignorance deserve particular attention. First, voters are not just ignorant about specific policy issues, but about the basic structure of government and how it operates (Neuman, 1986; Delli Carpini and Keeter, 1991 and 1996: ch. 2; Bennett, 1988). Majorities are ignorant of such basic aspects of the U.S. political system as who has the power to declare war, the respective functions of the three branches of government, and who controls monetary policy (Delli Carpini and Keeter, 1996: 707–771). This suggests that voters not only cannot choose between specific competing policy programs, but also cannot accurately assign credit and blame for visible policy outcomes to the right office-holders.[1]

Critiques like this ignore the fact that in many aspects of life, people use different kinds of memory and information to inform their decisions. This particular claim, for example, makes no reference to non-declarative memories—even though such knowledge influences political decisions. Gary Langer, one of America's foremost political pollsters, has called for writers and analysts to learn more about different kinds of knowledge:

> Knowledge reflects the ability to think—not merely to recite information, but to use it to draw connections and build concepts. You can have deep knowledge, but weak on-command recall. You can have terrific recall, but little knowledge. Life is not a game show.[2]

Following Langer's distinction, I refer to survey questions that measure specific components of a person's declarative memory as "recall questions." Recall questions measure elements of the knowledge that people bring to political tasks.

Conjectures like Somin's base broad conclusions about competence on answers to short lists of recall questions. These conjectures depend on the strong assumption that a person's ability to recall the types of questions asked on surveys is a necessary condition for having a broader knowledge of a given topic or competence at a given task. *When are such assumptions correct?* In part II, I show that many widely cited recall questions measure knowledge of facts that are neither necessary nor sufficient to increase citizens' competence at even very simple tasks. For now, I use a simple example to clarify the relationship between recall and competence.

In this example, a voter knows a set of 26 facts that we label A–Z. Suppose we can agree that knowing such facts allows the voter to accomplish a particular task competently. In other words, knowledge of these facts correlates with the voter's ability to cast a vote for the "best" candidate relative to criteria and standards to which we have previously agreed (I describe how we would reach such an agreement in chapters 9 through 13).

Is there knowledge of a different set of facts (perhaps a subset of A–Z) that would lead the voter to choose the same candidate? If the answer to the question is "no," then we know that knowledge of every fact from A to Z is a necessary condition for the voter to choose competently. In such cases, we can assess the voter's competence in a straightforward manner—measure her knowledge of A through Z. If she does not know (through either direct recall or use of procedural memories) even one of these facts, then we can declare her incompetent at the task at hand. To increase the voter's competence in this case, the voter must come to know—either directly through memorization or with a procedure that gives her the same ability—the facts of A through Z of which she is currently ignorant.

Many critics of public ignorance assume that they are in such a situation. Most are in error. The reason is that a sufficient condition for the assumption to be incorrect is knowledge of some other set of facts that also allows competent performance. In such cases, knowing A–Z is not necessary for competence.

The error manifests as follows. A critic claims that "person A does not know fact X, Y, or Z; therefore person A is incompetent at task T." For such a claim to be true, the critic must demonstrate that knowledge of X, Y, and Z is necessary for competence. In particular, they must be able to prove that no subset of these facts (say, knowledge of X and Y paired with ignorance of Z) or alternate set of facts (say, facts U and W, which are distinct from X, Y, and Z) also allows the voter to perform the task as she would have if she knew X, Y, and Z.

For many political decisions, however, there is no single set of facts that is necessary for competence. Instead, people make competent decisions using different kinds of knowledge. Non-declarative memories provide one such route to competence. Cues provide a different route and are one very common reason that the ability to recall a particular fact is unnecessary for important kinds of competence.

A cue is a piece of information that can take the place of other information as the basis of competence at a particular task.[3] It is an information shortcut—a simple way to draw complex inferences.[4] To see a common example of a cue in action, imagine that your task is to get from where you live to a nearby airport. For most people, multiple routes are available. One route involves a freeway. Another route involves only side streets. Other routes combine freeways and side streets. In my case, which involves driving from my Ann Arbor home to Detroit's international airport, my GPS tells me that there are thousands of possible routes.

Now suppose that you are quizzed on specific attributes of a particular route that goes from your home to your nearest airport. I, and most people that I know, know nothing about many of the possible routes. There will be routes that we have never traveled, routes we did not know about, and routes that we know to be inefficient. What can we infer from a person's ignorance of particular airport routes? Can we infer that because a person does not know all possible routes to the airport that they are incompetent at getting to the airport?

The answer can be "no" in both cases—as long as knowing every route to the airport is not a necessary condition for getting there. If you know how to get to the airport using a particular route, perhaps a side-streets-only route, then you are knowledgeable in the broader domain of "how to get to the airport." If you have the means for taking that route (i.e., a suitable mode of transportation), then you can be competent at getting there as well. You can accomplish the task of getting to the airport despite not being able to answer many of the types of quiz questions described above. Many critics proceed as if their favorite route to competence is the *only* one. But the assumption is true only if the facts on which they focus are a necessary condition for others' competence.

Educators need not repeat these mistakes. In many cases, educators can increase their effectiveness by checking on whether other—and perhaps more efficient—routes to competence are available. For many political topics, cues provide these routes. A common cue in political contexts is party identification. For many people, knowing whether a candidate is a Democrat or a Republican can help them cast the same votes they would have cast if they had access to sufficiently informative cues or knew many more relevant facts about the candidates.[5]

To get a broader view of how cues work in politics, consider the case of referendums, which ask voters to make a binary choice (e.g., vote "yes" or "no") on a specific statute or proposed constitutional change. In the United States, famous referendums have affected state tax rates, affirmative action in school admissions, and the legal status of same-sex marriage. In other democracies, referendums are used to settle significant constitutional questions.

For the purpose of example, let's for the moment focus on US state level referendums and define a competence criterion as follows:

- A competent vote is one that a person would cast
- if they could recall and apply to the question at hand
- the most accurate available information about whether a specific consequence of passing or defeating a given referendum
- would ever reduce state government budgets over the next 10 years.

In chapter 9, we address questions about who would choose this criterion—for now, this definition allows us to complete the example.

Two things about this situation are worth noting.

First, if our focus is on a person's competence with respect to this task, then we should evaluate her as competent regardless of "which route she takes." In this case, a competent person need not remember every potentially relevant piece of information about the referendum. What matters for competence is whether she makes the same choice that she would have made had she memorized the most accurate available information about the effect of passing or defeating a given referendum on the stated budgets. In other words, we are allowing for the possibility that a subset of available information may be sufficient for her to choose competently.

Second, once she chooses competently, additional information cannot increase her competence with respect to the task. To see why this is true, note that referendums do not offer voters opportunities to amend the wording that is placed on the ballot. The typical referendum restricts each person to vote "yes" or "no." So, even if the referendum is very technical, competence requires only that she know whether it is better or worse than the current law with respect to the next 10 years of state budgets.

As a result, if there is one and only one piece of information that will allow a voter to know whether the referendum is better or worse than the current law with respect to the stated criteria (i.e., if there are no cues), then knowing this piece of information is necessary for casting a competent vote. In such a case, an incorrect answer to a question that accurately measures the person's knowledge of this piece of information is sufficient to document their incompetence. For most referendums, however, the availability of cues means that individual pieces of information that may seem critical for competence are not, in fact, necessary for competence.

In referendums, valuable and widely used cues often take the form of endorsements. Interest groups, politicians, newspapers, and other entities take public positions for or against specific items on a ballot. These endorsements can facilitate competence. Consider, for example, a referendum on gun control that the National Rifle Association (NRA) opposes. For people who know that their preferences on such issues are parallel to those of the NRA, the endorsement can lead them to vote as they would have voted if they had committed to memory many details about the referendum's content.

This kind of cue usage is not unique to politics. In almost every aspect of our lives, we use cues such as the advice of others and rules of thumb to reach quick and often reliable conclusions about the consequences of our actions.[6] As the cognitive scientist Andy Clark describes, "Biological cognition is highly selective, and it can sensitize an organism to whatever (often simple) parameters reliably specify states of affairs that matter to the specific life form.... [Many organisms] rely on simple cues that are specific to their needs, and both profit by not bothering to represent other types in detail."[7] In the same way that drivers use the trajectory of oncoming headlights to draw accurate inferences about the future locations of other cars (i.e., when lights emerging from the darkness and changing shape provide information about cars, drivers, and speeds), and shoppers use brand names such as Mercedes-Benz and Coca-Cola to draw accurate inferences about qualities of certain consumer products, people use cues such as partisan identification and interest group endorsements to draw analogous conclusions about political phenomena.[8]

Cues do more than affect decision-making in the mass public. Many political "experts" also rely on cues. Members of Congress, for example, do not have the time to read every word of the thousands of bills and public comments that emerge in any given year. Hence, they regularly base their views on reports written by their staffs or by trusted advocacy organizations.[9] Without these brief reports, professional legislators would be overwhelmed by the enormity of their tasks. Indeed, research on Congress reveals that one of its main organizational objectives is to help busy legislators use information effectively.[10] As a result, when legislators rely on simple cues to inform their decisions (e.g., "ask my staff to summarize a piece of legislation," "vote as my party leader does unless I know of a very good reason to vote otherwise"), their inabilities to recall individual details of specific pieces of legislation may not reveal much about their competence at critical tasks.[11]

Because effective cues often exist for political choices, it is frequently false to say that competent performance at political tasks requires knowledge of "all the facts." Competence is the ability to perform a task with respect to a particular criterion. Thus, while competence often requires recall of some facts, the presence of cues and the potential effectiveness of non-declarative memories render declarative memory of many facts unnecessary for most kinds of competence.

5B. WHAT INFORMATION IS SUFFICIENT FOR COMPETENCE?

Knowing all the facts is unnecessary for many kinds of competence. Educators who distinguish between information that is sufficient and insufficient for a desired competence can increase that competence more effectively and efficiently. An experiment performed near Harvard University provides an interesting way to think about such distinctions:

> A researcher goes to Harvard Square in Cambridge, Massachusetts, with a tape recorder hidden in his coat pocket. Putting a copy of the *Boston Globe* under his arm, he pretends to be a native. He says to passers-by, "How do you get to Central Square?" The passers-by, thinking they are addressing a fellow Bostonian, don't even break their stride when they give their replies, which consist of a few words like "First stop on the subway."
>
> The next day the researcher goes to the same spot, but this time he presents himself as a tourist, obviously unfamiliar with the city. "I'm from out of town," he says. "Can you tell me how to get to Central Square?" This time the tapes show that people's answers are much longer and more rudimentary. A typical one goes, "Yes, well you go down on the subway. You can see the entrance over there, and when you get downstairs you buy a token, put it in the slot, and you go over to the side that says Quincy. You take the train headed for Quincy, but you get off very soon, just the first stop is Central Square, and be sure to get off there. You'll know it because there is a big sign on the wall. It says Central Square."[12]

Here, "educators" are attempting to increase the traveler's competence in getting to Central Square. What information is sufficient for this purpose depends on what the traveler already knows. The passersby gave more detailed information when they assumed that "first stop on the subway" would not be a sufficient cue.

What information is sufficient for competent performance? As the example suggests, the effect of almost any piece of information on a person's competence depends on what the person already knows.[13] To place this logic in a more political context, suppose that a person is voting in a local election. Suppose that her sole goal is to decrease violent crime in her city. A referendum on her ballot pertains to law enforcement. For the purpose of the example, I define her vote on the proposal as competent if it results in decreased violent crime in her city over the next five years.

Suppose that a group has conducted valid research on this proposal. The research proves that the proposal is necessary to decrease violent crime in the city over the next five years. But the researchers work in France. They have written their report in French. The voter does not understand French. Initially, she lacks the ability to translate the document.

Given her current knowledge, which does not include the ability to read French-language documents, the research is not sufficient for her to improve her competence. If she knew other things, such as how to read French or where to find a reliable translator, the same piece of information could be sufficient to increase her competence. (Moreover, if understanding the report were the only way to achieve this outcome, then access to the report would be a necessary condition as well.)

This example offers a simple way to demonstrate a general idea: What people learn from new information depends on what they already know and believe. An endorsement offered by, say, the Sierra Club or the NRA means nothing in isolation from other knowledge—such as what these groups stand for. When people know enough about these groups, learning about their endorsements can be sufficient for them to make competent choices.

To get a better sense of how seemingly simple cues can be sufficient for increasing important competences, consider a voter who must make a series of binary choices.[14] Such a circumstance is faced by a voter whose ballot has multiple contests in which pairs of candidates compete for each office. In such circumstances, there may be a good reason to judge a person's competence not just with respect to one decision, but with respect to the entire ballot that they cast. Suppose, for the purpose of example, that we set a high bar for calling someone competent. Let's say that the requirement is that the voter makes a competent choice (choose the best option with respect to a stated criterion) on every single issue on her ballot. Let N represent the number of decisions that the ballot asks her to make.

In such cases, the voter's task is more complicated than a simple binary comparison. If competence is measured with respect to a voter's choice in N two-candidate elections, then there are 2^N possible ways that they can fill out the ballot (i.e., two multiplied by itself N times). For example, if a ballot contains two binary choices, and assuming that the voter does not abstain, there are four ways for the voter to complete her ballot. If the first election is between candidates A and B and the second election is between candidates C and D, the four options are: vote for A and C, vote for A and D, vote for B and C, or vote for B and D. If a voter's competence depends on her casting the best of the four possible vote combinations, then simply flipping a coin to determine her vote in each of the two elections would lead the voter to make a "competent" choice approximately one out of four times. Compared to the case of a single binary choice, where a coin flip would produce competence half of the time on average, the requirement for competence in this example is higher.

The bar is raised further as the number of ballot choices increases. When a single ballot asks a voter to cast a vote in each of 20 two-candidate elections, the number of different ways that the voter can complete the ballot (excluding abstentions) is 1,048,576. For 30 elections, there are over a billion different ways to complete the ballot.

According to the competence criterion stated above, only one way of completing the ballot out of the million or billion possibilities qualifies as competent. If we want to judge a voter's competence in this way, it may seem very unlikely that the average person can be competent—particularly if the person pays little attention to politics.

Can a simple cue really help a vote make a competent one-in-a-billion decision? For some people, the answer is "yes." Voting according to a simple cue—say, knowledge of the political party to which each candidate belongs—can facilitate competence even with respect to the rigorous standard we have adopted for this example (cast the best vote in every circumstance). To see how, consider that numerous studies of American politics show that a congressional candidate's partisan identification is often a reliable indicator of the policy positions that he or she will support (I describe why that cue has such reliability later in this chapter). If the criterion for assessing a voter's competence is to choose a candidate whose policy positions are arranged in a particular manner, and if the candidate's partisan identification accurately signals their issue positions, then a person who uses partisan identification as a substitute for memorizing intricate details about these positions can complete a competent ballot even in the one-in-a-million and one-in-a-billion situations described above.[15]

In other words, if the competence criterion is to choose the candidate closest to a person's preferences on a set of N issues, and if it happens that a person always matches Democrats' positions on these N issues and never matches Republicans' positions on any of these issues, then voting for the Democrat instead of the Republican leads the voter to make the same choice she would have made had she been knowledgeable about the candidates' positions on every issue. If the voter knows enough to use a candidate's partisan identification in this way, the cue is sufficient for competent performance.[16] Simple cues can be very powerful.

Social scientists have sought many ways of clarifying the conditions under which cues have this kind of power. Experimental studies are particularly well suited for these purposes when they allow researchers to control what people do and do not know. Political scientists Richard McKelvey and Peter Ordeshook were early developers of such experiments.[17] They examined when uninformed voters can use cues from polls and endorsements to cast the same votes they would have cast if they were more informed and if they sought to use that information to vote consistently with certain values. Their findings clarified the extent to which less informed people make better choices after learning about others' views.

One experiment focused on whether cues could lead otherwise uninformed voters to think "if that many voters are voting for the [rightist candidate], he can't be *too* liberal" and then use that information to cast the vote that they would have cast if they knew enough factual information to cast a vote consistent with their own values. In McKelvey and Ordeshook's study, voter preferences were represented by points on a number line. Each "voter" was assigned a preference and paid for their participation. Their payment depended on choosing the candidate whose position was closest to their ideal point. So, if a voter were assigned the ideal point "7," if one candidate offered a policy represented by the number "5" and another offered a policy represented by the number "2," then the voter would be paid more when the first candidate won the election. If we assume that experimental subjects prefer to be paid more rather than less, then a "competent" vote is for the candidate that produces the higher benefit. Political economist Thomas Palfrey describes their main finding as follows:

> Perhaps the most striking experiment . . . only a few of the voters in the experiments knew where the candidates located . . . they proved that this information alone is sufficient to reveal enough to voters that even uninformed voters behave . . . as if they were fully informed.[18]

McKelvey and Ordeshook's experiments showed an unexpected range of conditions under which (a) uninformed voters vote competently, and (b) election outcomes are identical to what they would have been if all voters were sufficiently informed. Findings like these prompted a reconsideration of the role of cues in politics.

Subsequent research by Mathew McCubbins and myself, James Druckman, and Cheryl Boudreau, among others, identify many conditions under which people know enough to choose the cues that help them make the same choices they would have made if they knew much more and if they sought to use that information to act consistently with certain values.[19] This research shows that when information about the quality of cues is easier to acquire than information about policies, voters who appear to be uninformed can cast the same votes they would have cast if they had access to very detailed information.[20] Collectively, we found that the knowledge threshold for voting competently is lower than many so-called public ignorance critics had conjectured. Instead of being required to have detailed information about all consequences of their choices, it can be sufficient for the voter to know enough to make good choices about what cues to use.

Pursuing this topic further, political scientists Paul Sniderman and John Bullock have shown how electoral rules and norms affect informational needs associated with voting:

> [I]n representative democracies, citizens do not directly choose the alternatives. They only get to choose from among the alternatives on the menu of choices presented to them. That menu is simplified, coordinated, and advocated above all through electoral competition between political parties. Accordingly, we claim that citizens in representative democracies can coordinate their responses to political choices insofar as the choices themselves are coordinated by political parties.[21]

In other words, Sniderman and Bullock cite political party competition as a factor that produces effective cues. To see why party competition has this effect, it is useful to know that the best way to earn elective office in many democratic societies is to be the official candidate of a major political party.[22] In federal elections in the United States, for example, candidates who run in general elections without party endorsements almost always lose. This happens in part because many citizens have a difficult time understanding what these candidates would do if they were elected. Candidates who represent a major party, in contrast, are easier to associate with the positions that they are likely to pursue when in office.

Common legislative incentives—such as those that provide highly valued leadership positions to legislators who are steadfastly loyal to the party—increase the accuracy of these associations. Indeed, one reason that knowing a candidate's party identification can be so valuable is that once parties obtain control of a legislature or an executive office, they have significant collective incentives to govern in ways that protect and enhance the party's "brand name."[23] As a result, most individual legislators in many countries hew closely to the general principles with which most voters identify their party.[24] Indeed, individual candidates who go against their party's principles are often severely sanctioned. For this reason, individual legislators' "party loyalty" scores are extremely high in many countries.[25] With such loyalty incentives in place, knowledge of a candidate's partisan identification can be a powerful cue for voters. As Sniderman and Bullock describe:

> In our view, it is parties and candidates that do the heavy lifting.... They stamp a partisan and ideological brand on the arguments offered in their favor, signaling that accepting one means rejecting the other.... And much to the advantage of citizens. By structuring political choice spaces, parties facilitate citizens' reasoning consistently from basic principles.[26]

Similar dynamics affect the competence of civil juries. In a civil trial, a judge and a group of citizens hear evidence from plaintiffs and defendants. The judge instructs jurors about how to interpret evidence and then asks them to answer binary-choice questions about the defendant's guilt or innocence. If we define competence in these settings as convicting defendants who are guilty and acquitting defendants who are innocent, then simplifying the question in this way makes competence easier for juries to achieve. If prospective jurors are willing and able to follow the proceedings in a trial, the judge's instructions can help them be competent despite their lack of expertise in legal theories or canons.

Of course, that cues *can* have this power does not mean that they always *do*. As simple cues are applied to increasingly complex problems, the cues must "cut nature at its joints" if they are to increase complex competences.[27] Consider, for example, cases where a candidate's partisan identification provides very little reliable information to a voter. The partisan cue may not be informative because the candidate is a maverick who often votes against the party on issues that concern the voter, *or* the cue may not be informative because the two parties do not differ on issues that the voter cares about, *or* the cue may be less effective because the election in question is a primary election and all candidates are from the same party. Cues are also less likely to be sufficient for competence when voters cannot see that an often-useful cue does work in a particular circumstance. Political scientists Logan Dancey and Geoffrey Sheagly, for example, examined what people knew about occasions where their elected representatives voted against their own party—a rare event in many legislatures. Dancey and Sheagly not only find that many people have mistaken beliefs about these instances, but also that the people who are most interested in politics are both "the group most likely to know their senator's position when she votes with the party" and "*the group most likely to incorrectly identify* their senator's position when she votes against her party" (emphasis added).[28] Cues are no panacea. To increase competence, a cue's content must be sufficient to help the voter differentiate what he would and would not do if he knew enough other information to vote in accordance with the relevant competence criterion. In cases such as those described in this paragraph, educators may need to teach more than commonly used partisan cues to achieve desired levels of competence.

The fact that cues are not always sufficient for competence leads some critics to castigate cue-based decision-making as a whole. As columnist Rick Shenkman conjectures: "[W]hat the polls show is that Americans cannot make up for their lack of basic knowledge even if they shrewdly employ shortcuts."[29] This claim reflects a fundamental misunderstanding of how people use information.

In fact, every one of us is almost completely ignorant of almost every question about almost every political topic on which we could possibly be quizzed. Even on issues where we think of ourselves as expert, most of us know only a tiny fraction of all that is knowable. One consequence of this reality is that everyone uses information shortcuts in almost every decision that we make.[30] Much of what any of us consider to be our own knowledge is based on cues of one kind or another.

So, the right question to ask is not whether cues always (or never) yield competent decisions, because we know that the answer to both questions is "no." The constructive question to ask is, "Under what conditions are particular cues necessary or sufficient for competent decision-making?"

An important factor distinguishing cues that do, and do not, increase competence is whether a person can learn enough about the cue to make an informed judgment about whether to follow it. When people get reliable feedback about cues, they can use them more effectively. Such feedback is more likely when choices are binary or simple. Without such feedback, or when applied to more complex problems, simple cues can lead people to make bad decisions.[31]

5C. HOW MUCH INFORMATION DOES COLLECTIVE COMPETENCE REQUIRE?

In some cases, an educator is interested in improving an individual's competence. In other cases, an educator seeks to improve a group's competence. In other words, an educator seeks to help a group make a "better" decision with respect to a competence criterion. Consider, for example, a political outcome that depends on a majority vote. If an educator seeks to improve the electorate's competence in such cases, then it will be sufficient if a majority of the electorate makes decisions of a certain quality.

To clarify the relationship between information and competence in such settings, let's consider a simple example.[32] The example returns us to the context of referendums. Many established national democracies, most US states, and thousands of local governments use ballot initiatives and referendums to make important policy decisions. In these elections, citizens vote for or against specific policy proposals. If a proposal earns a certain number of votes, it becomes law. Suppose that an electorate's choice is competent if it is the same choice that a majority would have made if everyone in the electorate knew a particular set of highly salient facts about the consequences of the choice (whether this is an appropriate criteria—and how to defend it if it is—is the subject of chapters 9 through 13).

How competent are electorates to make such decisions? The answer to this question is heavily influenced by the fact that the typical ballot measure offers a binary choice. As mentioned before, a binary choice is one with two options. In almost all initiatives and referendums, voters get to vote "yes" or "no." They do not get to propose alterations or support their own preferred amendments in the voting booth. Since the choice is binary, even if the proposed law and the current law are very complex, a competent electorate needs only to figure out which of the two alternatives is better than the other with respect to the criterion. Seen in this way, our competence question becomes "Can the electorate choose the better of the two alternatives?"

To clarify the example, suppose that one of the two alternatives is truly better according to the criteria previously stated. Let's call the better alternative "heads" and the other alternative "tails." So, if a majority were to choose "tails," then by this criterion, we would agree that the electorate had made an incompetent choice.

To provide more insight as to when an electorate can make a competent choice, suppose that we allow chimpanzees to determine the election outcome. Suppose further that instead of reading books, watching videos, and talking to others, each chimp bases their voting decisions on a coin flip. What can we say about this electorate's competence?

In this scenario, a single chimp with a fair coin can make a competent choice (heads) 50 percent of the time on average. In many decision-making venues, a 50 percent success rate is regarded as a good thing. Baseball players are considered among the top in their sport if they get a hit even 30 percent of the times that they step up to the plate. In politics, by contrast, people often want voters to have a higher competence rate, something approximating 100 percent. If this is true, then one chimp with a fair coin does not meet the standard.

Now let's change the example a bit by giving each chimp a nearly fair coin. This new coin lands on heads 51 percent of the time. This is not much greater than 50 percent and far short of the 100 percent correct rate that people might desire.

Table 5.2 shows the results of making the decision in this manner. When compared to one chimp with a fair coin, a group of chimps with 51 percent correct coins is far more competent. This example's logic follows

TABLE 5.2. **Probability that a Majority Chooses Competently Using Coins that Give the Right Answer 51 Percent of the Time**

# voters	Probability of correct majority decision
1	.51
305	.61
1 million	.9999
10 million	.9999...

from the Generalized Condorcet Jury Theorem.[33] The theorem states that if each voter in an electorate is more likely than not to make a correct choice, then as the number of voters increases to infinity, the probability that a majority makes the correct choice goes to 100 percent. In other words, the 51 percent coin-flipping chimp electorates make competent choices almost all of the time.

We can use this idea to evaluate the competence of larger electorates. Suppose that one electorate has one million chimps (the approximate size of electorates in many US states) and that another electorate has ten million chimps (the approximate size of electorates in the largest US states). The Generalized Condorcet Jury Theorem tells us that a majority of either electorate makes competent choices approximately 100 percent of the time. Put another way, for electorates of the size of most US states, even one populated by 51 percent coin-flipping chimps, majorities would choose competently about 100 percent of the time.

The outcome changes even more if we allow the coin to be correct more often. If each chimp's coin is right 55 percent of the time, a majority of a 399-member electorate chooses competently 98 percent of the time. If each coin is correct 60 percent of the time, then majority rule groups of size greater than 41 choose competently nine out of 10 times. If the coin is right 70 percent of the time, it takes only 11 voters to achieve a 90 percent chance of a majority choosing competently.

If an electorate of chimps with slightly-to-moderately unfair coins chooses the best alternative approximately 100 percent of the time, what does this imply about the competence of human voters in binary choice elections? Are real voters dumber than coin-flipping chimps?

While this question may seem fanciful at first, the human voters' superiority cannot be taken for granted. The chimps have at least one advantage that human voters do not. The coins do not try to mislead the chimps.

The coins do not generate bumper stickers or banner ads with catchy slogans. The Jury Theorem's apparent magic is based on the assumption that every voter on average is more likely than not to be correct, that any voter errors occur at random, and that errors are not caused by a common factor. If large segments of the electorate are easily or systematically led to vote against their interests, then the group's aggregate competence is imperiled (Althaus, 2003).

This brief example shows that not everyone in a group must be well informed, very knowledgeable, or individually competent for an electorate as a whole to make competent choices. Knowing this much can help educators increase important competences with greater efficiency. In other words, educators who seek to improve a group's competence may not need to provide the same information to all voters. Of course, this example focuses on competence with respect to a single issue. If the information in question increases other valuable competences, then there may be good reasons to provide more common information to more group members. I discuss this topic further in chapter 12 where I focus on how individuals' diverse political roles affect the kinds of information that are most useful to them and the communities to which they belong.

5D. THE TUESDAY PROBLEM

> Citizen: "Can you tell me how to get to my polling place?"
> Well-intentioned information provider: "Tuesday."

In many cases, some people have problems that they want to solve and others have information that they want to give. People who give information to others have various motives. Unfortunately, many people who give information for generous reasons are mistaken about the kinds of information that others value. As is the case in the "Tuesday" example, people sometimes give others information that they do not want or need. In education, desirable motives need not produce desired outcomes.

This chapter clarifies kinds of information that are necessary or sufficient to increase competence. Figure 5.1 integrates this chapter's main conclusions with those of chapter 3. The figure traces a path from available

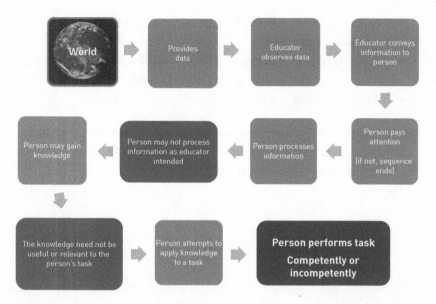

FIGURE 5.1. How Information and Knowledge Affect Competence: A Global View.

information to a prospective learner's competence at a given task. The figure reinforces the following ideas:

- Some information is necessary for obtaining knowledge.
- Many kinds of information are not useful for obtaining certain kinds of knowledge.
- Some information is false.
- Knowledge is an attribute of memory.
- A person can be competent at many things while being ignorant of many things.
- If a piece of information is necessary for competence, then no other cues are sufficient substitutes for that information.
- In many cases, a particular piece of information is not necessary for competence.
- Educators can convey information directly but not knowledge. Knowledge comes from a combination of the content of information and how the prospective learner processes the information.
- How people process information depends on what they already know. A piece of information that is sufficient to increase one

person's competence may have no effect on another person's competence.

- If people have different kinds of prior knowledge, then increasing competence may require giving different kinds of information to different people.

Educators who understand these lessons can spend less time responding "Tuesday" to inquiries about important topics and can spend more time providing information that makes a difference.

6

Lost in the Woods

Chapter 5 offered a logic that clarifies the kinds of information that can increase knowledge and competence. In the coming chapters, I explain how educators can more effectively communicate this kind of information to others. From this point forward in part I, I focus on the time after an educator has identified information that can increase desired knowledge and competences. An educator in this situation faces an important challenge: Just because information can increase knowledge and competence does not mean that it will do so. For information to have these effects, prospective learners must think about the information in certain ways. For example, if a piece of information is to increase another person's competence, that person must pay attention to the information. If the prospective learner ignores the information or processes it in ways that an educator did not anticipate, then the information may not have the educator's desired effect.

In chapters 6 to 8, I use insights from research on information processing to describe two necessary conditions for persuading an audience to think about information in ways that increase knowledge and competence. These conditions are *gaining an audience's attention* and *having sufficient source credibility*. I focus on these conditions not only because of their logical necessity, but also because they are two factors over which educators often have some degree of control.

"Not so fast!"

This is a reaction that I sometimes get when suggesting that we base educational strategies on basic facts about attention and credibility, rather than continuing to rely on often-faulty intuitions about how others learn. Indeed, I have met many educators who initially argue that: "Being an expert in (say, deliberative democracy) makes me persuasive. Citizens and policymakers should respect me and be interested in what I have to say." This is an attractive notion. It is also an illusion in many cases.

Learning is a process that has knowable biological and psychological properties. A fundamental implication of these properties is that people ignore almost all of the information to which they could attend and people forget about almost all of the information to which they pay attention. No expert, advocate, writer, or speaker is immune from these facts. Even educators with the most benevolent intentions are affected. That said, we can use lessons from research on attention and source credibility to help educators convey valuable information to more people more often.

Attention research clarifies when, and to what type of stimuli, people do (and do not) pay attention. This research alerts us to the fact that educators are usually competing with a myriad array of potential distractions when they offer potentially valuable information to an audience. In chapter 7, I use this research to help educators increase their odds of success in winning the ever-present battle for prospective learners' scarce attention.

Credibility research, the subject of chapter 8, clarifies conditions under which an audience will believe, rather than reject, information that an educator is offering. In that chapter, I explain why educators who want to increase knowledge or competence in political circumstances often have to express themselves differently than they would in nonpolitical conversations. The reason for this difference is that political situations have special properties that make credibility particularly important to establish. For example, when politics gives prospective learners reasons to question the truthfulness of the information being offered, what they believe about the motives of the provider of that information can influence what the prospective learner does with the information.

Chapters 6 through 8 establish a simple but important idea: *the value of seeing things from an audience's point of view*. To attract a prospective learner's scarce and often fleeting attention, and to gain the credibility that is needed to get that person to believe the content of an educator's presentation, educators need some understanding of how audiences perceive different kinds of information. The main lesson of chapters 6 to 8 responds to this need. It can be stated as follows:

> An effective educational strategy requires more than the provision of information that is logically connected to a desired form of knowledge or competence. Prospective learners must also perceive the information as so relevant to their values and aspirations that they not only pay attention to it but also work to integrate its content into their own beliefs in ways that are consistent with the educator's goals.

The full meaning of this statement and its implications for educational strategies will become clearer in the coming pages. As an initial way to give the idea more force, I offer a short vignette called "A Walk in the Woods." Many people with whom I work on improving educational effectiveness find it to be a useful starting point.

A WALK IN THE WOODS

Some educators will not have the time to read the entire book. I take no offense. Ample research on information processing reveals just how scarce a resource human attention is. So, in an important sense, I am grateful that you are reading even this page.

With these attention limits in mind, I seek to convey one of the book's most important points using a short story that I call "A Walk in the Woods." I tell this story when addressing larger audiences. I find that it gives many people a comfortable way to place important themes of the book within the contexts of their own experiences and educational aspirations.

Suppose that there are woods with which you are very familiar. Perhaps you grew up near these woods. As a child or as an adult, you had reasons to explore the woods in great detail. It is reasonable to say that you know all about them. No one would doubt that with respect to these woods, you are an expert.

Now suppose that one day you are walking through these woods with a friend or another person about whom you care a great deal. Maybe it is your best friend. Maybe it is a child. Maybe it is a vulnerable adult who has put their trust in you.

A storm occurs. The wind blows violently. Trees fall. You are forced to seek cover. Your friend also seeks cover. You are separated from your friend.

You are able to make it out of the woods. Your friend does not. Your friend is lost in the woods. (It is worth noting that this saying, "lost in the woods," is often used to describe people who lack relevant knowledge.)

At this moment, you may think that while your friend is lost in the woods, she is in a good situation. After all, *you are an expert on the woods.* You have explored the woods in great detail. You know every tree, every path, and every stream within the woods. Who better to rescue your friend than you?

But the woods are dense. You can't see your friend. The storm is such that you cannot physically get to where she is. But she can hear you. So, you shout directions.

The main lesson of the following chapters comes in what happens next. To get your friend out of the woods, you must know two things. First, you must know enough about the woods to be able to describe effective ways out. This is the kind of thing that an expert typically knows. Second, and this is just as important, *you must know where your friend is and what she can do.* This is the point at which many educators' best-laid plans collapse. Indeed, I have met many educators with great expertise and passion for their cause who base their communication strategies on assumptions about "where their audience is" and "what prospective learners can do given where they are" that have little or no basis in truth.

So, in the woods, you shout, "Take three steps to the left!" You imagine that this advice helps your friend. You imagine her taking the steps. You imagine that each step gets her further from being lost in the woods and closer to the place where you want her to be.

Instead, you have made an incorrect assumption about where she is. So, she is falling into a pit or a river or she is walking straight into the trunk of a large and unforgiving tree.

Through these misadventures, you remain an "expert" ... and your friend remains "lost in the woods."

To get multiple friends out of the woods, moreover, it is not enough to care about them or to be an expert. You must also account for the possibility that they may not all be in the same place and that they may have different abilities. Some friends may have physical limitations. Others may have events in their pasts that make them hesitant or unable to move in certain directions. In such cases, giving the same set of directions to all of your friends is not the best way forward. You may need to give different directions to different friends.

What should you do? If you gather information on your friends' circumstances as seen from their points of view, you have greater potential to give them the kinds of information that get them from where they are (lost) to where you want them to be (with you). Such knowledge can empower you to ask questions such as "What can you see?" and "In what directions can you move?" before shouting instructions that your friends cannot use—or offering instructions that lead them to go in unwanted directions. The following chapters are designed to help educators avoid common mistakes and, as a result, empower them to lead important audiences "out of the woods."[1] In the pages that follow, we will find that educators who find ways to relate their information to an audience's abilities, aspirations, and fears can become more effective and efficient as a result.

7

Attracting Attention

Educators seek to convey information that increases knowledge and competence. A necessary condition for accomplishing these goals is to attract attention to their information. Attracting attention can be difficult. Other people, nature, and many variations of consumer society and pop culture compete for a prospective learner's attention. People can also pay attention to things that are not "in the room" when an educator is presenting potentially important information. Prospective learners can think about events that happened in the past or events that could happen in the future. At any moment, there are many things to which people can pay attention.

In this chapter, we will review basic facts about how people direct their attention. To this end, I establish simple principles that educators can use to make their presentations more memorable to more people. Individually and collectively, these principles are not an automatic recipe for success, but they can help educators avoid common mistakes in how they convey information to others.

The chapter's main lessons are as follows:

- Learning requires attention.
- Human attentive capacity is extraordinarily limited.
- For an educator to get a prospective learner's attention,
  the prospective learner must perceive the information as

something they can use to achieve highly valued aspirations. These aspirations can include making bad things go away.

- A phenomenon called motivated reasoning sometimes leads people to pay attention to information because of how it makes them feel, rather than basing their attention on the information's true relationship to their aspirations. Educators can benefit from considering the concept of motivated reasoning when choosing how to convey information.
- Many educators overestimate the amount of information to which prospective learners are willing or able to pay. Correcting these estimates can help educators increase knowledge and competence more effectively.

The chapter reaches these conclusions in the following way. Section 7A offers basic definitions that clarify attention's role in learning. Section 7B shows how challenging earning attention can be. Section 7C explains how to make information more memorable for more people. Section 7D concludes.

7A. UNDERSTANDING THE PROBLEM

For most educators, having their audience learn from the information they provide is the initial outcome they hope to achieve. While an educator's larger motivation may be to increase another person's knowledge or competence, neither outcome is possible unless learning happens first.

Learning is a process of forming new memories. For example, to say that a person learned that George Washington was the United States' first president is to say that they were exposed to information that led them to have a memory that they did not have before. Prior to the learning event, the person would not remember "George Washington" when asked about the nation's first president. After learning, they would have this memory. Learning occurs when new memories are formed. These new memories can be declarative or non-declarative.

Learning often manifests as a belief change. By belief, I mean a cognitively stored association that relates objects and attributes (e.g., "Anne believes that the climate is changing").[1] A person can hold a belief with certainty (i.e., they believe that the association in their memory is unconditionally true) or with uncertainty (i.e., they believe that an association in their memory is possibly true).

Many educators are motivated not by a desire to teach a prospective learner random facts but by a desire to change specific kinds of beliefs. History teachers seek to change beliefs about historical events, mathematicians seek to change students' beliefs about certain mathematical properties, and campaigners seek to change citizens' beliefs about whether or not to vote for a candidate.

By belief change, I mean an outcome of learning attempts that relates objects and attributes differently after an exposure to information than they were related before the exposure (e.g., "I used to believe that the sun rotates around the earth, now I believe the opposite"). Belief change refers not only to a mind that believes different things than it did before exposure to information, but also to a belief that is held with more (or less) certainty than before ("I used to believe that the earth rotates around the sun, now I am more certain"). For an educator's information to increase another person's knowledge (i.e., to cause new factive memories to form), belief change must occur.

Belief change is a product of biological processes within a brain. It requires alterations in the structure or performance of neurons within neural networks. For example, if you think "red" when I say "wagon," your reaction is a manifestation of a physical and chemical relationship between clusters and networks of brain cells that store "wagon" and "red" as relevant attributes.[2] So, if you did not initially know that a wagon could be red, and my presentation helps you to realize and later recall that a wagon can be red, the subsequent recollections are a consequence of networks and clusters of red-attribute-representing brain cells changing their physical or chemical relationships to networks of wagon-attribute-representing brain cells.[3]

Belief change occurs only if parts of these associational networks receive an electrochemical stimulus that produces physical growth in some of the networks' brain cells or changes in chemical activity within and across these networks.[4] This fueling process is propagated by blood flow variations that are propagated by the manner in which a person perceives stimuli. In other words, learning requires changes in physical objects and chemical relationships within a brain. If an educator provides information to a person and these physical and chemical changes do not occur, then belief change and learning do not occur.

Why is this information about cells and blood flow worth discussing? The answer is that it sets core biological ground rules about learning to which every educator is subject. So, if an educator wants her information to become another person's knowledge, the information must induce this kind of fuel to go to the needed brain areas.[5] While this fueling process has complex properties, one property deserves our focus. *Fuel requires attention.*

If, for example, we can get a prospective learner to pay attention to an educator's claim about a behavior that makes a cancer less likely, clusters of brain cells that represent the behavior are being simultaneously activated with clusters of brain cells that represent the prospective learner's existing knowledge about cancer avoidance. Attention provides the fuel that can make cancer avoidance come to mind *the next time* the prospective learner thinks about the behavior.

When a person devotes mental effort to thinking about an association, this effort can change the properties of physical structures and networks within their brains. If this explanation is too technical, a different way to think about it is to treat learning like exercising. When a person does certain types of exercises, muscles get bigger and corresponding muscle systems react with greater speed and force in subsequent activities. Physical properties of learning have similar attributes. In learning, the mental "exercise" associated with paying attention to a stimulus can make memory of the stimulus a bigger part of their subsequent beliefs. This change allows learners to access and use the information with greater speed and force in subsequent activities.

In sum, for educators to provide information that becomes valuable knowledge and competence for others, the information must attract enough attention to allow their audience to change relevant beliefs.

7B. ATTENTIONAL CAPACITY IS EXTRAORDINARILY LIMITED

In this section, I examine challenges associated with getting prospective learners to pay attention to new information. A key conclusion is that people ignore most of the information that is presented to them. This outcome does not indicate a character flaw. It is better described as a matter of biology. In other words, people can't help but ignore almost all the information to which they are exposed.

One way to understand the limits of attention is to examine studies of *working memory*.[6] Working memory is a brain system that provides temporary storage for new information while a person is processing it. Working memory's capacity is very limited. As neuroscientists Earl Miller and Timothy Buschman (2015: 122) describe:

> Working memory holds the contents of our thoughts. It acts as a mental sketchpad, providing a surface on which we can place transitory information to hold it "in mind." We can then "think" by manipulating this information, such as by combining it with other items or transforming it into something new.... Given its fundamental role in thought it is surprising that working memory has such a severely limited capacity: we can hold only a few thoughts in our consciousness at once. In other words, the surface of our mental sketchpad is quite small.

Scientists have evaluated working memory's limits in many ways. One famous study used reading comprehension tests to produce a widely cited result: seven plus or minus two chunks.[7] While other evaluations of working memory produce different estimates, all estimates find its capacity to be of similar magnitude.[8] An implication of research on this topic is that all people, whether experts or novices in a particular field, can pay attention to only a small number of stimuli at any time.

A chunk is a conceptual unit—a memory or belief that is recognized without further processing. The unit can represent a single attribute of a single object or it can bring to mind a particular relationship between attributes and objects (e.g., instantly seeing "Mickey Mouse" when exposed to a particular arrangement of white lines and black circles). What differentiates experts and novices is that an expert's few chunks store more information about pertinent relationships than do a novice's few chunks. Experts outperform novices at tasks not because their working memories produce more chunks, but because a typical expert's chunk carries more relevant information than a novice's chunk.[9]

A chess expert, for example, instantly draws inferences from an arrangement of pieces on a chessboard that a novice does not. Producing beliefs about "next moves" is likely to require fewer of an expert's chunks than a novice's. For example, an expert can look at a chessboard and instantly imagine their next three moves. A novice can look at the same board and ask themselves "What do I do with piece that looks like a horse?"

Put another way, there are some conclusions about next moves that would require a novice to piece together and process relatively elementary information about the game—as in effortful attempts to remember the distinctive moves that different chess pieces are allowed to make. Such processing would involve multiple chunks. An expert would have the sensation of simply knowing these conclusions (as a result of previous learning). This realization would involve fewer chunks.

So, when an educator attempts to convey a particular piece of information to another person at a particular moment, the information is competing for one of the person's few available open slots in working memory with all other phenomena to which that person can pay attention. However, some educators believe that, because their motives are so benevolent or because their expertise is so great, the laws of nature that govern human attention—and limit chunk capacity—will make an exception for them. They believe that audiences will "hang on my every word." *In most cases, such an outcome is a physical impossibility.* Regardless of how hard prospective learners try, they can pay attention to relatively few things at any one time.

An implication of working memory's limits is that prospective learners are forced to ignore almost every piece of information to which they are exposed. This implication makes it physically impossible for an audience to "hang on a speaker's every word" (except in cases when a speaker says almost nothing). These limits also prevent prospective learners from paying attention to most of what is said or shown during a presentation.

To see just how limiting this cognitive attribute is, imagine that I am onstage giving a presentation and you are in the audience. At every moment, I am competing for one of the seven-or-so slots in your working memory. The competition is fierce. Seminar rooms have many other things to which attention can be paid, such as light fixtures, signs about safety on the walls, floors or rugs that have interesting designs, other people in the room, things that other people are wearing, things that other people are doing, how other people smell, seats with multiple moving parts, the hum of a heating source or air conditioner, or the hum of a projector, and so on. If any of these attributes of the room capture your attention, it takes one of the seven-or-so parking spots in your working memory and makes it harder for you to pay attention to me.

But the competition is fiercer than this. Not only is my presentation competing for attention with myriad objects in the room, it is also competing with objects outside the room. These objects include: what you had for dinner last night, details about an appointment later in the day, a call that you need to make, a vacation that you would like to go on, or perhaps a scene from a movie that you saw last week. Even if you are engaged in some aspect of my presentation, I may use a phrase or show you an image that brings some of these other things to mind. If you think of them, they take one or more of the seven-or-so parking spots and make it harder for you to attend to other things.

Things that I have recently said or shown also compete with what I am saying or showing at any particular moment. From the perspective of working memory, what I am saying to you "right now" is competing with what I am saying to you "right now" and what I am saying to you "right now." So, if during "right now" number 1, I said something very interesting that you attempted to relate to your previous beliefs, that attempt is taking up one or more of the seven-or-so spots. If you are sufficiently engaged with the content of the first "right now," it will be difficult, if not impossible, for you to pay attention to the content of my subsequent utterances. For all presentations that are longer than a few seconds, even the most committed listener can attend to only a fraction of the content. Moreover, even the most committed listener can remember only a fraction of any content to which they attend. No educator is exempt from these limits.

Human brains have evolved to direct attention to a select set of environmental stimuli and to block out just about everything else.[10] Similar biological processes cause people to forget almost everything to which they have paid attention.[11] These facts of human cognition are the result of basic biological forces. They are not changeable. This is our reality as educators. Now the question is, "How should we respond?"

7C. CORE CONCERNS

To what information will prospective learners pay the most attention? Many educators with whom I have worked share a theory about this topic. They base their presentational strategies on the theory that if they tell an audience what they know, the inherent quality and virtue of their claims will automatically lead the audience to pay attention. But, as we know, audiences cannot pay attention to all available information. *We need a different theory.*

I offer an alternative theory. It is based on the premise that information is more likely to earn another person's attention if a prospective learner perceives it as providing sufficient net benefits. Educators can generate this perception and increase their odds of increasing others' knowledge or competence by presenting information in ways that prospective learners perceive as directly relevant to their immediate needs or core concerns.[12]

Supporting this theory are decades of research on the brain's automatic and executive control functions. For example, when a person perceives a threatening stimulus, these functions induce selective attention to external stimuli associated with the threat.[13] Information that a person perceives as being immediately relevant to their ability to achieve high-value aspirations or ward off significant threats is far more likely than stimuli lacking these attributes to win their attention.[14] People are hardwired to attend to stimuli that that they perceive as very likely to vastly increase their pain or pleasure. Hence, increasing knowledge or competence requires educators to present materials in ways that induce these perceptions.

At the same time, many educators want their presentations to stay true to the content of a particular knowledge base. Consider, for example, the challenges faced by educators who seek to convey scientific information to broader audiences. There are many instances in which science helps people produce substantial individual and social benefits. However, scientists who attempt to convey such insights are often ignored.[15]

In some cases, the science communicator's challenge is easily explained. Scientists think about important phenomena in complex ways. When discussing these phenomena with one another, they develop new language or use existing language in unusual ways. Although such conversations allow scientists to have very precise conversations, the same conversations are often impossible for non-scientists to interpret.

As a result, descriptions of scientific activity that scientists see as groundbreaking can be perceived by others as disconnected from the real world and as "failing to get to the point."[16] Prospective learners who have this view have less motivation to pay attention.[17] When such motivations are absent, the seeds for communicative failure are sown. Many educators who are not scientists encounter a similar situation—they understand topics in great detail, but encounter audiences with limited interest in detailed explanations.

Educators are more likely to gain others attention if they convey material in ways that speak directly to prospective learners' fears and aspirations.

It is important not just to present information that is correct, but to present it in ways that an audience perceives as directly relevant to their core concerns. By *core concerns*, I mean the concerns that prospective learners enter a room with and concerns for which new information has the potential to cause outcomes that the prospective learners recognize as substantially beneficial.

Consider, for example, scientists who want to persuade broad audiences that climate change is relevant to certain lifestyle choices and policy decisions. Scientists who work in this field know that climate systems and climate-weather relations are complex. If an educator's objective is to increase particular competences related to knowledge of climate and weather, success depends on the extent to which (a) the audience perceives the information as sufficiently beneficial to their core concerns to prompt attention, and (b) the information to which they attend is necessary or sufficient to increase the competence at hand.

With such goals in mind, it can be a mistake to use an abstract presentation (say, about global climate theories) to convince people to make concrete lifestyle changes. To most individuals, the benefits of responding to global trends by reducing their own emissions will initially seem to pose definite costs in exchange for distant, abstract, and uncertain benefits. For most people, carbon dioxide and other greenhouse gases are largely invisible. Melting polar ice caps are far away from where they live and work. Moreover, there is substantial disagreement among the most respected climate modelers about what would happen if emissions were cut by 20 or 50 percent today (i.e., how long it would take for currently deleterious effects of emissions to dissipate). Asking people to make certain and concrete sacrifices (e.g., paying higher costs for electricity) in exchange for distant, abstract, and uncertain benefits is not typically an effective recipe for belief change. It's a bit like asking a farmer to give up his only cow in exchange for "magic beans." So, if the information is presented too abstractly, prospective learners are likely to ignore it.

If the information is also threatening, people may also generate counterarguments. In a phenomenon commonly called *motivated reasoning*, people process information in accordance with what they want to believe about it.[18] In other words, prospective learners actively interpret new information as confirming what they already believe (e.g., "global warming is a hoax").

Educators can increase their odds of winning battles for attention, and of more effectively managing the effects of motivated reasoning, by presenting materials that are directly relevant to an audience's core concerns.[19] Using human scale examples, analogies, and metaphors as foundational components of educational strategies can be powerful means of achieving these ends.[20] One example of such a strategy, developed by Climate Central, a nonprofit science communication organization on whose board I serve, seeks to draw attention to possible effects of climate change on local communities. One of its topical emphases is the human consequences of rising sea levels. Although rising seas can be described as an abstract global phenomenon, scientists can also use models to estimate the effect of sea level rise on specific neighborhoods and communities.[21] I encouraged the organization in its early days to present these effects at the most local levels possible. I offered evidence that people would be more likely to pay attention to the information if they could identify potential effects of climate change on places about which they have strong feelings—places like their home, their children's schools, and other emotionally salient landmarks.[22] Climate Central's success at conveying these increasingly personal climate change implications has gained new attention for this kind of information in a number of high-traffic communicative environments.[23] These presentations have also helped many members of the media explain how rising seas are linked to the probability of hurricanes and other extreme weather events that have wreaked havoc on large metropolitan areas.[24]

In sum, learning requires attention, and attention requires that a listener see a piece of information as directly relevant to a choice or outcome about which they care. Educators who understand these requirements should be motivated to take time to learn about an audience's concerns (i.e., where "in the woods" prospective learners are starting out). Educators who obtain such knowledge will have an increased capacity to discover their prospective learners' unachieved aspirations, unresolved fears, and related phenomena. If an educator uses that knowledge to provide information that an audience perceives as essential, then the educator is more likely to have an audience that is paying attention.

Alan Andreasen reaches similar conclusions.[25] His examinations of communication organizations that seek to improve health outcomes reveals a common attribute of organizations that, while well-intentioned, are ineffective. He finds that:

> Too many organizations . . . are really mired in an organization centered mindset that sees their mission as inherently good and their lack of success as their customer's fault.[26]

These are organizations that conceive "of the customer as a target whose behavior is to be shaped to fit the organization's goals."[27] He compares these organizations to ones that see prospective learners as having "unique perceptions, needs and wants to which the marketer must adapt."[28] While this social marketing literature tends not to deal with the logic of competence described in earlier chapters or many of the challenges that politicized environments bring to educational contexts described here and in chapter 8, educators who focus on health-related topics may find Andreasen's studies useful.

More generally, the "sweet spot" for an educator is to offer information that is not only necessary or sufficient to increase a valuable type of knowledge relative to their competence criteria, but also perceived by prospective learners as sufficiently beneficial.[29] This perception is required even when the information is highly accurate and potentially relevant to the prospective learner's quality of life. If information has these qualities but a prospective learner does not perceive them, the information is likely to be ignored.

7D. WHY SOME EDUCATORS STRUGGLE TO UNDERSTAND ATTENTION

Attention is a necessary condition for learning. Attentive capacity is scarce when compared to the range of things to which prospective learners can pay attention at any moment. As neuroscientists Earl Miller and Timothy Buschman describe:

> We have seen that despite our impression that we can store and perceive a significant amount of visual information at once, this is not the case. We can only simultaneously think about a very limited amount of information. Our brains knit together these sips of information to give us the illusion that we have a much larger bandwidth.[30]

Hence, a critical challenge for educators who want to increase others' knowledge and competence is to simply break through—to offer the kinds of information that will induce people to turn away from all the other stimuli that could occupy their thoughts. By paying attention to the topic of attention, educators can learn to present information that makes their knowledge more relevant and more memorable for more people.

If this conclusion seems obvious or easy to reach, then a lingering challenge for those of us who seek to improve various kinds of civic education is the fact that our target audiences appear to ignore many, if not most, of our attempts to convey information that we believe can increase their knowledge and competence. When confronted with communicative failures of this kind, some educators have a simple explanation: "It's them."

If only the audience had better character.
If only the audience was less apathetic.
If only the public would get up off its collective "couch" and see the
    importance of the information that we are conveying.

My experience with these claims is that they do not stand up well under examination. These expressions are often attempts to absolve the claimant of responsibility for a communicative failure. More importantly for our purposes in this book, these claims are of little help in improving educational outcomes. Educators who want better outcomes can achieve them by aligning their strategies with the realities about attention described above.

Still, some critics of the public's political knowledge and competence persist in claiming that those of us who want to increase others' knowledge and competence needn't be concerned with conveying information in ways that reflect the biological and psychological properties of attention. As columnist Rick Shenkman contends:

> Studies show that students who take civics courses in high school usually forget what they learn after a few years. This is an argument in favor of doing more civics not less. Students should be required to take civics courses not only in high school but in college as well.[31]

This is an odd bit of logic when you consider the fact that the same students do not forget other things learned in school—such as how to add.

Like all of us, students are more likely to remember information that they perceive as advancing their core concerns. This part of human biology does not change its rules for civics teachers or science experts. Part of the problem facing civics education today is inconsistent effort put toward presenting information in ways that are relevant and memorable to prospective learners. What we know about attention and belief change tells us that forcing students to do more of what hasn't worked in the past is not likely to improve educational outcomes.

Why is it so tempting for experts in various fields to have misleading intuitions about why prospective learners are uninterested in their information? A common source of such errors is the visual and oral cues that people offer one another when communicating.[32] People nod at certain moments to signal that they are paying attention to a speaker and comprehending their message. When others are speaking, for example, we often nod after they pause and occasionally interject with phrases like "yes" and "uh huh." We sometimes augment these signals with eye contact (well, some of us do).

But people who seek to act in socially desirable ways, or people who believe that offering an affirmative comprehension signal will allow them to leave an unwanted conversation, also send such signals.[33] In other words, people who have become inattentive to the content of a speaker's utterances, and who recognize that the speaker has paused or stopped speaking, often give visual cues to suggest that they are paying more attention than is actually the case. As a result, speakers sometimes mistake inattention for attention and become overconfident about the extent to which others are truly paying attention to them.[34]

Feeding this overconfidence further are phenomena such as elevated social status. For example, many people who seek to increase others' knowledge and competence view themselves as being knowledgeable and competent in their domain of expertise. Many people earn higher status within organizations because they actually possess these attributes. In some cases, this knowledge and expertise induce others *to appear to be very attentive* to the presentations of high-status experts. This is particularly true of people who need the expert's support for a desired promotion or other personal or career advancement.

In some cases, experts become accustomed to being in the company of people who already agree with them, or who have incentives to appear agreeable as a way of advancing their own agendas. An expert who spends a lot of time in such company may come to believe that they are especially good at gaining the attention of intelligent people. As a result, they may conclude that they are naturally entitled to an audience's sustained attention when discussing the subjects of their expertise.

If an expert has such beliefs and comes to disdain broader audiences who pay less attention to them than their supporters and sycophants—if they treat audiences who are less attentive to them as an aberration in a natural communicative order in which they *deserve* others' attention—they may forfeit valuable opportunities to offer valuable information to others. In other words, when an expert is in the frequent company of people who have incentives to present themselves as being more interested in the expert than they actually are, the expert can form false beliefs about how others are receiving his information. These false beliefs, in turn, can limit the expert's communicative effectiveness.[35]

I am no stranger to this phenomenon. As a college professor, I am regularly in the presence of people who have strong incentives to pay attention to what I am saying. Students, younger faculty, people whose research I may be able to support, and so on perceive that their grades, tenure, pay raises, and future professional opportunities depend on staying in my good graces. They pay attention to me much more than they would absent the dependencies, and some have incentives to appear to be paying more attention to me than they actually are. I accept that this is my reality, but I try to stay grounded by remembering this fact when attempting to read others' reactions to my presentations. In general, I believe that it is important for people who spend time in high-status contexts to realize that many of our audiences are effectively captive—and to use that information to calibrate our expectations when providing information to "non-captives."

When attempting to convey information to less-captive audiences, you and I and everyone else are participating in a battle for attention. If we want to earn another person's attention, we need to learn enough about their fears and aspirations to provide information that they can't help but want to think about. We need to understand the kinds of information that reflect their core concerns. Providing information that has these qualities increases the likelihood of winning needed attention competitions—and provides opportunities for educators to convey information that increases valuable forms of knowledge and competence.

7E. CONCLUSION

Many educators believe that if they tell an audience what they know, the inherent quality and virtue of their claims will automatically lead the audience to change what they do. In this sense, educators sometimes think of the things that they want others to know in the same way that many people think about their new cars. Many new car owners admire and enjoy the beauty of the instruments they have acquired. They spend time imagining the wonderful places that their new cars can take them. They are sometimes inspired to go for rides just to show off their new machines to other people.

While some people are car enthusiasts, most people spend little time thinking about cars. Even for people who do think about cars, most do not spend time thinking about all cars or about a stranger's passing car. Think for a moment about your car, if you have one. The fact of the matter is that nearly all the time, nearly all people are spending no effort thinking about your car.

You may say, "This makes sense. Why would I spend any time thinking about a stranger's car? It is irrelevant to me." That is a good point. Keep it in mind because it is exactly the kind of point that many educators can benefit from contemplating with respect to their own areas of expertise.

Just as new car owners may think of the heads that will turn as their shiny new vehicles roll down the street, many educators are convinced that their ideas are so powerful and attractive that heads that will turn and minds will change as soon as they put their ideas on display. However, if an educator cannot present his wares in ways that reflect the audience's aspirations and concerns, then the audience will treat an educator's information as they treat most strangers' cars—as not worthy of their attention.

In general, the audience is the ultimate arbiter of what is relevant to them. To the extent that paying attention to information requires a conscious commitment to do so, the decision to pay attention is ultimately theirs. This is why "the sweet spot" is the target at which educators should aim. To increase competence, educators need information that has two attributes: It should be necessary or sufficient to increase competence if it received sufficient attention *and* it actually elicits the needed attention.

In sum, the importance of a piece of information to an educator, and the logical relationship of that information to a desired knowledge or competence, *is irrelevant* to increasing a prospective learner's competence if that learner never sees the information as worthy of their attention. There are always multiple phenomena competing to get through any person's very limited attentive bottlenecks. Therefore, for any of us to educate others, battles for attention must be waged—and won.

8

Building Source Credibility

If a person pays attention to a piece of information, they form a judgment about it. In many cases, the judgment is that they do not need to pay more attention to it. In some cases, however, the judgment is that they want to think more about the new information and attempt to integrate its content into what they already believe. What judgments prospective learners form about information affects when and how an educator can increase others' knowledge and competence.

Many civic educators struggle with the fact that information in politicized environments is often judged differently than information offered in other environments. Words and images in politicized environments are scrutinized, interpreted, and attacked in ways that rarely, if ever, occur in other educational settings. Educators who are used to communicating in nonpolitical environments, and who then wade into a politicized environment, often find these dynamics surprising. Actually, "surprising" is a gentle way to put it.

Many educators learn that educational strategies that work well in classrooms or at professional conferences are disastrous when attempted in more emotionally charged and politicized environments. Many educators who venture into more politicized contexts find that their information is ignored. Others find their words misinterpreted and twisted. Many have difficulty explaining why their attempts to convey their expertise to others in these important environments were not more constructively received.

In this chapter, I examine how communication dynamics change as learning environments become more politicized. To help educators better manage these dynamics, I highlight two factors that affect source credibility in political contexts. These factors are *perceived common interests* and *perceived relative knowledge*.[1] Each factor has significant effects on how prospective learners interpret words and images. Educators who understand these dynamics can better identify information that prospective learners are—and are not—likely to believe. Such knowledge can help educators increase knowledge and competence more effectively—and reduce unwanted surprises.

The chapter's main lessons are as follows:

- When prospective learners can interpret information in multiple ways, their perceptions of an educator's motives and expertise can affect whether or not they pay attention to the information and what inferences they draw from it.
- If a prospective learner perceives an educator as benefiting from the same types of outcomes as they do, and as knowing more than they do about how to achieve those outcomes, then the learner has greater motive to believe the educator's information.
- When a prospective learner's perceptions of an educator's motives and expertise differ from the educator's true motives and expertise, the perceptions prevail in affecting how the learner treats the information.
- An implication is that educators can more effectively increase others' knowledge and competence by presenting information that is not only factually accurate, but that also helps to establish their own credibility.

8A. THE CHALLENGE OF "MORE THAN ONE MEANING"

Though our perception convinces us beyond doubt that we see the visual world as one coherent whole, we actually see a series of snapshots from which we construct a unified view of the world in our brains. Wurtz (2015: 32).

If an educator is to increase another person's knowledge or competence, the information that they provide must produce certain changes in the other person's brain. These changes require altered activation patterns within and across networks of brain cells. If a presentation of information does not cause such alterations, audiences do not form or reinforce memories of the information to which they are exposed. When no memories are formed or reinforced, learning does not occur.

As described in the previous chapter, these alterations require attention. In this chapter, I start from the point at which a person is paying attention to a piece of information that an educator is conveying and then focus on what happens next. To get a sense of the options available to prospective learners at such moments, consider the image in figure 8.1. My first question to you about the figure is: "What is it?" Here is a hint. It is an image whose earliest appearance is traced to the October 23, 1892, edition of a German satirical publication called *Fliegende Blätter* ("Flying Leaves"). A similar image also featured prominently in work by the psychologist Joseph Jastrow in 1899 and by Ludwig Wittgenstein in his 1953 book *Philosophical Investigations*.[2]

The answer to the question is that the image is a rabbit-duck. To see that it's a duck, notice that the curvature of the right side of the image is the back of the duck's head. The two parts of the image projecting out to the left are the duck's bill. To see that the image is also a rabbit, notice the small break in the curvature on the right side of the image. The area above that break is the rabbit's nose. The two parts of the image projecting out to the left are the rabbit's ears.

I show you this image because it has multiple meanings. This is an unusual attribute for an image to have. Typically, we are used to an image having a single meaning. When you see a photo of a colleague's head and shoulders, you typically think "that's my colleague."

Such exact relationships (one meaning to one image) stand in contrast to how we interpret most words. Consider, for example, the word "duck." One meaning of this word describes the animal that you may have seen in figure 8.1. The word has other meanings—including what a person does when trying to avoid being hit by a flying object. Words often have multiple meanings. Simple dictionaries reveal as much.

When a word has multiple meanings, educators cannot always assume that the thoughts that they have when using particular words (e.g., global warming) will correspond to the thoughts that other people have when they react to these words. Herein lies a critical challenge for educators.

FIGURE 8.1. Image from *Fliegende Blätter*, October 23, 1892. Source: http://diglit. ub.uni-heidelberg.de/diglit/fb97/0147?sid=8af6d821538a1926abf44c9a95c40951&zooml evel=2.

When interpreting new information and attempting to assign meaning to it, people compare attributes of the information to attributes of beliefs and concepts that they already have in their minds.[3] In other words, what a person learns from information is influenced not only by the information's content, but also by their prior memories.[4] This is one reason why people who are very knowledgeable about a subject can learn different things from a single piece of information than can people who are less knowledgeable. These effects increase as a person finds information difficult to understand. If, for example, a person sees information as too abstract or as not "getting to the point", the beliefs and feelings that they had prior to encountering the information have a larger effect on how they interpret the new information—if they pay attention to such information at all.[5]

If, in addition to seeing information as abstract, a prospective learner sees information as threatening, a common reaction is to ignore it.[6] This reaction is like a flight response to a threatening stimulus. A related reaction to threatening information is to generate internal counterarguments. That is, individuals search their memories for reasons why it is okay to discount, reinterpret, or ignore information that is potentially threatening and not clearly necessary (from their perspective) to accomplish vital goals.[7]

When information can be evaluated in different ways, prospective learners look for environmental signals about which interpretation is in their interest to adopt. For many prospective learners, beliefs about an educator's motives and expertise can influence their interpretation. In the next section, I show that whether a prospective learner interprets information as an educator intends, or interprets it in a way that is contrary to an educator's objectives, depends on the extent to which a prospective learner views the educator as *credible*.

8B. BUILDING CREDIBILITY

Because so much of what people learn from new information depends on how they interpret it, educators who are attempting to convey information to unfamiliar audiences are often surprised at how their information is received. This is particularly true of educators who seek to increase knowledge and competence in politicized environments.

By politicized environments, I mean the forums that societies build to deal with questions about social organization and collective action that are not easily resolved through less formal interactions. Educators can benefit from understanding that many issues that are labeled "political" are not inherently political. An issue is political because salient social disagreements about it persist.[8] When issues cease to have this quality, they lose their "political" character.

Child labor, for example, was once a contested political issue in American politics. It was political because people held and were willing to publicly voice different points of view about the propriety of American children working long hours in factories.[9] Because this notion is hard for some people to fathom today, let me briefly describe the competing arguments for and against child labor from its "political" era.

Prior to the industrial age, American children worked on family farms and helped with other endeavors critical to life. Many people who were familiar with these practices argued that it was natural, and even developmentally beneficial, to extend the tradition of children contributing to family income by having them work in factories and mills. It is worth noting that this tradition was widespread, and available evidence suggests that it was broadly accepted.

Over time, however, a social consensus emerged that working in factories was too dangerous and left children prone to many forms of exploitation. This consensus became codified in law and policy and eventually implemented in practice. Now, few people consider the issue politicized. It became a broadly consensual moral issue, rather than a political issue. Indeed, if a major politician in America today were to propose employing 7-year olds in factories and paying them $1 per hour as a way to grow the economy, they would be roundly ridiculed. Even though factories are safer today than they were in the 19th century, there is no tangible support for even discussing such proposals in modern political contexts.

What about educators who find themselves in situations where issues relevant to their attempts to increase knowledge and competence are seen as "political" rather than as strictly moral or ethical? How can they provide information that helps others? The rest of this chapter focuses on how educators can build and maintain the type of credibility that can help them achieve their educational goals in more politicized environments. To achieve this goal, I draw on a large body of research that examines how people choose what and whom to believe in situations where information can be interpreted in different ways. Today, many educators forfeit opportunities to increase others' knowledge or competence because they have incorrect beliefs about how others judge and interpret different kinds of information. This section of the book offers information that can help educators reduce the range of circumstances in which incorrect beliefs about credibility cause them to effectively defeat themselves.

For example, many educators assume that elements of a speaker or writer's true character (e.g., honest), demographic attributes (e.g., female), or academic pedigree (e.g., "I have a Ph.D. in physics" or "I have written highly cited work on climate change") are sufficient for a person to be considered a credible source of information. *These assumptions are incorrect.* Although there are conditions under which such factors correlate with source credibility, these factors do not determine source credibility.

Source credibility is more accurately described as a perception that is bestowed by an audience.[10] Source credibility represents the extent to which an audience *perceives* a communicator as someone whose words or interpretations they would benefit from believing. A wide range of studies show that when an audience's perception of an educator differs from the educator's true attributes, the perception, and not the reality, determines the extent to which the audience will believe what they are reading, seeing, or hearing.[11]

Analyses of such situations show that if a prospective learner perceives a speaker to have sufficiently conflicting interests or no expertise on the issue at hand, then they will discount or ignore any utterance from that speaker.[12] The basic idea is that if someone whom you trust knows things that you do not, then you have an incentive to believe what they say. If either condition fails to hold, the incentive dissipates.

Diverse kinds of research on the topic of source credibility document this correspondence.[13] Mathew McCubbins and I, for example, examined a range of interactions between speakers and listeners.[14] In these experiments, the speaker is the "source" and "credibility" reflects the extent to which the listener believes what the speaker says. Listeners face a decision (e.g., to support or oppose a particular policy proposal) that the speaker may be able to influence. The speaker may possess information that helps listeners make a competent decision. A focal variable in the analysis is the speaker's stake in the listener's decision. The speaker may, for example, benefit from leading listeners to make decisions that they would *not* make if they were better informed. In other words, there are some conditions in which speakers have incentives to mislead listeners (e.g., the choice that is best for the listener is worse for the speaker and vice versa). In other cases, the speaker is motivated to convey truthful information.

This kind of analysis produces testable hypotheses about conditions under which listeners find speakers credible. To describe these findings with greater accuracy, a few definitions are needed. *Commonality of interests* is the extent to which the listener and speaker want similar outcomes from the speaker's communicative attempt. For example, the speaker seeks to tell the listener about facts that will not only help the listener make a competent choice, but also make the speaker better off as well. Another critical factor is perceived relative expertise. *Relative expertise* refers to the extent to which the speaker knows things about the consequences of the listener's choice that the listener does not know.

The main implications of our work for source credibility are as follows:

- Actual relative expertise is neither necessary nor sufficient for source credibility.
- Actual common interests are neither necessary nor sufficient for source credibility.
- The following conditions are individually necessary and collectively sufficient for source credibility: A listener must perceive the speaker as having sufficiently common interests *and* relative expertise. Interest perceptions can come from speaker attributes or from external forces that affect their incentives—forces such as sufficiently high penalties for lying.

The intuition is that if someone wants outcomes that also benefit you and if they know things that you do not, then you have an incentive to believe what they say. If either condition fails to hold, the incentive dissipates. For example, if you believe that you and I have the same preferences regarding the frequency of a particular toxin in a given water supply, and if you believe that I have knowledge on this topic that helps you make better decisions, then you will interpret my claims differently than if you believed me to be ignorant on this topic or believed us to have conflicting interests. By similar logic, my interpretation of your claim about the effectiveness of a policy may depend on whether I know you to be conservative or liberal.

This type of analysis implies that if a prospective learner *perceives* an educator to have sufficiently conflicting interests or no expertise on the issue at hand, then they will discount or ignore any utterance from that educator on that issue. Note that the key word in this sentence is *perceives*. As mentioned above, when an audience's perception of an educator differs from the educator's true attributes, the perception, and not the reality, determines the extent to which the audience will believe what they are reading, seeing, or hearing.

The last bullet point on the list above describes *external forces* that can affect a prospective listener's perceptions of an educator's interest commonality and relevant expertise. Penalties for lying, the possibility that others can verify whether a speaker's claims are true or false, and factors that make communication costly can affect a speaker's motivation and incentives.

These factors can induce a speaker who might otherwise try to mislead a listener to speak the truth instead.

Consider, for example, a listener who encounters a speaker in a courthouse where there are significant penalties for lying, such as perjury fines. A listener in this context can make one of two inferences from a speaker's claims. One inference is that the speaker is telling the truth. The other inference is that the speaker is telling the kind of lie that benefits them more than the risks and costs associated with perjuring themselves. In this context, the prospect of perjury penalties can substitute for the perception of common interests and give the listener sufficient reason to believe the speaker. This effect can occur, for example, when the perjury fines render the most damaging lies not worth telling.

Experimental research demonstrates the predictive accuracy of the conditions for credibility just described.[15] While much of this research takes place in laboratories, other research occurs in more realistic environments. In one experiment, I randomly exposed 1,464 participants in a nationwide survey experiment to different combinations of well-known political commentators (e.g., Rush Limbaugh) and issue positions (e.g., supporting or opposing expanded spending on prisons or no position).[16] Subjects were then asked to state their own positions on the issues and to answer questions about the commentator to whose issue position they were exposed. I found that subject perceptions of the commentator's interest commonality and relative expertise on the issue were the primary determinants of whether or not the subject's issue position followed that of their randomly assigned speaker. Other factors commonly associated with political persuasiveness, such as partisan identification or political ideology, *had no significant explanatory power once perceived common interests and perceived expertise were accounted for.* The opposite was not true. Perceived common interests and perceived relative expertise had significant associations with following the speaker's advice even after accounting for party or ideology. These results attest to the centrality of perceived common interests and perceived relative expertise in explaining source credibility. If partisanship, ideology, ethnicity, or other factors are not signaling common interests or relevant expertise to prospective learners then they are not contributing to a speaker's credibility.

Collectively, this research shows that perceptible speaker attributes (such as partisanship or celebrity status) affect credibility *only if* they change prospective learners' perceptions of a speaker's common interests or relative expertise. These findings imply that educators can establish greater credibility with prospective learners by relating their interest in an educational topic to their desired audience's likely interests. An example of this strategy is found in the opening minutes of the Geoffrey Haines-Stiles-produced television program "Earth: The Operator's Manual." Geologist Richard Alley is the program's host. The program is an accessible and visually striking presentation about climate change's causes and consequences.

In the program's opening minutes, Alley describes his background and why he cares about the topic. This vignette is structured to establish Alley's credibility—particularly among potentially skeptical audiences. In the introduction, Alley reveals himself to have valuable expertise on the topic, as well as common interests with some typically skeptical groups:

> I'm a registered Republican, play soccer on Saturday, and go to church on Sundays. I'm a parent and a professor. I worry about jobs for my students and my daughter's future. I've been a proud member of the UN Panel on Climate Change and I know the risks. I've worked for an oil company, and know how much we all need energy. And the best science shows we'll be better off if we address the twin stories of climate change and energy. And that the sooner we move forward, the better.[17]

Key moments in this introduction are Alley's identification as a Republican and his description of himself as doing things that are associated with people who are often skeptical of such science (e.g., working for an oil company). Actions like Alley's can help an audience discover common ground with an educator and establish credibility-boosting perceptions.

Reinforcing this strategy was the producer's decision to focus the segment following Alley's introduction on the acceptance of key parts of climate science within the US military. In the second segment, a high ranking official cited military acceptance of core tenets of climate science as being so comprehensive that important strategic decisions regarding troop location, supply routes, and certain intelligence projections are based on it.

Conveying such facts can help counter stereotypes of climate scientists as too liberal or too idealistic to convey the research's implications objectively. Consider, in contrast, a presentation on the same topic that does not divulge this type of information about the people presented as experts in the documentary. Absent this information, the experts' motives would be more likely to remain a mystery—and the audience would be more likely to fill the void with their own stereotypes about people who make claims about climate. This is why Haines-Stiles's decision on how to open his documentary as he did gives it greater potential to reach new audiences. If an audience is not predisposed to perceive climate scientists as credible, the opening moments of a presentation can give them a new reason to do so.

Frank Luntz's *Words That Work* (2007) offers parallel lessons. Luntz is, in many respects, America's most influential political wordsmith. He has worked mostly with Republican candidates and conservative organizations to develop ways of describing issues that move people to feel differently about them. While Luntz's work often infuriates liberals (e.g., coming up with the term "death panels" to describe entities that make decisions on which health procedures to pay for), I know many people on the left who wish Luntz was on their side instead.

Luntz's writings offer advice about how to convey certain types of political information more effectively. His advice includes principles such as "use small words," "use short sentences," "credibility is as important as philosophy," and "speak aspirationally". His mantra ("it's not what you say, it's what people hear") is consistent with the main lessons of this chapter and book: Speak directly to people's core concerns in ways that motivate them to connect the content of new information to the beliefs and feelings they already have. This is more effective than hitting an audience with a list of technically correct but dry and abstract claims.

My final example in this chapter is a personal one. Beyond the models, experiments, and surveys that I have conducted on this topic, I have worked with a diverse range of organizations to help them convey information (mostly from science) in politicized environments. It has been a life-changing experience, and the evidence suggests that I have been able to help a good number of people communicate important ideas more effectively. On one such occasion in 2005, I gave an opening presentation at a conference in Aspen, Colorado. The conference included many of the country's leading climate scientists, representatives from industry, the media, leaders of both major political parties, and leaders from a number of national religious organizations.[18]

After my talk, a number of the religious leaders approached me. One asked, "If you were going to write a sermon about climate change, how would you do it?" This particular leader was from a denomination that, at the time, was known for its skepticism about climate change being real and human-caused. Before I tell you how I answered that question, I should note that I grew up in a small town. There are many important topics on which I do not consider myself an expert—organized religion is among them. In fact, I had never been asked for any kind of advice by a major religious leader before. I was aware of these facts about myself at the moment I was asked the question. My memory of the sequence remains vivid. Despite these doubts, I recognized that my opening presentation was being very well received. My adrenaline was flowing. Moreover, it was clear that these gentlemen really wanted my advice. I, in turn, respected what they were trying to accomplish. So I gave it to them. My response to his question was, "I wouldn't do it."

Then, after a pause, I remember saying something very much like this:

> ... because your congregation probably does not perceive you as an expert on climate or science. So, if you told them that you were going to give a sermon about climate science, they might be confused and question whether you were really qualified to talk about the subject. Moreover, if you started discussing science terms and climate-related abstractions, a lot of your congregation would probably "tune out."[19]
>
> But would you consider a different idea? Do you have any sermons about shared responsibility of God's creations? Do you have one that every time you give it, the congregation is right there with you? Every time you deliver a punch line [yes, I am almost certain that I used this word—please accept my apologies], you can feel the energy in the room. You can sense that everyone in the chapel thinks that you are speaking directly to them as an individual and speaking directly to the wonderful things that you as a congregation share. I think that you should give a sermon about that. But when you get to one of the final punch lines—after you have been telling the story of shared values and shared responsibility for 10 or 20 minutes—then add "and that means that we are responsible for all of God's creations as well, including the environment." Then, talk about climate change and its potential effect and what your ministry can do to protect in a way that is completely in line with your faith's strong values.

I remember describing to the pastor and the other leaders the difference between "building a long bridge" to get you to where you want to go and "building a short bridge" to exactly the same place. In this case, the "long bridge" was the pastor attempting to convince his congregation that he was a credible source of information on climate science. The "short bridge" is the pastor reminding his congregation of their deeply shared interests and how those interests inform environmental stewardship. On the short bridge, the connections to what prospective learners already believe is readily apparent and they, in turn, don't have to work as hard to get to the pastor's desired destination.

The group of us then worked on variations of this idea throughout the day. At this time, I learned that other people were having similar conversations. They developed the relationship that I described in more powerful ways than I could have imagined at that moment. Within a few years, a number of religious organizations for whom environmental stewardship is a core concern used this strategy to more effectively relate climate matters to their faith (see, e.g., The Evangelical Climate Initiative, 2006). Credibility matters.

8C. CONCLUSION

The requirements for educational success in political environments can be very different than in environments that many educators find more familiar. Given the frequent presence of deep value conflicts among political combatants, understanding how to build source credibility is critical for those who seek to increase knowledge and competence in politicized environments. If a prospective learner perceives an educator as lacking sufficient credibility, then she is less likely to take the educator's information seriously. This is true even if the educator actually possesses information that can increase the prospective learner's competence at a highly valued task. That is why many educators can benefit by understanding where source credibility comes from. That is also why this chapter offers advice about how educators can build and maintain credibility-boosting perceptions.

Educators who demonstrate that they share important interests with their audiences, and who conduct themselves in ways that audiences correlate with expertise, give audiences a reason to believe their explanations. Research on topics such as reputation and interpersonal influence imply that consistent demonstrations of common interests and relative expertise are effective ways to maintain a credible reputation.[20] For educators in politicized environments, few assets are more valuable than this kind of reputation.

With this basic set of insights about credibility in hand, I would like to close this chapter with advice that I am often asked to give. The background for these requests is that I am often asked to speak to, or work with, people who want to educate others about some matter of politics or science. In these settings, I am often asked for strategic advice. I get questions like "How can we get an audience to be interested in X"? or "How can we get people to pay more attention to Y"? In almost all of these cases, the person or group asking the question has a story they want to tell. They want others to pay more attention to that story than they are currently doing.

One answer I often give is that "the audience is not intrinsically interested in having you tell *your* story. What they really want is for you to tell *their* story." In other words, *Can you stay true to the content of what you are trying to convey, but tell the story in a way that relates to your audience's core concerns and immediate needs?* Can you tell your story in ways that allow them to link your content to aspirations that you can help them achieve and to fears that you can help them mitigate?

My reason for giving advice like this is not moral or ethical, it is biological and psychological. For every person at every waking moment, attention is an incredibly scarce resource. Conscious and subconscious processes combine to give us amazing powers to ignore almost everything around us. Attention is directed only to phenomena that a person recognizes as highly relevant to their wants and needs. This is as true when we are the intended recipients of information as it is when we are attempting to educate others.

Regardless of how benevolent we perceive our motives to be, this part of human biology makes no exceptions for those of us who wish to provide others with important information. To educate, we have to break through these barriers to attention. Moreover, when we do break through, we have to offer information in ways that people find credible—something about the information has to trigger recognition of common interests or relative expertise. There is no other way to educate.

Note that my advice is not to "dumb down" what you are trying to convey. It is to "smarten up" about how your information will be received. This means learning enough about your audience to weave your information into the concerns that they had before they met you and the concerns to which they will return when your encounter ends.

For people who want to educate students, my advice means finding the intersection between your content and your prospective learners' desire to get a better grade, get a job, or change the world. For people who are seeking to educate working parents, it means finding the intersection between your content and their desire to make ends meet or provide for their children's future. For people who want to influence policymakers, it means finding the intersection between your content and the types of information that they need to more effectively serve their constituents and improve their leverage in legislative or bureaucratic negotiations. For scholars, this means that presentations that are well received at academic conferences almost certainly need to be altered for nonacademic audiences. I say none of this to devalue technical and academic presentations—*though a lot of them could use a little work*. I say this to help people become much more effective in offering information that can be of great value to others. (For further advice on this topic, see Lupia, 2013, or my National Academy of Science video at www.youtube.com/watch?v=UsYFa_abIeQ.)

The next chapters of this book offer additional ways for educators to provide information that matters. Specifically, chapters 9 through 13 provide a set of insights that can help educators more effectively draw prospective learners' attention and affect important judgments. In these chapters, I identify factors that are common to political environments and that affect how people perceive the benefits of learning various kinds of information. Combining that knowledge with an understanding of the logic of competence described in chapter 5, the need to get attention described in the previous chapter, and the importance of credibility described in this chapter can empower educators to convey more information of more value to more people.

9

The Politics of Competence

To increase another person's knowledge or competence, it is necessary to attract attention to the information and for attentive persons to find the information credible. What attributes of information induce an audience to respond in these ways? To answer this question, I offer a framework called the *politics of competence*. This framework offers a way to organize and use information about psychological and contextual factors that affect how prospective learners think about what information is worth learning.

The politics of competence has four components: *value diversity, issue complexity, political roles, and learning costs*. Individually and collectively, these four components affect what educational strategies are feasible, unfeasible, successful, and unsuccessful. They have this power because they produce divergent views of what strategies, knowledge, and competence are beneficial. They lead people to reach different conclusions about educational strategy questions such as "What information should educators convey?" and "*Who* should know *what*?"

Educators can benefit from understanding the politics of competence. To see how, consider that a necessary condition for an educational endeavor to increase knowledge or competence is that prospective learners choose to participate. Some educators also need people to support their educational endeavors with money or labor. To draw the needed participation, potential learners, partners, and supporters must perceive that the endeavor will produce sufficiently positive net benefits. That is, all who are asked to sacrifice something of value as a means of advancing an educational endeavor must see the newly created knowledge or competence as providing benefits that are large when compared to the personal costs of achieving these goals. If sufficiently few people perceive an educational venture in this way, they will not participate. When success depends on producing outcomes that offer substantial net benefits from the perspective of essential participants, educators can benefit from understanding how the politics of competence affects the kind of information that different people find valuable.

Designing educational endeavors that can deliver such benefits can be difficult. People who have gone a lifetime without knowing much about a particular issue may wonder why they need to learn about it now. Others may want to learn new things but may doubt that a particular educator's book, article, advertisement, website, or course is an effective way to obtain knowledge that they would value.

To motivate participation and address doubts, educators need to explain the net benefits of their endeavors. In this chapter, I describe how educators can more effectively make such arguments in a range of environments. Here is a summary of chapter 9's main argument:

- Competence exists not only with respect to a task, but also with respect to a set of values.
- Many issues are perceived as *political* because they are associated with deep or longstanding value conflicts in a population.
- People vary in their civic responsibilities and, hence, the outcomes they can effect. These variations can cause people to value information and knowledge differently.
- Competence and knowledge can be costly to obtain. Here, costs are measured not just in terms of money, but also in terms of effort and foregone opportunities.
- For the reasons listed above, endeavors that provide net benefits to some people can impose net costs on others. As a result, people sometimes disagree about answers to the questions "What information should educators convey?" and "*Who* should know *what*?"

- These disagreements can affect who participates in an educational endeavor, who pays attention to its content, and who finds its information credible.
- For these reasons, the politics of competence affects the kinds of outcomes that an educator can achieve.

In other words, understanding the politics of competence can help educators more effectively design and better defend educational strategies that produce the outcomes that they desire in more situations.

The chapter continues as follows. In section 9A, I open the argument by showing that many judgments about civic competence are heavily subjective, rather than being based exclusively on facts or logic. Such subjectivity is present even among people who believe that their judgments abot others' competence are strictly factually oriented. This subjectivity, if unrecognized, can lead educators to make mistakes about whether and for whom their educational endeavors truly provide benefits. In section 9B, I introduce the politics of competence. I explain how its four components cause disagreements about what kinds of information, knowledge, and competence are valuable. In section 9C, I describe how the politics of competence affects the kinds of information that audiences perceive as addressing their core concerns and the kinds of educators whom audiences perceive as sharing common interests. Because information that a prospective learner will not pay attention to, or perceive as credible, cannot increase knowledge or competence, I conclude by encouraging educators to learn about the politics of competence as a means for developing more effective strategies.

9A. SUBJECTIVITY AND COMPETENCE CLAIMS

Educators have an audience and a knowledge or competence aspiration in mind. The audience consists of those people whom an educator believes would make better decisions if they knew things that they do not presently know. The aspiration is to help the audience execute important tasks more competently.

What information is valuable for educators to provide? In politics, people often answer this question differently. Some differences in answers arise from misunderstandings about the logic of competence. Specifically, some people are mistaken about whether particular pieces of information are necessary or sufficient for changing performance at a valued task. Consider, for example, cases where a critic claims that other people "must know" a particular set of facts to be competent when at the same time he fails to recognize that cues or other facts are sufficient for achieving the same outcome.

In other cases, different answers to claims about what is worth knowing are a consequence of subjectivity. By subjective, I mean that the claim reflects attributes of the subject making the assessment as opposed to being based exclusively on attributes of the objects (e.g., candidates or issues) being assessed. When evaluating works of art, for example, subjective assessments are common. Although one person may find the mix of surrealism and religious imagery in Salvador Dali's work to be of unusual and broad-ranging cultural depth, another person may find it sacrilegious or distasteful. Just as many claims about art reflect not just the work but also the tastes and perceptions of the person judging the work, many claims about what information is valuable to citizens also entail subjective components.

Claims about what others should know about politics often come with a point of view attached.[1] This attachment occurs because politics involves making tradeoffs between what different people want. No government can fulfill every individual and collective desire. Since politics is how we manage these limitations, politics confronts educators with situations where arguably objective facts about "what exists" and "what causes what" are deeply intertwined with arguably subjective statements about "what is important" and "what is valuable."

Similarly, claims about which political choices are "well-informed" or "competent" often combine evidence-based statements of fact with subjective value-based statements. Subjectivity about what facts matter fuels disagreements about whether to continue wars, increase funding for public schools, limit tax rates, and so on. Subjectivity affects opinions about what is desirable. Subjectivity arises in claims about competence because ours is not a world in which a neat and organized pile of objective facts sits separately from a neatly organized pile of subjective value statements.

As we will see many times throughout the rest of this book, subjectivity is present in most civic competence assessments—including those offered by individuals who see themselves as thoroughly objective and unbiased. When I have made this argument in the past, some people have responded that the claim does not apply to them. Many people see themselves as completely objective and interested in "just the facts." At the same time, they describe their causes as "right" and "just." They do not understand why they or anyone else should spend any time thinking about alternative points of view—particularly perspectives that they believe to be based exclusively on ignorance. They assume that their political opponents simply misunderstand the true nature of a topic or problem. They contend that others would be well informed only if "others" knew and valued the same facts that they know and value. Usually, these "others", who are cast as the "ignorant" opposition, view themselves differently. In many cases, they also view themselves as "right" and "just" and cannot understand how their opponents could act differently than they do.

How can educators defend the value of an educational endeavor in such circumstances? The logic of competence introduced in previous chapters provides a baseline for progress. Educators who understand how cues and procedural memory affect competence can explain why certain pieces of information are (or are not) or sufficient means for achieving certain outcomes. But many educators need more. For example, educators who need others' financial or logistical support and prospective learners' participation and attention may need to demonstrate that increasing a particular competence is not only logically possible, but also worthwhile. It is at this point where the politics of competence becomes useful.

9B. COMPONENTS OF THE POLITICS
OF COMPETENCE

The politics of competence are four factors that lead people to have different views about what types of things are valuable to know. These factors also cause people to draw different conclusions about which educational endeavors confer positive net benefits. The four factors are value diversity, issue complexity, political roles, and learning costs.

Value diversity. By values, I mean "(a) concepts or beliefs, (b) about desirable end states or behaviors, (c) that transcend specific situations, (d) guide selection or evaluation of behavior and events, and (e) are ordered by relative importance" (Schwartz and Bilsky 1987: 551). Value diversity infuses conclusions about information's net benefits with subjective assertions about what matters. In chapter 10, I show educators how to better anticipate and respond to questions about an educational strategy's net benefits in these circumstances. Such knowledge not only helps educators develop competence criteria that are easier for diverse people to accept, it can also help educators establish common interests, and hence better credibility, with their audiences.

To see the kinds of challenges that value diversity can pose for educators, observe for a moment how partisan combatants sometimes describe their opponents' mental states. After one US state banned same-sex marriages in its constitution, the pro-LGBT New Civil Rights Movement claimed that "ignorance and hate has enveloped ordinary citizens." They explained support for the amendment as evidence of how "ill-informed, mis-informed and just plain ignorant the citizenry . . . truly are."[2] Supporters of traditional marriage saw things differently. They argued that "the irony of the gay marriage debate is that traditionalists are making arguments based on reason and nature, while secular culture is now largely irrational . . . the severing of faith and reason has led to a nihilism wherein the greatest good is the fulfillment of whatever desires among consenting adults."[3] In cases like this, hearing the opinions of "the other side" in a debate can make participants angry or anxious. So, a common reaction is to find a way to absolve themsleves of having to contemplate others' views.[4] By attacking the mental capacities of their opponents, advocates of each position on same-sex marriage seek absolution for having to directly defend their own positions against others' views. But absolution is not a solution for educators who want to work with value-diverse political audiences. So, whether one agrees with one, both, or neither of the claims about the mental state of same-sex marriage debaters, they are precisely the kind of arguments that value diversity can bring to political settings. Chapter 10 shows educators how to adapt educational strategies to such circumstances.

The politics of competence's second component is *issue complexity*. An issue is complex if it can be divided into multiple parts. Complexity can cause disagreement about which of an issue's multiple parts should be emphasized in educational strategies. Consider for, example, a debate on federal income tax rates. To say that one position (e.g., supporting a particular rate increase) is "more competent" than another implies a specific answer to questions like "Is it more important to evaluate a tax rate change with respect to its effect on GDP, income inequality, neither, or both?" and "If both, how should GDP and income inequality be weighted relative to one another in the competence criterion?" People can agree on general economic principles—even to the extent of being common ideologues. At the same time, they can disagree about what parts of a given issue are most important. Chapter 11 offers advice about how to develop educational strategies that others will see as credible in such circumstances.

In chapter 12, I examine how educators can use knowledge of *political roles* to target information more effectively. A political role refers to a citizen's opportunities to affect decisions or outcomes. Some individuals are in roles of great authority (i.e., such as the president, a governor, or other people whose singular actions can change laws or policies). Others have different roles (e.g., being one of several million voters in a two-candidate election).

To see how knowledge of political roles can make educators more effective, suppose that an educator is working toward a particular political outcome. Suppose, for example, that an educator seeks to have bill X become law (perhaps because it is more consistent with a knowledge base that her audience values than the status quo policy). If she wants to develop an efficient educational strategy, should her strategy include informing everyone about the bill? In many cases, the answer is "no." In such cases, targeting information with respect to people's different roles (i.e., giving people with different roles information that each can use) can make the strategy more effective and efficient.

The politics of competence's fourth component is *learning costs*. The costs are in terms of money, effort, and sacrifices that come with devoting time to teaching or learning. When we take these costs into consideration, the net benefits (i.e., benefits minus costs) of attempting to increase another's competence become relevant.

When attention turns to *net benefits*, questions arise about whether it is really worthwhile for anyone to pay the costs of improving a given competence. In some cases, the question answers itself—as occurs in discussions of whether it is worthwhile to provide an audience with information that they can never use. In other cases, the question is harder to answer.

Consider, for example, cases where many people agree that there is a net societal benefit from increasing a competence at a given task. To make the example more concrete, let's say that changing the math curriculum in a local school in a particular way would achieve the objective. At the same time, people disagree about who should pay the costs associated with this change. These questions become more sensitive when childless adults, who may see themselves as having less of a stake in the issue, are asked to learn more about it. Related challenges arise when beneficiaries of a particular competence are disliked—as can occur when residents of one community are asked to learn things that provide benefits to residents of another community. In such cases, the people who are asked to learn may ask why they—rather than someone else—should pay these costs. In chapter 13, I explain how educators can build educational strategies that provide greater net benefits.

9C. IMPLICATIONS OF THE POLITICS
OF COMPETENCE

Individually and collectively, the politics of competence affect who benefits and who pays when an audience learns something new. Understanding these factors can help educators convert strategies that do not increase competence into strategies that do. To see how, recall that achieving many knowledge- or competence-related goals requires multiple kinds of people to participate in the endeavor. Prospective learners must choose to pay attention to information and view it as sufficiently credible. Educators who understand the politics of competence are better equipped to offer information that has these attributes.

Suppose, for example, that an educator discovers that a particular plan for conveying a particular set of facts to a particular audience does not provide positive net benefits to the constituency whose participation is needed. If an educator can use knowledge of the politics of competence to identify an alternate plan that produces the desired competence at a lower cost (perhaps involving more cues and fewer abstract or technical facts), and if the alternate plan confers sufficiently higher benefits to the needed constituency (perhaps it helps the audience achieve additional goals), then the alternative can offer greater net benefits to the constituents. In such cases, knowledge of the content of chapters 9-13 can help educators obtain the participation that the success of their educational strategy requires.

Unless politics is occurring in situations where the four factors of the politics of competence are not present, there will be disagreements about what actions are competent and what facts are worth knowing. As James Madison (1787) put it in *The Federalist #10*:

> As long as the reason of man continues fallible, and he is at liberty to exercise it, different opinions will be formed. As long as the connection

subsists between his reason and his self-love, his opinions and his passions will have a reciprocal influence on each other; and the former
will be objects to which the latter will attach themselves.

As a result, you, as an educator, may encounter people who question whether
you are thinking about knowledge and competence *in the right way*. Your
questioners will ask why you are not paying more attention to topics or
points of view that are important to them. Prospective sponsors want to
understand why, how, and to whom an educational strategy provides benefits. Prospective employees of, or volunteers in, educational efforts will want
to know whether participating in an educational endeavor is a good use of
their time and energy. An educator's answer to these questions can be the
difference between whether or not he or she obtains the participation that
an educational plan needs.

Prospective learners are another constituency. While citizens sometimes seek out learning opportunities, others who have found politics
unpleasant in the past want to know "what's in it for them" when an educator invites them to learn about a particular subject. In such cases, educators
benefit from being able to explain why taking the time to learn this information will provide a tangible and worthwhile benefit to them.

Indeed, when potential sponsors, employees, volunteers, or audiences
suspect that an educator does not understand or respect their values, the
complexity of relevant issues, their political roles, or their costs of learning,
they can become skeptical of the benefits of participating in an educational
endeavor. If the skepticism is sufficiently widespread, an endeavor that is
beneficial in theory will fail in practice.

In the remaining chapters of part I, I seek to help educators better
develop and defend the criteria that they use when explaining to others
why certain kinds of information are valuable for others to know. By "better," I do not mean the ability to develop criteria that everyone will accept.
As chapter 4's "silver bullet" example foreshadowed, there are times when
no such answers exist. By "better," I mean criteria that can be defended as
providing positive net benefits to increasingly broad audiences.

10

Value Diversity and How to Manage It

Value diversity causes people to give different answers to questions like "What information is most valuable to convey?" and "*Who* needs to know *what*?" I define values as do Shalom Schwartz and Wolfgang Bilsky (1987: 551). By values, they mean "(a) concepts or beliefs, (b) about desirable end states or behaviors, (c) that transcend specific situations, (d) guide selection or evaluation of behavior and events, and (e) are ordered by relative importance." By value diversity, I refer to the different values that people have. This chapter is about how value diversity affects claims about what is worth knowing and, hence, an educator's ability to get prospective learners and supporters to participate in an educational endeavor.

Some critics and educators regard values as a nuisance—particularly the values of those with whom they disagree. These critics want people to teach a particular set of conclusions about a subject that matters to them. They often see others' values as illegitimate and as getting in the way of a rational conversation about issues that they consider important. These claims manifest as advice for others to focus on "just the facts." I will show that these critiques often reflect a misunderstanding of how values affect learning. I will also show how to overcome these misunderstandings in ways that enhance educators' abilities to increase many kinds of knowledge and competence.

Here is a short summary of the chapter's main conclusions:

- Values affect how people perceive and process information.
- Values drive individuals to embrace certain types of information and reject others.
- Values often have these effects before prospective learners are conscious of them, and they have these effects even if prospective learners have trouble describing them.

In other words, values affect the types of information prospective learners are willing to pay attention to and regard as credible. As attention and credibility are critical assets for educators to possess, and as political situations often include people with different values, educators who understand how values affect learning can make more effective choices about what information to convey.

The chapter's most important lesson is that educators who wish to increase competence effectively and efficiently must provide information that accomplishes two things. First, the information must be necessary or sufficient to increase knowledge that is itself necessary or sufficient to increase the competence. Second, the information must be sufficiently consistent with a person's core concerns that they will pay attention to it and think about it in ways that lead them to the desired knowledge or competence. Values affect how people connect information to their core concerns. Therefore, if educators offer information that can increase a competence, and if prospective learners see the information as sufficiently related to their values, then prospective learners will have greater motivation to use the information in the way that the educator desires.

Here is a summary of the argument in this chapter that leads to its main lesson:

- For most adults, many values are effectively hardwired—they cannot be changed by the types of information that most educators are able to offer.
- Value diversity affects perceptions of who needs to know what. It can cause some people not to participate in educational endeavors that confer positive net benefits to others. Nonparticipation can limit educators' abilities to increase knowledge and competence.

- This implication of value diversity for educators' strategies depends on whether they operate in "small" or "big" tents.
- "Small tents" contain people who share many values. Educators in small tents produce positive net benefits by providing information that is necessary or sufficient for increasing competences that reflect the shared viewpoint.
- "Big tents" contain people with diverse values who can benefit from certain types of collective action. Educators who want to increase competence in big tents must find information that is not only necessary or sufficient for increasing the competence, but also information that the target audience perceives as sufficiently credible and beneficial.

Understanding how values affect learning can empower civic educators, and other people who care about the effectiveness of civic education, to increase a wide array of knowledge and competence in many political settings. Such an understanding also casts a number of civic ignorance critiques in a different—and more constructive—light. For example, we will discover in the pages that follow that when many critics cite "ignorance" as the reason that other citizens make decisions they disagree with, the evidence for such claims is often misinterpreted, sparse, or nonexistent. Indeed, many "ignorance" critiques are really about one person demanding that others privilege his values over their values. In other words, many critics of others' knowledge or competence attribute to "ignorance" disagreements that are deeply rooted in values. Hence, one more implication of the chapter's main lesson is that:

- Many claims about others' political ignorance are not logically defensible or empirically grounded statements about what information is necessary or sufficient to increase or achieve well-defined competences. Instead, they are a product of subjective assertions about what values "others" *ought* to have. As a result, many such claims are poor guides to the kinds of information that can actually increase broadly beneficial competences.

Throughout the chapter, I explain why many experts and advocates fall into this kind of trap, and I explain how future educators can avoid repeating those mistakes.

To reach the conclusions listed above, the chapter proceeds as follows. In section 10A, I explain how values affect learning. In section 10B, I evaluate strategies for describing what information is important to convey when prospective participants have diverse values. In section 10C, I describe three psychological processes that lead people to blame "ignorance" for differences caused by value diversity. Because these errors often limit educators' abilities to convey important information to others, this section also offers ways for educators to avoid repeating these mistakes. In section 10D, I reexamine four prominent "public ignorance" claims. I then show how an appreciation of value diversity can help us increase the accuracy and practical relevance of many such claims. Section 10E reviews lessons learned and offers a more effective way forward for different types of educators.

10A. VALUES ARE REAL

Values have a strong and deep effect on how people see the world. They influence choices about who people will listen to. They influence what types of information people are willing to regard as factual and what kinds of claims they reflexively reject. Values cause people to feel things, and to draw strong conclusions, about information even before they realize they are doing such things. Values sometimes cause people to react quickly and viscerally to factual information that could help them. Any of these reactions can limit an educator's ability to convey beneficial information.

To clarify how educators can adapt to these challenges, it is important to understand where values come from. For this reason, I now offer a short description of cognitive development that is pertinent to an understanding of how values affect learning.

The manner in which every person interacts with and understands their environment is heavily influenced by a process that began very early in cognitive development.[1] This process starts before birth and has conscious and subconscious elements. This process manages correspondences between environmental variations and bodily systems.[2] It causes people to experience their bodies' interactions with their environments as varying levels of warmth and cold, hunger and satiation, comfort and discomfort. Before birth, the fetus begins to associate some of its bodily reactions with external variations in sound and light. A fetus can sense variations in light at about 15 weeks and can sense some external variations in sound soon thereafter.

After birth, there is more cognitive development and environmental variation.[3] With such inputs, an infant develops a broader set of associations. She associates sounds and smells, such as that of her mother, with her own feelings and sensations. With sufficiently many or sufficiently strong associations, reoccurring sounds and smells can trigger the feelings that co-occurred with the associations. As Thomas D. Albright, director of the Salk Institute's Vision Center Laboratory, describes (2015: 32):

> Sensory associative learning is the most common form of learning: it inevitably results when stimuli appear together in time, and particularly so in the presence of reinforcement; it can occur without awareness ("classical conditioning") or with ("instrumental conditioning").

Soon thereafter, an infant realizes that she can affect her environment in ways that affect her own pleasure, pain, hunger, thirst, warmth, cold, comfort, and discomfort. She learns that crying or making noises at certain times corresponds with relief of hunger and other pain. She learns that she can move objects with her hands and arms and that moving some objects affects her sensations.

Through these processes, infants and young children start to have beliefs and feelings about more objects and concepts. As patterns across these relationships become more recognizable, conceptual categories emerge. With these categorical tools, children start to build frameworks for understanding their world and their roles in it.[4]

Feelings about categories come from memories of associations between early icons of the emerging categories and basic sensations like warmth and hunger.[5] Children come to feel affection for those who care for them and objects that give them pleasure. They come to feel anxiety about objects that cause them pain and correspond to discomfort. Hence, children develop feelings about certain categories of people, noises, toys, and food. These feelings manifest as preferences for certain toys, food, and people and as fears of other objects.

As a child grows, she comes to understand a larger and more expansive set of categories. She also learns about more complex relationships among these categories. Children learn about subcategories (black cats) and super-categories (felines). They come to have feelings about increasingly abstract categories.

These more complex feelings do not arise completely anew.[6] Beliefs and feelings that we have about newly encountered objects heavily reflect previous feelings and associations.[7] Feelings and beliefs about more complex concepts are built from feelings and categories that the child has already developed.

Children then become adults. The processes previously described cause adults to have strong beliefs and feelings about things they will never experience directly (e.g., the outer reaches of the universe or subatomic particles) and about abstract concepts like common notions of what is liberal and what is conservative. Adults have beliefs and feelings about a great many things, including many invisible and abstract phenomena.

Some feelings and beliefs are widely shared among adults. For example, fire burns everyone. As a result, most adults will make significant efforts to avoid being burned or have others suffer the same fate. How different people perceive and sense things like fire is so common that it is reasonable to expect that almost everyone will experience these phenomena in the same way. This commonality explains a great deal about why whether or not fire burns people *is not* considered an appropriate topic for political debate.

For other objects and concepts, diverse feelings and beliefs emerge. Sometimes, these differences are very deeply felt. This diversity can arise from differences in individual physiology, differences in experiences, or both. For example, two people with different bodies can experience a common stimulus in different ways. A tall person may experience the tops of door frames in ways that a short person does not. A person who is tall enough to bump into door frames may develop anxieties and feelings about such objects that a short person does not. Differences in the inner ear canal, the functioning of rods and cones in the eyes, and many other physical variations can lead people to experience common objects in different ways. Objects that one person finds visually exciting or aurally pleasing may cause others to experience anxiety or pain. Seemingly simple differences in bodies can cause people to have very different feelings and beliefs about common objects.

Experiences also matter. A person who has had only experiences with friendly dogs will grow to have different expectations about dogs than would a person who has had very painful dog experiences. Timing also matters—the experience of traumatic events as a child or teenager often produces different developmental consequences than when similar events are first experienced later in life.[8]

These processes and sequences produce people who have values: concepts or beliefs about desirable end states or behaviors that transcend specific situations, guide selection or evaluation of behavior and events, and are ordered by relative importance. By the time that adulthood is reached, and for many of their values, the supporting beliefs and feelings are effectively hardwired.

As a result, we often perceive our values as fundamental and unchangeable parts of ourselves. Such perceptions are not wholly unreasonable. The neural foundations of many of our values have a longstanding physical instantiation within our bodies. The clusters and networks of axons and dendrites that produce these values are, from a physical perspective, very much like other parts of our bodies—they can remain functionally stable for long periods of time.

One implication of values having these attributes is that they often act beneath our conscious ability to perceive them. Values often affect our responses to new information before we realize that they are having this effect. We often have trouble putting these parts of ourselves into words. Moreover, our values need not be consistent with one another. If we are never in a situation where we observe and suffer from a conflict between our values, we may not recognize the contradiction or work to resolve it.[9] For all of these reasons, we feel our values, and they affect how we process information, but we often struggle to explain them.

These hardwired differences in values or preferences, in turn, can cause people to disagree about what kinds of outcomes, competences, knowledge, and information are beneficial. To see how these disagreements appear in political contexts, it is useful to take a moment to understand the relationship between values and two concepts that also appear in conversations about how people feel about politics. These concepts are *preferences* and *attitudes*.

Following communication scholar Daniel O'Keefe (2002: 6), I define an attitude as "a person's general evaluation of an object." Following work with James Druckman (2000: 3), I define a preference as:

> a comparative evaluation of (i.e. a ranking over) a set of objects. A preference serves as a cognitive marker that reminds people how to interact with various aspects of their environment. Preferences are stored in memory and drawn on when people make decisions. When, for example, people say that they prefer Lincoln to Douglass, they identify an aspect of their environment that, in their mind, provides them with greater benefits than other environmental aspects.

The relationship among the three concepts is: attitudes are beliefs and feelings that pertain to objects, preferences are beliefs and feelings that pertain to comparisons over multiple objects, and values refer to feelings and beliefs that transcend these comparisons. Values provide a structure that helps to organize a person's attitudes and preferences. Because values are more general and held more deeply than many attitudes or preferences, they also tend to be more resistant to change.

Now, suppose that we encounter people whose attitudes and preferences over wide ranges of issues can be traced back to a particular moral commitment. Suppose that this commitment was forged by a set of powerful experiences when they were younger. A common example is people who believe that certain types of public and private decisions should align with a particular theology or religious text. Chances are that these people are not rethinking these commitments as we speak to them, nor have they rethought these commitments in a very long time. The same holds true for many people who believe that decisions in a broad policy domain should be based on a particular set of scientific findings—a belief that can also manifest as a strong moral commitment. For some people, even people who see themselves as rational scientists committed to high standards of logic, evidence, and inference, these feelings are best described as values.

All people have values, even those with whom we disagree. For reasons stated in the previous pages, people can have different values for honest and legitimate reasons. Although this is not to say that all publicly expressed beliefs and feelings are honest or legitimate from every point of view, it *is* to say that our differences with others need not be the exclusive products of ignorance. This insight, as we shall see, can help educators who seek to increase beneficial competences by providing information to which value-diverse populations will want to attend.

10B. TENT SIZE, COMMON GROUND, AND THE EFFECTIVENESS OF EDUCATIONAL STRATEGIES

With basic information about values in hand, I turn to how we can use knowledge of value diversity to make an educational strategy more effective. I begin with a simple proposition: An educator operates in a big tent or a small tent.

In a small tent, people have broad agreement on what kinds of outcomes are valuable. So, when developing an educational strategy for a small tent, the objective is clear: provide information that produces knowledge that increases competence from the perspective of the small tent's shared values.

In a big tent, values are more diverse. This diversity can lead people to disagree about what outcomes are valuable, what actions are competent, what knowledge is beneficial to know, and what kinds of information are worth conveying.

Across issues and over periods of time, people move back and forth between big and small tents. For example, a likeminded subset of a large tent may choose to break away from the larger group. If a breakaway group has a sufficiently strong and comprehensive foundation of shared values, they are likely to view their shared cause as moral rather than political. Such self-perceptions are not exclusive to faith-based groups; many experts, science-based educators and partisan advocates also view their attempts to inform others in strongly moral terms.

When people view their motives as moral rather than political, they sometimes interpret their own values-based standards as universal. As psychologist Linda Skitka (2010: 269) describes, these groups see their shared principles as "absolutes, or universal standards of truth that others should also share" and perceive their values-based views as "objective—as if they were readily observable, objective properties of situations, or as facts about the world." In these cases, there is little internal motivation to compromise with others.[10] Every potential point of contact with outsiders represents a zero-sum or negative-sum engagement. In the extreme, there is no information that simultaneously benefits the small tent's members and its adversaries.[11] Such feelings can lead people to seek out small tents.

In contrast, when people come to learn that they have more shared values with "others" than they previously thought, they can be motivated to move from small tents to big ones.[12] Learning in big tents is different than learning in small tents. In small tents, educators can identify information that is not only logically necessary or sufficient to increase a competence but also consistent with the small tent's shared values. In a big tent, educators who want to increase knowledge and competence face a more complex problem. *The rest of this section focuses on increasing knowledge and competence in a large tent.*

When value diversity is present, but not in amounts that preclude members of a large tent from taking mutually beneficial actions, an educator has to adopt a point of view. Deciding not to decide (e.g., imagining that weighting multiple perspectives equally is a value-neutral default position) is still a choice.[13] In such cases, any point of view necessarily privileges some values relative to others and can prompt questions about what is worth knowing. As political scientists John Patty and Elizabeth Maggie Penn (2014: 38) describe in their research on how collective decisions come to be seen as legitimate:

> When confronted with the task of furthering various criteria [decision-making bodies] could likely make a number of reasonable decisions. No given decision, however, can be deemed "perfect" because each decision will involve a compromise with respect to one or more goals.

What point of view regarding criteria, reasonable decisions, and goals should an educator adopt?

One common idea is to propose as a point of view measuring success in terms of what is best for a group's "average member." This seemingly simple solution, however, can be problematic when it is easy to make a true claim about an average group member that does not describe any individual member's actual truth. Suppose, for the purpose of making a simple example, that we can accurately gauge and monetize the individual benefits of a particular increase in competence for members of a big tent. Suppose that half of the members receive a $1,000 benefit and the other half receive a $3,000 benefit. Here, we can correctly claim an average benefit of $2,000. We can also have every single person in the big tent deny that our claim reflects their circumstance.

Another oft-proposed point of view characterizes big tent competence with respect to the relative numbers of people who hold certain types of preferences. Consider, for example, a big tent consisting of three equally sized groups of citizens. Their values are such that two groups prefer government action A over government action B. The remaining group prefers B over A. If we agree that competence should be defined with respect to these preferences, a debate can still ensue about what government action constitutes a competent choice.

One can argue that the answer is A. Is this a valid claim? If the question is: "Which government action is supported by a *majority* of the big tent's members?" then A is correct. But that was not the original question. The question was about which choice to label as "competent."

To pursue the matter further, suppose that the groups that prefer A over B have only a mild preference for A over B. At the same time, suppose that the group that prefers B over A holds this preference very strongly. To members of this third group, action B is equivalent to a life of unquestioned eternal bliss, while action A is akin to eternal torture. And, for the purpose of the example, let's suppose that this analogy is not just rhetoric. Suppose that these descriptions truly represent what the group members believe and feel. What point of view should an educator adopt about which choice to label competent? If it were possible to measure how strongly each voter feels about each action, it is possible that we would reach the conclusion that the big tent as a whole gets greater aggregate benefit from choosing B. Still, this description does not accurately represent the views of a majority of groups within the tent. It remains the case that two out of three groups prefer A.

In short, when value diversity leads people to prefer sufficiently different outcomes, there is no way to draw a conclusion about what choice is most competent without inserting a subjective claim about how to weigh the choice's implications for different types of people.[14] Value diversity often forces educators in big tents to base competence criteria on subjective decisions about how much to count various individuals' feelings and situations.

When I raise this point in classrooms, I am sometimes asked whether just counting all individuals' preferences equally would solve the problem. This is not always a harmless position to adopt. Children, the elderly, victims of violent crime, handicapped persons, war veterans and other members of the military, and people who have suffered from racial discrimination or religious persecution are commonly singled out as having special needs in many situations. When the plights of the groups listed above are compared with those of other groups that have not made the same sacrifices, or who seem less deserving, people can have very visceral reactions to "equal treatment" proposals. In general, when people in big tents make claims about what choices are competent, they may, whether they realize it or not, be making strong assumptions about how much to value one person's feelings or well-being relative to the feelings or well-being of others.

This section's principal advice is for educators to recognize that strong subjective assumptions are often nested within claims about which choices are and are not competent. I contend that educators who recognize this fact will be better positioned to legitimate their own claims about what things are worth knowing.

For example, when an action makes one subset of a group better off at the expense of another, getting others to accept the action as legitimate requires an explanation of why this tradeoff is preferable to other tradeoffs that could be made (Patty and Penn, 2014). One argument of this kind is that the "payers" should see, from their own values perspective, that the beneficiaries' benefit is very large relative to their personal costs and is therefore worth pursuing. Another argument is that the proposed tradeoff can or will be bundled with other tradeoffs in ways that make the payers better off when they view all of the tradeoffs in the aggregate.

Consider, for example, a situation in which achieving an educator's objective requires two individuals to participate. Suppose that the two have an adversarial relationship on one issue, that they can both benefit from acting collectively on a second issue, and that the desired outcome on the second issue requires compromise or collaboration on the first issue. In such cases, the "sweet spot" for an educator is to identify information that is (a) necessary or sufficient to increase competence on the second issue, and that (b) reflects both individuals' common interests on the second issue to such an extent that any disagreement on the first issue is outweighed by the benefit of their collaboration on the second.

These examples show how big tent educators can benefit by using knowledge of value diversity when developing educational strategies. This knowledge can sensitize educators to prospective learners' and supporters' perspectives on what kinds of information, knowledge, and competence are beneficial. Educators who have such insights will be better equipped to explain the benefits of their endeavors to increasingly diverse audiences. This skill, in turn, can empower educators to recruit learners and supporters from increasingly diverse populations. That is, educators can learn to develop educational strategies in which people from multiple value orientations will want to participate. For these reasons, educators can use knowledge of value diversity to increase the range of tents in which they can increase beneficial kinds of knowledge and competence.

10C. HOW INFORMATION PROCESSING BIASES TRANSFORM VALUES INTO "IGNORANCE"

Educators who ignore the challenges of value diversity are vulnerable to a critical error—interpreting disliked political outcomes as being the exclusive product of others' ignorance rather than an outcome that also reflects diverse values or preferences. The error is critical when it leads educators to misread the relationship between information and competence and then to offer information that others neither want nor need.

In this section, I describe three concepts from psychology that lead some critics and educators to conclude that others who disagree with them do so out of simple ignorance. The concepts are *attribution error, out-group stereotyping*, and *motivated reasoning*. In previous chapters, I discussed how processes like these affect the kinds of information to which people attend. Here, I explain that they have parallel effects on critics and educators and, if unrecognized, can limit an educational strategy's effectiveness. In particular, I show that learning about attribution error, out-group stereotyping, and motivated reasoning can help educators understand when value diversity, rather than simple ignorance, produces different views about "What information is most valuable to convey?" and "*Who* needs to know *what*?" Educators can use this knowledge to more effectively develop educational strategies that offer positive net benefits to diverse members of a large tent.

Let's start with attribution errors. When one person sees another trip over a sidewalk, a common reaction is something like, "What a klutz." The inference drawn when the stumbler is a stranger is that the person is prone to such acts. In other words, an observer views the outcome as being caused by a longstanding personal trait.[15]

When we observe our own actions, in contrast, we know more about our history. We know that situational factors affect our behaviors. When we trip over a curb, we know that it is an unusual occurrence that happens only when we are severely distracted. More generally, when people do something for which they might feel shame, they often instinctively attribute the occurrence to circumstance rather than to themselves.[16] For example, a person who trips over a curb in front of others may think, "I'm not a klutz. This was an unusual circumstance. Normally, I navigate curbs very well. In this instance, I was distracted."

Attribution errors can cause people to draw inaccurate conclusions about others' competence. A critic may see a citizen make a choice that is different than the choice that they would make. The critic concludes that the citizen is incompetent. But the citizen may be making a decision that would produce the best outcome for the critic, if the critic were in the citizen's shoes. Suppose that this is true. If the competence criterion is achieving the most preferred outcome from the citizen's perspective, then following the critic's advice, and making a different choice because of it, would reduce the citizen's competence. In such cases, the critic is inaccurately characterizing the citizen as incompetent because he is ignorant of meaningful differences between them. In sum, attribution errors can cause critics to conflate difference and incompetence. Differences in personal circumstances and other sources of value diversity can lead people to use and value information in different ways.

The second psychological concept is out-group stereotyping. People often identify themselves as members of groups, such as women, or Democrats, or hunters. To preserve self-esteem and to facilitate various forms of social coordination, people seek to establish the legitimacy and superiority of groups to which they belong. These motivations can lead them to denigrate competitive groups, also known as "out-groups."[17] In America, for example, many Democrats see Republicans as an out-group, and vice versa.

A common manifestation of out-group bias is the stereotyping of out-group members.[18] A common attribute of an out-group stereotype is that all members of an out-group are unthinking, unsympathetic to important concerns, and "all the same."[19] These groups are compared unfavorably to members of a person's in-group, who are often characterized as dynamic, diverse, and intelligent.

I see such stereotypes before and after major elections. People voice views about the competence and knowledge of people who voted differently than they did. These advocates stereotype their opponents as ignorant and do not allow for the possibility that value diversity could lead others to cast different votes than they did. I often see such claims after the writer's favored candidate or cause has lost an election. Winners, in contrast, tend to talk about "mandates" and praise the electorate for being well informed.[20]

Consider, for example, this comment published on a blog after North Carolina passed a constitutional amendment preventing same sex-couples from legal marriage:

> And what's really sad is they won. There (sic) dumb ignorant and they won this one. We can pants them in any intellectual argument but when it came to the ballot box we lost.... These are our opponents, willfully ignorant and proud, and we are losing ground to them.[21]

The actor Jon Voight made a similar argument at about the same time, though from a different perspective:

[T]hey've got to open their eyes because they don't know anything, that's the trouble with most of the people on the left. . . . They don't know anything because the media that they're being fed and the friends that are feeding them stuff, they are not getting information. They don't know anything about Barack Obama, except what he says he is and they buy it.[22]

In other words, while participants in political debates are often skilled at explaining their own beliefs, they often revert to general "ignorance" claims when seeking to explain the beliefs and actions of those with whom they disagree.[23]

Such stereotyping is also present in academic debates. Adherents of one scholarly approach often portray adherents of other approaches as all the same and as following simplistic rules (see, e.g., Pious, 2004). At the same time, people who share a scholarly approach tend to view one another as diverse and vibrant.[24] As in the case of racial stereotypes, simple and sweeping "they're all the same" edicts are often used to relieve those who voice them of having to actively contemplate the possible legitimacy of other ways of thinking. People often use such characterizations to absolve themselves of having to justify their own views relative to others.

Out-group stereotyping that uses ignorance to explain opponents' actions is rampant in politics. A widely seen example occurred the day after George W. Bush defeated John Kerry in the 2004 US presidential election. *The Daily Mirror*, a popular British newspaper, posted the headline "How Can 59,054,057 Be So Dumb?" alongside a photo of a smiling President Bush. The number was the official tally of Americans who had voted for the president. The headline reinforced the idea that all who voted for Bush were the same and simply ignorant. While no one who seeks to reconcile their claims with logic and evidence can deny that there were many things Bush voters were ignorant about, the same has to be true for Kerry voters, given the kind of infinite ignorance that I described in chapter 1.

One of my favorite pieces of writing on the topic of out-group stereotyping in modern politics is a column by A. Barton Hinkle of the *Richmond Times-Dispatch* (2012). It is titled "The Wrong Side Absolutely Must Not Win." It was written in the heat of the 2012 U.S. presidential election and begins as follows:

The past several weeks have made one thing crystal-clear: Our country faces unmitigated disaster if the Other Side wins. No reasonably intelligent person can deny this. All you have to do is look at the way the Other Side has been running its campaign. Instead of focusing on the big issues that are important to the American People, it has fired a relentlessly negative barrage of distortions, misrepresentations, and flat-out lies. . . .

The column goes on to contrast the many virtuous ways in which "My Side" is waging the campaign with the smarmy and undesirable way the "Other Side" is proceeding. The entire column, however, is a satire. Every paragraph describes an identical action by each side, but describes each action from a strictly partisan point of view. For example:

I recently read about an analysis by an independent, nonpartisan organization that supports My Side. It proves beyond the shadow of a doubt that everything I have been saying about the Other Side was true all along. Of course, the Other Side refuses to acknowledge any of this. It is too busy cranking out so-called studies by so-called experts who are actually nothing but partisan hacks. This just shows you that the Other Side lives in its own little echo chamber and refuses to listen to anyone who has not already drunk its Kool-Aid.

If these examples are not sufficiently compelling, I ask that you set this book down for a moment and go to any political news website or blog that has a "comments section"—the area below the main article where readers (often anonymous) add short commentaries and address comments written by others. Whether the topic is international nuclear agreements or small-town politics, you will often see partisans on each side in political debates declare that those who disagree with them are ignorant and simple-minded. Educators who base strategies on these stereotypes will have limited ability to develop defensible big tent competence criteria.

Motivated reasoning is a third factor that inhibits seeing value diversity. Motivated reasoning is the practice of paying attention to, and seeking to inflate the importance of, information that is consistent with a point of view that a person already holds. It also entails ignoring or minimizing the importance of information that challenges a person's existing views. A less technical term for this phenomenon is "hearing only what you want to hear."

Psychologists Lisa Sinclair and Ziva Kunda (1999) offered a classic example of motivated reasoning. They asked experimental subjects to complete a few tasks. An "authority figure" evaluated the subjects' work. The researchers varied whether the authority figure was black or white.[25] All of the subjects were white. The researchers also varied whether the authority figure praised or criticized the work. The black and white authority figures (whose feedback was conveyed through scripted videos) used identical language to praise or criticize the subjects. After the evaluation, the subjects were asked to evaluate the authority figure. The scholars found that when the authority figure praised subjects, the subjects reciprocated by describing him positively. When the authority figure was critical, subjects went out of their way to diminish him, with some referencing unfavorable stereotypes as a rationale for such diminishment. In general, motivated reasoning resembles the fight-or-flight responses that are basic to human decision-making. When encountering a threatening stimulus, people seek to distance themselves from it or make it go away (when possible).

Motivated reasoning can lead people to elevate the importance of statements by those they agree with, while simultaneously ignoring or uncharitably reinterpreting the other side's words.[26] It can cause partisans to see their side's electoral victories as broad mandates for change and their defeats as temporary setbacks that are caused by bad luck, unusual circumstances, or an opponent's misdeeds. As Susan Jacoby puts it, "In today's America, intellectuals and non-intellectuals alike, whether on the left or right, tend to tune out any voice that is not an echo."[27]

In fact, everybody has engaged in motivated reasoning and is likely to do so again. If you are now trying to convince yourself that you are immune to such ways of thinking, then you are almost certainly engaging in motivated reasoning. None of us is immune from this bias, but we can learn to recognize it and adapt to the problems that it causes.

Attribution errors, out-group stereotyping, and motivated reasoning lead critics, citizens, and some educators to ignore, or reinterpret, information about why others act differently than they do. The histories of movements designed to assess others' competence are riddled with such practices. Many otherwise-intelligent people mistake their ignorance of others' thoughts and behaviors for evidence of an out-group's lack of intelligence.[28] A book by psychologist Robert V. Guthrie details a particularly damaging set of such practices. It describes how early 20th-century psychology was interpreted to support discrimination against American blacks. The title represents the problem well: *Even the Rat was White* (1998). In it, self-pronounced experts concluded that others were ignorant or unskilled because they did not know the same things, or have the same physical attributes, as the white experts' peer groups. Attribution errors, out-group stereotyping, and motivated reasoning led these individuals to equate difference with ignorance. We now know that those who were quick to see ignorance in others were far less knowledgeable than they imagined. Educators can avoid these mistakes.

Understanding these three processes and looking inward for traces of these biases can help educators better understand the desires of people who are unlike them. For educators in big tents, such reflections can serve as the foundation for more effective strategies. By thinking about the values that might have led others to reach different conclusions about social issues, an educator may be able to find common ground. When this happens, an educator has a basis for building new coalitions around educational strategies that can provide positive net benefits to new and broader combinations of people.

10D. ARE GENERAL IGNORANCE CLAIMS REALLY ABOUT WHAT VALUES OTHERS "SHOULD" HAVE?

Many people seek to support their own agendas by drawing attention to the ignorance of their opponents. In previous chapters, I showed that many such claims are based on a misunderstanding of the logic of competence—in particular, a failure to understand whether certain pieces of information are really necessary or sufficient for having the knowledge or competence in question. Now, I will show that many claims about others' ignorance are not only indefensible as logical statements about the relationships among information, knowledge, and competence, but are also a product of heavily subjective assertions about what values others ought to have. As a result, these ignorance claims are often poor guides to the kinds of information that educators should convey or that audiences should learn to increase broadly beneficial competences.

I present four such ignorance claims for us to evaluate. Two are by academics and two were written in the wake of electoral defeats. These claims are rare for how articulate they are, but they are not rare with respect to their content. Thousands, if not millions, of similarly themed statements appear daily in editorials, blogs, and the comment sections of online publications. Scores more are offered hourly at dinner tables, hallways, and barstools around the world.

If you are a partisan or consider yourself a liberal or conservative, then you may find at least one of these quotes to be the product of ignorance itself. If you have a particular religious background, you may find one or more of the arguments offensive. If you are having these reactions, let me suggest that you read them with an eye toward what the four writers have in common. If you think that even one of these arguments is on the right track and provides a constructive means of defending claims about what others should know, then I ask you to think about the following question: "Why do the other arguments not have the same power?" Differences in values are often the answer.

The first example comes from an essay published on slate.com on the day after Democrat John Kerry lost the 2004 US presidential election to Republican George W. Bush. In this example, the number "55 million" is a reference to the approximate number of people who voted for Senator Kerry in the election. The term "red states" refers to the states in which President Bush earned a majority of votes—and where Republican candidates often win majority support.

> The election results reflect the decision of the right wing to cultivate and exploit ignorance in the citizenry. I suppose the good news is that 55 million Americans have evaded the ignorance-inducing machine. . . . Ignorance and, bloodlust have a long tradition in the United States, especially in the red states. . . . The error that progressives have consistently committed over the years is to underestimate the vitality of ignorance in America. Listen to what the red state citizens say about themselves, the songs they write, and the sermons they flock to. . . .
>
> Here is how ignorance works: First, they put the fear of God into you—if you don't believe in the literal word of the Bible, you will burn in hell. Of course, the literal word of the Bible is tremendously contradictory, and so you must abdicate all critical thinking, and accept a simple but logical system of belief that is dangerous to question. A corollary to this point is that they make sure you understand that Satan resides in the toils and snares of complex thought and so it is best not to try it [sic]. . . . The history of the last four years shows that red state types, above all, do not want to be told what to do—they prefer to be ignorant. As a result, they are virtually unteachable. . . . [M]ost important, when life grows difficult or fearsome, they (politicians, preachers, pundits) encourage you to cling to your ignorance with even more fervor. But by this time you don't need much encouragement—you've put all your eggs into the ignorance basket, and really, some kind of miraculous fruition (preferably accompanied by the torment of your

enemies, and the ignorant always have plenty of enemies) is your only hope. If you are sufficiently ignorant, you won't even know how dangerous your policies are until they have destroyed you, and then you can always blame others. (Jane Smiley, "The Unteachable Ignorance of the Red States," November 4, 2004)[29]

The second example is, in some respects, a mirror image of Smiley's critique. It comes from a press release by a polling firm that was circulated in the days after Republican John McCain lost the 2008 US presidential election to Democrat Barack Obama. A debate ensued about whether this poll was nationally representative, so there are questions about whether the quote's numerical claims are accurate. I recommend treating the claims as very rough approximations. Even then, the study conveys tangible evidence about things that many 2008 supporters of then-Senator Obama appeared not to know.

> Just 2% of voters who supported Barack Obama on Election Day obtained perfect or near-perfect scores on a post-election test which gauged their knowledge of statements and scandals associated with the presidential tickets during the campaign, a new Zogby International telephone poll shows. Only 54% of Obama voters were able to answer at least half or more of the questions correctly.
>
> "After I interviewed Obama voters on Election Day for my documentary, I had a pretty low opinion of what most of them had picked up from the media coverage of the campaign, but this poll really proves beyond any doubt the stunning level of malpractice on the part of the media in not educating the Obama portion of the voting populace," said [John] Ziegler.
>
> Ninety-four percent of Obama voters correctly identified Palin as the candidate with a pregnant teenage daughter, 86% correctly identified Palin as the candidate associated with a $150,000 wardrobe purchased by her political party, and 81% chose McCain as the candidate who was unable to identify the number of houses he owned. When asked which candidate said they could "see Russia from their house," 87% chose Palin, although the quote actually is attributed to Saturday Night Live's Tina Fey during her portrayal of Palin during the campaign. . . .
>
> Obama voters did not fare nearly as well overall when asked to answer questions about statements or stories associated with Obama . . . 83% failed to correctly answer that Obama had won his first election by getting all of his opponents removed from the ballot,

and 88% did not correctly associate Obama with his statement that his energy policies would likely bankrupt the coal industry. Most (56%) were also not able to correctly answer that Obama started his political career at the home of two former members of the Weather Underground. (Zogby International Press Release, November 18, 2008)[30]

The third critique is offered by a scholar. Political scientist Robert Luskin claims (2002: 282) that "by anything approaching elite standards most citizens think and know jaw-droppingly little about politics." He continues:

> The mass public contains ... a great many more people who know next to nothing about politics. ... The average American's ability to place the Democratic and Republican parties and "liberals" and "conservatives" correctly on issue dimensions and the two parties on a liberal-conservative dimension scarcely exceeds and indeed sometimes falls short of what could be achieved by blind guessing. The verdict is stunningly, depressingly clear: most people know very little about politics. ... (Luskin, 2002: 284)

Questions to ask about each claim include "To whom is knowledge of such facts valuable?" and "For what competences are such facts necessary or sufficient?"

In part II, I will show that the types of questions referenced in the last two claims as evidence of general ignorance are neither broadly representative of general knowledge nor necessary for even very basic competences. For present purposes, however, what unifies these three statements is that the writer puts forward a subjective assessment about the value of certain kinds of information. In some cases, the assessment has an ideological origin—as occurs when the liberal critic claims that citizens are making bad decisions because they do not appear to privilege her way of thinking. In other cases, the bias originates in the writer's professional incentives—as occurs when the academic critic, whose own credibility depends on being well versed in abstract representations of political debate, claims that bad decisions are being made because citizens do not recognize these abstractions. Value diversity prompts disagreements about which political actions are competent and what information is valuable to know.

The fourth and final example is more detailed. I use it to show how considering value diversity changes the meaning of a widely cited claim about voter ignorance. In an article called "Homer Gets a Tax Cut: Inequality and Public Policy in the American Mind," political scientist Larry Bartels (2004: 4) argues that "most Americans support tax cuts not because they are indifferent to economic inequality, but largely because they fail to connect inequality and public policy." In its attempt to explain the American public's thought process, the article characterizes the opinions of "ordinary people" as being "unenlightened" and the result of "simple-minded and sometimes misguided considerations of self-interest."

The data for this article come from the 2002 edition of the American National Election Studies (ANES), a well-regarded survey with measurements of "political knowledge" that I describe more thoroughly in chapters 15 through 18. This particular survey was conducted several years after Congress passed and President George W. Bush signed a change in tax rates that came to be known as "the Bush tax cuts." The ANES asked questions about inequality in general and the Bush tax cuts in particular. In that survey, two-thirds of respondents who offered an opinion about the tax cut approved of it. Bartels (2005: 24) explains the result as "entirely attributable to simple ignorance."

The ANES collects information on many variables. To find that support for the tax cuts was "entirely attributable to simple ignorance" requires ruling out other reasonable explanations for the patterns in the data. Bartels measures the "effect of political information by comparing the views of better and worse informed respondents in the ANES survey using a measure of political information based on interviewers' ratings of respondents" (chapter 17 focuses on the quality of this measure). Bartels's "simple ignorance" claim comes from the fact that people who scored lower on the ratings that he used were more likely to support the tax cut than those who scored higher.

After Bartels's paper was published, my research team and I wanted to see if we could replicate his findings using the same data (we could not) and examine the extent to which his conclusions depended on what struck us as an extreme assumption about the relationships among information, competence, and values. In the remainder of this section, I summarize our findings. Lupia et al. (2007) offers a full account of our methods and additional findings.

Our reanalysis of Bartels's data showed that for a large and politically relevant group of respondents—people who described themselves as conservative or Republican—higher information ratings either had no significant effect on support for the tax cut or they corresponded to increased support for the cuts. This is true even after accounting for reasons that conservatives or Republicans might be more likely than others to support tax cuts (e.g., higher income). No matter how we sliced it, the ANES provided no direct evidence that these groups' support for the tax cuts was "entirely attributable to simple ignorance."

Bartels's findings depended on a strong assumption. His analysis restricted *all respondents*—whether liberal or conservative, Republican or Democrat—to draw identical conclusions about the tax cuts from higher information levels. This assumption eliminates the possibility that, on issues such as the merit of a tax cut proposal, people with diverse values can use new information to reach different conclusions about how economic equality should be weighed relative to other concerns such as economic growth.[31]

To see why Bartels's assumption is problematic, suppose for a moment that we gave respondents more information about the tax cuts. Suppose, moreover, that this additional information revealed that the tax cuts would spur long-term economic growth at the expense of greater economic inequality in the short run. Bartels's assumption requires liberals and conservatives (and Republicans and Democrats) to react to this information in the same way. In this respect, Bartels writes as if there is only one conclusion about the tax cuts that a highly informed respondent can reach. But often in politics, value diversity produces different views on such matters.

Figure 10.1 shows the findings of a reanalysis of the same ANES data from my 2007 article (Lupia et al., 2007). The reanalysis could have verified Bartels's assumption that higher information ratings affect the tax-cut opinions of all political ideologues or partisans in the same way—but it did not. The figure shows that, for the sample as a whole, people are less likely to support the tax cut as they reach higher information levels. However, this effect of changing information levels is quite small. About 70 percent of people in the highest information group supported the tax cut compared to about 67 percent of people in the lowest information group. This is not a big difference. This comparison offers evidence against the claim that "better-informed respondents were much more likely to express *negative* views about the 2001 tax cut."

Moreover, and as previously mentioned, increasing information ratings affected liberals and conservatives (and Republicans and Democrats) very differently. Figure 10.2 depicts the information level/opinion relationship for different partisan and ideological groups. Of interest here are

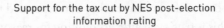

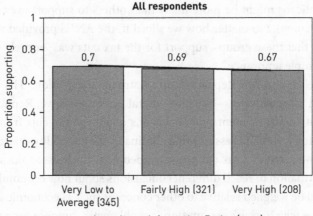

FIGURE 10.1. Support for the Tax Cut by ANES Post-Election Information Rating. *Figure previously published in Arthur Lupia, Adam Seth Levine, Jesse O. Menning, and Gisela Sin, 2007. "Were Bush Tax Cut Supporters 'Simply Ignorant?' A Second Look at Conservatives and Liberals in 'Homer Gets a Tax Cut,'"* Perspectives on Politics 5: 761–772. *Reprinted with permission.*

respondents who label themselves conservative when asked about their ideology (top) or Republican when asked about their partisanship (bottom). For these individuals, the relationship between information rating and tax-cut opinion is just the opposite of what Bartels claims. As members of these groups achieved higher information scores, their support for the tax cut increased.

For self-identified conservatives, 82 percent of respondents whose information rating was "average" or below supported the tax cut. This compares to 88 percent of those who received an information rating of "very high." For Republicans, the corresponding statistics are 89 percent support for respondents rated "average" or below and 96 percent support for the tax cut for those rated "very high." Among these groups, there was a clear consensus in favor of the tax cut—particularly for those with the highest information scores.

Figure 10.2's left side focuses on liberals and Democrats. For these groups, support for the tax cut declines as information ratings increase. Roughly half of these respondents supported the tax cut when their

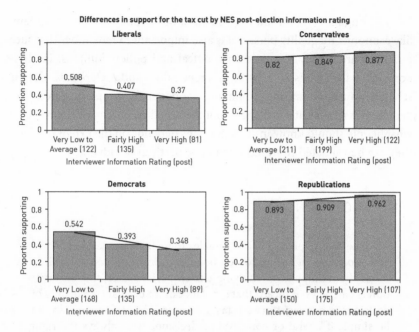

Differences in support for the tax cut by NES post-election information rating

FIGURE 10.2. Differences in Support for the Tax Cut by ANES Post-Election Information Rating. *Figure previously published in Arthur Lupia, Adam Seth Levine, Jesse O. Menning, and Gisela Sin, 2007. "Were Bush Tax Cut Supporters 'Simply Ignorant?' A Second Look at Conservatives and Liberals in 'Homer Gets a Tax Cut,'"* Perspectives on Politics *5: 761–772. Reprinted with permission.*

information rating was "average" or below and over a third continued to support the policy when rated "very high." For liberals, higher information ratings corresponded to more tax-cut opposition. It should be noted, however, that even among the most highly rated liberals and Democrats, there existed diverse opinions about the tax cut—which further undercuts the credibility of "simple ignorance" explanations. While Bartels concludes that "public support for President Bush's tax policies derived from 'unenlightened' considerations of self-interest," the data are also consistent with the conclusion that value diversity fuels opinion differences.

Elsewhere in Bartels's article, citizens are described as "superficial" and "lacking a factual or moral basis" for not thinking about the 2001 tax cut in a particular way. Like the three statements about citizen ignorance described earlier in this section, these claims are a product of heavily subjective assertions about what values others ought to have.

Although it is important to raise questions about why social problems like economic inequality persist, it is also important to remember that such problems are largely managed in political and policy domains. In these domains, participants enter with different values and preferences. Careful scholarship can contribute to making life better for people in poverty or people with similar life challenges, but the broad credibility of claims about what people should know in such domains depends on the extent to which they can be validated from more than one partisan worldview.

10E. CONCLUSION

> The stuff of politics is contestable. There is no single right way to vote, no single right position on issues, no single right set of beliefs. From the standpoint of studying citizen performance, this observation is bad news. It means that scholars cannot evaluate the quality of decisions in a straightforward fashion. Assessing performance would be simple if liberal or conservative decisions were always the right decisions or if a select group of individuals who were known to "get it right" always agreed. For scholars who study such things, unfortunately, neither is the case. (Kuklinski and Quirk, 2001: 285)

The quote highlights why coming to grips with value diversity can help educators provide real benefits to diverse audiences. In many situations, there are no universal criteria that will be accepted as "best" by everyone. There are no silver bullets.

If such an outcome seems unsatisfying, that's politics—the means by which societies attempt to manage conflicts that are not otherwise easily resolved. Issues that people typically perceive as "politicized" are ones over which salient social disagreements persist.[32] When issues cease to have this quality, they tend not to be viewed as political. Recall from a previous chapter that child labor was once a contested political issue in American politics. It was political because people were willing to voice different views about the propriety of young children working long hours in factories. Today, few if any Americans are willing to endorse American children as factory workers. Hence, few consider that issue to be political.

While much of what we consider political is a product of value diversity, diverse societies can come to realize that certain actions produce widely valued benefits. When such realizations emerge, so can broad-based agreements on what competence means. When it can be demonstrated that what a certain audience does not know is preventing a broadly valuable competence from occurring, a sweet spot for educators can emerge. This sweet spot entails identifying information that is not only necessary or sufficient to increase the competence, but also sufficiently beneficial to gain needed attention from prospective learners with diverse perspectives. That is, it is not enough for the information to be factually accurate. To obtain the attention and credibility that increasing knowledge or competence requires, the information must reflect the common interests that exist within the diverse group. With such insights, educators can increase valuable competences in increasingly bigger tents.

11

Complexity and Framing

Politics includes issues of varying complexity. By complex, I mean issues that have multiple and possibly interrelated attributes.[1] While it is arguable that all issues have multiple parts, I use the notion of issue complexity to draw attention to the fact that some issues have so many attributes that educators must make decisions about which parts to emphasize. Consider, for example, the Patient Protection and Affordable Care Act, which the United States passed in 2010. If you haven't heard of this bill, you may know it by another moniker: "Obamacare."

One measure of this law's complexity is its length. It is 906 pages long.[2] The law's table of contents alone is nearly 12 pages.

At 906 pages, and given its frequent use of technical language, it is likely that few citizens, including many candidates for office, are knowledgeable about every part of it. It is inevitable that many, and perhaps most, of the people who express public opinions on this issue base their arguments on knowledge of only a few of the law's many attributes. (This fact, by the way, does not stop people from labeling as "ignorant" others who disagree with them about this law.) In all such cases, experts, advocates, and interested citizens encourage their audiences to weigh certain attributes of the law more (or less) than others when making decisions about it.

Insights from previous chapters can help educators make choices about which of a policy's or candidate's many multiple attributes to emphasize when attempting to improve others' knowledge and competence. From chapter 5, for example, we know that just because an issue is complex, it does not mean that an audience's decision task is complex. Suppose that the task is whether to vote for a specific candidate for office who promises to defeat the healthcare law in its entirety or a candidate who makes the opposite promise. Suppose that we have consulted the relevant range of values and from that consultation we can define a competent choice in the election as the vote that a person would cast if they understood a specific and large set of facts about the law. Given this task, prospective learners may not need to memorize and comprehend all 906 pages of the law to make a competent choice. Each person's task is to cast a single vote with respect to the stated criteria. Since the choice is binary, a child with a fair coin can make the competent choice half the time by voting for the first candidate when the coin lands on heads and not voting for that candidate when it lands on tails. So complex issues need not imply complex tasks—educators can help prospective learners cast competent votes in this case by offering cues that are necessary or sufficient for the voter to make the binary choice that is most consistent with how the continuation of "Obamacare" relates to the facts and values named above.

When issues and prospective learner's choices are complex, educators must make decisions about what information to convey about them. If an issue has 20 parts and attention limits mean that prospective learners can think about far fewer than 20 parts at any given moment, educators who want to earn prospective learners' attention have to decide which parts to emphasize.

The chapter's main lessons are as follows:

- When issues are complex, educators must make choices about which attributes to emphasize. This practice is called *framing*.
- Educators can use "frames" to increase knowledge or competence if two things are true. First, the frame must draw sufficient attention—which it can do by connecting an issue to the values that a person already holds. Second, the frame must contain information, or cause pursuit of additional information, that is necessary or sufficient for the desired knowledge or competence to increase.

This lesson implies that values can affect which framing decisions attract needed attention. This happens because values can affect prospective learners' perceptions and feelings about various issue attributes. In some cases, this role of values in information processing will make it difficult for educators to distinguish between value diversity and issue complexity. People's values and other reasons for focusing on parts of an issue often become fused in memory.[3] So, even if we ask prospective learners to help us separate the two components, many will have difficulty finding the words to do so.[4]

I advise people who are attempting to develop effective educational strategies to think about the relationship in the following way: If values drive attention to certain parts of an issue, then learning about these values can help educators choose the types of frames that can help them more effectively and efficiently increase knowledge and competence on complex issues. In this respect, this chapter can be considered an extension of the previous chapter. In other cases, however, understanding values will not be sufficient to choose an effective frame. In such cases, additional knowledge about how framing works can help educators offer information that is more likely to hit the "sweet spot" described in earlier chapters. This chapter is dedicated to helping educators develop that knowledge.

The chapter continues as follows. In section 11A, I show how issue complexity leads to debates about what information to convey to prospective learners. In section 11B, I describe findings in the scholarly literature on framing effects. In section 11C, I describe how different kinds of educators have put these findings into practice. In section 11D, I address the claim that certain political proposals are "better for everyone" and that for such cases, topics like framing, issue complexity, and value diversity are irrelevant. I show how effective framing can be critical to increasing knowledge and competence even in these cases. Section 11D is a brief conclusion in which I offer additional advice about how to choose frames.

11A. WEIGHTS AND VALUES

For educators, this section's main advice is that when an issue is complex, subjective weighting decisions need to be made. By weight, I mean the relative importance that a person assigns to various parts of an issue when defining competence criteria. An educator assigns heavier weights to parts of a problem that are more important components of a competence criterion. Less important parts receive less weight.

Weighting matters because decisions about which parts of an issue are more important than others are often needed to support arguments about what is worth knowing. An example from a debate on policy responses to climate change presents such a situation.

In 2000, a group of conservative evangelicals issued the Cornwall Declaration. John Copeland Nagle (2008: 62), who has written on the role of religion in environmental law, describes the declaration as identifying "three areas of common misunderstanding." The first misunderstanding was the failure to recognize people as "producers and stewards," as well as "our potential, as bearers of God's image, to add to the earth's abundance." The second misunderstanding was a failure to favor "active human shaping of creation" over "leaving nature untrammeled by man." About the third misunderstanding, Nagle says:

> The Cornwall Declaration's third claim sought to distinguish environmental concerns that "are well founded and serious" from those that "are without foundation or greatly exaggerated," listing "fears of destructive manmade global warming, overpopulation, and rampant species lost" among the latter." (Nagle, 2008: 62)

Other evangelical leaders made similar claims. They advised Christians to explore biblical principles regarding creation before offering opinions about environmental policy. Jerry Falwell (2007), for example, preached that "[t]he alarmism over global warming . . . is Satan's attempt to re-direct the church's primary focus."

With such forceful arguments put forward against climate change, it is difficult to imagine how an educator who seeks to define competence in ways that are consistent with the scientific consensus on the existence of manmade climate change could possibly defend competence criteria that evangelicals could accept. But a powerful counterargument emerged.

Instead of attempting to persuade evangelicals to trust the science, a group called the Evangelical Climate Initiative developed alternate competence criteria. They developed their criteria from a point of view about the importance of various issue attributes that many evangelicals could accept. The Initiative's mission statement reads as follows:

> With the same love of God and neighbor that compels us to preach salvation through our Lord Jesus Christ, protect the unborn, and preserve the family and the sanctity of marriage. That same drive which

compels us to take the Gospel to a hurting world brings us together with others of like mind to pray and to work to stop global warming.

Pollution from vehicles, power plants, and industry is already having a dramatic effect on the earth's climate. The vulnerable are being hurt by the early impacts of climate change. Left unchecked, global warming will lead to more severe droughts, more intense storms, and more devastating floods, resulting in millions of deaths in this century. Prudence and compassion require us to act.

As Christians, we seek to learn what we can do as individuals, families, churches, and communities. We pray for wisdom and courage as we face the difficult choices and issues related to climate impacts. And we call upon our leaders in government and business to act boldly and to set a new course.

We believe that working together and with God's help, we can make a difference. Please join us. (Downloaded August 21, 2011, from http://christiansandclimate.org/about/)

Note that in the first paragraph of this statement, the Evangelical Climate Initiative's leaders are not only reminding potential supporters of their shared values, but also proposing a means of weighting decisions that are consistent with those values.

The Cornwall Declaration and the Evangelical Climate Initiative offer competing competence criteria. While both sets of criteria refer back to a common value orientation, they differ in how they weigh the relative importance of particular tenets of their faith. The presence of multiple attributes of an issue, mixed with some amount of diversity within the faith community, led two subsets of evangelicals to disagree about the kinds of climate-related actions that are more and less competent.

This debate within the evangelical community in some ways exemplifies the larger debate on whether and how governments should attempt to mitigate or adapt to climate change. Proposed policies differ in how much they cost to implement, who should pay these costs, and which statistical climate models are being used as a basis for estimating the various policies' benefits and costs. While there is a scientific consensus on the occurrence of climate change and on humankind's hand in it, the consensus does not extend to who should pay to change current behavior and it has not converged on a single "best model" for projecting how a particular change in policy or human behavior will affect many important aspects of future climates.

Consider, as a parallel to the climate-related debate within the evangelical community, scholarly debates about which statistical models should be used when estimating predicted effects of climate change on sea-level rise.[5] Each statistical model is really a set of assumptions about how to weight different kinds of data. While the models all refer back to a common value orientation (i.e., the proposition that science is a valid way to explain climate change and its effects), they differ in how they weight the relative importance of particular tenets of their knowledge base and methodology. The presence of multiple attributes of an issue combined with some methodological diversity within the scientific community led different groups of scientists to disagree about the kinds of climate-related claims that are more and less accurate.

As a result, claims about what behaviors are competent in places where politics and climate science interact have led some of the most esteemed scientific experts to make subjective weighting decisions about various components of policy proposals. These decisions pertain to whose interests in society are more important than others', how much we should value marine life relative to human life, and what parts of climate-related scientific phenomena are more important than others, and so on.[6] For these reasons, even with seemingly technical issues such as science policy, and even for experts who agree on the general direction in which policy ought to move, there can be large disagreements about which of the issue's moving parts and which of the issue's many constituencies are most important to consider. As ecologist Thomas Dietz (2013) argues,

> It may be that much opposition to taking action on climate change is based on beliefs that government action is ineffectual and intrusive, and interferes with self-interest and traditional values. In that case, more evidence about climatology won't matter but evidence about the nature and performance of public programs might.

For issues like climate change, appeals to scientific facts can play a critical role, but they are not sufficient to define competence in contexts where people must make policy tradeoffs. Educators whose aspirations require the participation of others can benefit from gathering knowledge about what attributes of an issue are commensurate with prospective learners' values. Educators can then use this knowledge to identify information that is capable of earning desired participants' attention.

Consider, for example, arguments about what types of voting behaviors constitute competent behavior by poor people. Poor voters in the United

States are often castigated for voting Republican.[7] These claims are typically built on the assumption that many Democrats pursue social programs and progressive taxation that offer benefits to the poor. But if at least some of the poor care about factors instead of or in addition to their own economic plight, then it may be wrong to conclude that all or even most poor voters should prefer Democrats. In other words, the poor may not have different economic policy preferences than critics imagine, but they may weight the importance of various policies or parts of policies differently than critics understand. Given that most citizens in most elections are not afforded opportunities to cast issue-by-issue votes (they are typically given choices among candidates or parties that represent inseparable bundles of policy positions), the poor may vote Republican because there is something that they care more about than poor-directed social programs and progressive taxation.

To cite just one example, for those among the poor who are deeply religious, who hail from religious traditions that hold the sanctity of human life as a paramount value, and who see abortion as the most serious and frequent threat to that value, drawing a conclusion about what candidate or political party the voter should prefer based only on economic factors assumes a stark moral or ethical tradeoff to which the voter would not consent. So, even if we were to agree that poor voters receive economic benefits from Democratic policies, the validity of claims about which candidate or party represent "a competent vote" for such people depends on strong stated or unstated assumptions about what values are more important than others and what parts of an issue are more important than others.

Even when it comes to the issue of abortion itself, issue complexity affects claims about what "competent" citizens should know. As mentioned in chapter 4, many pro-life advocates claim that information about the fetus should be first and foremost in any discussion of abortion's legal status. They present true technical facts about abortion (e.g., the time in the developmental cycle when a heart begins to beat) to support competent decision-making from this perspective. Many pro-choice advocates, in contrast, claim that information about a pregnant woman's health and freedom of choice should be paramount. They too present true technical facts (e.g., stories about women who were forced to carry pregnancies to term under terrible circumstances). From moral and ethical worldviews that are held by hundreds of millions of people, each set of claims has validity.

Moreover, what is beyond debate in the contemporary politics of abortion is that each side in the debate can present facts in support of its arguments. Where debaters often disagree is on what values and parts of the issue to prioritize. On this topic and many others, there is not as yet a universally accepted measure of which facts or values are more important. Given the fundamental, deeply felt, and culturally instantiated values inherent in the different points of view, and given the diverse ways in which the issue can be evaluated, a universally accepted competence criterion for abortion-related decisions in the United States seems unlikely in the near future.

For many issues that are recognized as political, if someone is making a claim about what a competent citizen should know, they are also arguing for the prioritization of certain issue attributes and values over others. For educators, this fact is important, as it should alert them to the need to answer questions about the weighting decisions that are implicit in their own choices about what kinds of information prospective learners will perceive as offering positive net benefits. Educators who have this skill can help prospective learners, and potential supporters of labor or capital for their educational endeavor, see the benefits of their plans of action. Such clarity can persuade prospective learners and potential supporters that an educator's competence-increasing endeavor is worth pursuing.

11B. FRAMING EFFECTS

Many educators believe that their decisions about which issue attributes to emphasize have a large effect on prospective listeners' subsequent thoughts. Interest in how to choose which parts of an issue to emphasize often manifests as claims about *framing effects*. Political scientists Dennis Chong and James Druckman (2007: 104) define framing as "the process by which people develop a particular conceptualization of an issue or reorient their thinking about an issue." In other words, framing is an attempt to influence the manner in which others weight an issue's various attributes in their subsequent thinking.

A substantial academic literature and a consulting industry have been built around the concept of framing. Their work reveals conditions under which emphasizing certain parts of an issue can increase attention to an issue and can change how an audience subsequently thinks about an issue.[8]

An iconic experiment by psychologists Amos Tversky and Daniel Kahneman (1981, 1986) reveals the potential power of framing effects. They asked experimental subjects to choose one of two ways to manage a deadly disease. The experiment varies how the two options are framed. One group received this frame:

- If Program A is adopted, 200 people will be saved.
- If Program B is adopted, there is a 1/3 probability that 600 people will be saved and a 2/3 probability that no people will be saved.

When described in this way, 72% of the subjects chose Program A. Another group received this frame:

- If Program A is adopted, 400 people will die.
- If Program B is adopted, there is a 1/3 probability that nobody will die and a 2/3 probability that 600 people will die.

When described this way, 78% of the subjects chose Program B. Note, however, that programs A and B are identical in their effects. The difference between the two frames is whether they emphasize *lives saved* or *deaths caused*.

Results like these have led many people to believe that effective framing is easy. Generally speaking, it is not. James Druckman (2001a), for example, identifies source credibility as a severe limit on framing effects. A key premise for his work (2001a: 1061) is that "nearly every time scholars look for a framing attempt, they tend to find it. There has been an almost exclusive focus on successful framing attempts." Working from ideas about credibility described in chapter 8, Druckman finds (2001a: 1050) that "a perceived noncredible source cannot use a frame to affect opinions . . . or the perceived importance of different considerations." In other words, if an audience does not perceive the source of a framing attempt as having common interests and relevant expertise, then the source's framing attempts have little to no effect.

Values are also an important limiting factor. Some studies have shown that when people are presented with frames that contradict their values or preferences, framing effects dissipate. Druckman (2001b), for example, reran the Tversky-Kahneman experiment. His version randomly assigned subjects to one of six experimental groups. Two matched Tversky and Kahneman's experimental groups. One group was told about the two options in terms of lives saved, while the presentation to the other group emphasized the number of deaths. Druckman's findings for these two groups replicate the original Tversky and Kahneman study.

In the third and fourth groups, Program A was relabeled the "Democratic proposal" and Program B was called the "Republican proposal." In the fifth and sixth groups, the names were reversed. So, in the third and fifth groups, both proposals are described in terms of lives saved. In the fourth and sixth groups, the description emphasizes deaths caused. Also, in a pre-experimental questionnaire, Druckman asked subjects to identify their partisan leanings.

Druckman finds that once the Tversky-Kahneman programs gain partisan labels, framing effects fall significantly or disappear. This work implies that when values-based information is available, more abstract framing attempts lose their force. Druckman (2001b: 77) shows that "[i]nstead of basing their preferences on arbitrary question wording, people tend to rely on what they believe is credible information."[9]

Other scholars have identified methodological problems in claims about the size of framing effects. When claiming that a particular frame has influenced an audience, for example, it is important to account for the possibility that the effect is an illusion. To clarify this point, political scientist Daniel Hopkins examined framing effects in the debate that followed the passage of the Affordable Care Act. He finds that

> supporters at the elite and mass levels alike emphasized the expansion of insurance and increased access to health care. Yet supporting citizens used these arguments to explain their views *even before the health care reform debate came to dominate headlines*, a fact which suggests the limited influence of elite rhetoric." (Hopkins, 2013: 23–24, emphasis added)

In other words, advocates may choose a frame not because it will move an audience, but because the frame reflects and follows the way the audience is already thinking (Bovitz, Druckman, and Lupia, 2002). So when a correlation between a frame and public opinion is observed, it can be hard to differentiate whether the correlation reflects framing effects changing opinions or opinions influencing an advocate's framing choice.

One implication of these mixed findings about framing effects makes a popular conjecture about civic incompetence harder to reconcile with the evidence that is alleged to support it. Political scientists Paul Sniderman and Sean Theriault (1999: 158) describe this conjecture (to which they do not subscribe) in their review of a large literature on public opinion:

> According to the framing theory of public opinion, citizens are not capable of political judgment: the very same person will approve a course of government action or oppose it depending on how the action happens to be framed at the moment of choice. . . . They are instead puppets, voting thumbs up or down depending on how issues are framed, their strings being pulled by elites who frame issues to guarantee political outcomes.

At least two sets of framing-related research findings contradict this view. One set of findings is reflected in the results described above: Framing effects depend on source credibility. If citizens do not believe that a source shares their values and has relevant expertise, then framing attempts are less effective or completely ineffective. The second set of findings shows that some framing effects are larger not for relatively uninformed "puppets," but rather for people who are relatively well informed about an issue. Chong and Druckman (2007: 112), for example, have found that greater knowledge of an issue can enhance framing effects "because it increases the likelihood that the considerations emphasized in a frame will be available or comprehensible. . . ." In other words, framing affects are different from manipulating "puppets." Some framing effects work because prospective learners already have substantial knowledge about the issue at hand. In sum, framing can have powerful effects on how prospective learners think about a candidate or issues—but these effects occur only if certain conditions are met.

11C. FRAMING EFFECTS IN ACTION

In the previous section, we identified conditions under which framing effects can affect attempts to increase knowledge and competence. As Chong and Druckman (2007: 111) conclude, however, "there is nothing inherently superior about a [successful] frame other than its appeal to audiences." The key for educators is to find a sweet spot—information that not only increases competence if sufficient attention is paid to it, but is also framed in a way that draws the necessary attention.

An example where advocates used a framing change to induce people to rethink their position on a focal issue involved same-sex marriage. At one time, advocates for legal same-sex marriage emphasized that LGBT persons should have the same rights as heterosexuals. They argued that withholding marriage rights from this population denied them important legal and economic benefits (such as being covered by a partner's health insurance). Advocates and other researchers began to collect data on how heterosexuals thought about the issue. They found that many people who had mixed feelings about same-sex marriage (a.k.a. "the middle") resisted these "rights-and-benefits" appeals.[10] As Lanae Erickson (2011:3) explains:

> Extending marriage to gay couples is in some ways about rights, and there are myriad legal protections that arise from marriage, but that is not how people see their own marriages. Most Americans think that marriage is about love, commitment, obligation, and respon-sibility. That is why the solemnity of the ceremony and vows are so important—because they represent a one-of-a-kind promise of life-time commitment and fidelity, made publicly in front of family and friends. Yet advocates have often focused on rights and benefits, not commitment, when talking about why gay couples want to marry. This mismatch may have exacerbated an existing disconnect in the minds of the middle, perpetuating the notion that gay couples want to marry for different reasons than other couples or, worse, implying that gay couples don't truly understand what marriage is about.

Erickson's think tank Third Way ran additional studies. They examined whether different frames could move the middle and induce them to become more supportive of same-sex marriage. In one study, they asked respondents to choose the most important reason why "couples like you" want to get married. Fifty-eight percent of their respondents chose the response "to publicly acknowledge their love and commitment to each other." Only 22 percent chose a response that focused on "rights and ben-efits." Respondents were then asked why they believed gay couples wanted to marry. Of those who gave an answer, half said "rights and benefits" and half said "love and commitment."

Third Way discovered that over 60 percent of respondents who saw gays as seeking rights and benefits reported being "uncomfortable" with same-sex marriage. In contrast, over 60 percent of respondents who saw these couples as seeking love and commitment supported marriage at the highest levels that the question wording permitted. Third Way used these results to propose a change in strategy (Erickson 2011:4):

> To move the middle, we must convince them that gay people seek similar things in marriage as they do. Leading with commitment will show the middle that gay people want to join the institution of marriage, not change it. And our research found that when voters thought gay couples were seeking to join marriage, not change it, support burgeoned.

Research like this allowed a range of organizations to identify a new sweet spot that increased their effectiveness.[11]

With respect to whether this example describes an increase in competence, value diversity at the time that I wrote this book continues to produce divergent views on same-sex marriage. There is, at present, no universally accepted value orientation that renders this example one of increased or decreased competence. What is clear is that the empirical discovery of a belief about marriage (the primacy of love and commitment) that transcended specific situations (i.e., a value) produced a frame that conveyed knowledge in ways that other strategies had not. For all sides of the same-sex marriage debate, the emergence of the love and commitment sweet spot means that subsequent educational strategies to reach the middle will require information that not only connects to their values, but also builds upon—or counters—the attachment to love and commitment that many gay and straight people share.

A second example of framing's potential importance to contemporary society can be seen in attempts to communicate information about vaccines and public health. Many vaccines reduce the spread of contagious diseases. Their effectiveness depends not just on individuals receiving vaccinations, but on significant proportions of large populations doing the same. In many cases, contagion risk is minimized when everyone is vaccinated. If a public health goal is to minimize the spread of diseases, and if there is broad acceptance of a criterion that measures competence in terms of how few cases of diseases arise, then many countries have been successful at achieving high competence levels. Even the United States, where mid-level celebrities have helped to spread false information about links between vaccines and autism, education has kept vaccination rates high. According to the World Health Organization's most recent estimates, vaccination rates in the United States for the most common vaccines maintained their post-2000 average of over 90 percent and saw declines of less than 1 percent with respect to those averages.[12]

Yet more can be done. A challenge for educators who want to increase this type of competence is to get more people to vaccinate. To achieve this outcome, educators should not simply convey dry facts about vaccination and herd immunity. For example, important work by political scientists Brendan Nyhan and Jason Riefler (2010, 2015) has identified several instances in which members of the public hold false beliefs about things like flu vaccines. They have run experiments in which subjects receive true information that contradicts the false beliefs. They report that:

> Corrective information adapted from the Centers for Disease Control and Prevention (CDC) website significantly reduced belief in the myth that the flu vaccine can give you the flu as well as concerns about its safety. However, the correction also significantly *reduced* intent to vaccinate among respondents with high levels of concern about vaccine side effects—a response that was not observed among those with low levels of concern. This result, which is consistent with previous research on misperceptions about the MMR vaccine, suggests that correcting myths about vaccines may not be an effective approach to promoting immunization. (Nyhan and Riefler, 2015: 459)

Instead, educators must also find ways to present vaccination's net benefits in ways that hesitant populations will find sufficiently credible. Following themes established in previous chapters, one way for educators to break through is to learn more about the target population's values and use that knowledge to find common interests. This means proceeding differently than doctors and media personalities who, by simply scoffing at citizens who disagree with them, may be hurting rather than helping their professed cause of greater immunity. As noted health communications scholar K. Vish Vishwanath describes:

> Calling them anti-vaxxers is not helpful. Trying to persuade them that they are wrong is only going to reinforce their attitudes. With them, you have to explore other ways of reaching out and explaining why this process is safe.[13]

Vishwanath and a growing number of health communication scholars are increasing their use of the kinds of methods described in this book to learn more about the values and core concerns of diverse populations.[14] These organizations are identifying factual information about the net benefits of vaccination that intersects with prospective learners' priorities. These are constructive and promising approaches to the cause of greater immunity.[15]

11D. BUT I'M "RIGHT," SO NOTHING IN THIS CHAPTER APPLIES TO ME

Over the years, I have run across educators who believe that they are immune from having to account for others' values or consider framing as a strategic response to issue complexity. These educators see themselves as outside of or above politics. They are trying to "bring reason" to some aspect of social life. They want to make things "better for everyone."

There are indeed debates in which broad populations agree that a certain principle is the only legitimate means by which to evaluate a behavior as competent. In these cases, a "bringing reason" frame can be a broadly acceptable description of what an educator is trying to do. However, as we move from such consensual domains, the need to subjectively weigh an issue's multiple components reappears.

When I lived in San Diego, California, for example, the area was growing in population. There were ongoing political debates about how to use the increasingly scarce undeveloped land. Some people wanted to use the land to build new houses, office buildings, freeways, and shopping malls. Others wanted to keep the land in its natural state.

People who wanted to develop the land ran political campaigns. One campaign posted advertisements in support of a development proposal that included the tag line, "It's better for everyone." The tag line often appeared above a picture. The picture showed about a dozen people of different races and ethnic groups wearing different types of clothes. The clothes suggested that they held different kinds of jobs and were from different socioeconomic backgrounds. The individuals were facing the camera, and by extension looking straight at the viewer of the picture. Every one of these people who were looking at me and other viewers appeared to be very happy. The tag line and image suggested that this development proposal could benefit everyone.

I did not know "all the facts" about this development proposal. The information that was most easily available to me was supplied by the campaign's combatants. I struggled to find less biased information about the proposal's economic impact (this was at a time before such information was

regularly posted on the Internet). I also lacked information on other factors, such as whether any environmental damage or displacement would
result from the proposed construction. But I did know one thing. Given
the fact that the matter had to be settled in a long series of political battles,
and given that there was a very visible and organized opposition to these
plans—it had to be the case that not everyone in San Diego agreed with the
tag line.

It was California, after all. Clearly, there were some people who felt that
placing a freeway, office parks, tens of thousands of homes, and dozens of
strip malls in places where horse pastures and undeveloped hills now stood
was a bad thing. Had everyone agreed on which attributes of this complex
issue were most important, the promoters would not have had to go through
a long series of political maneuvers and wage an expensive PR campaign.

When presented with the idea that competence criteria can include
subjective assertions about what parts of an issue are most important, many
people deny that this idea applies to *their situation*. They see themselves as
pursuing a goal that is defensible from any reasonable point of view. Some
want to claim that what they want is better for everyone. While we can
think of many things that are better for everyone, when an issue is such that
it needs to be resolved politically, better-for-everyone claims deny the reality of value diversity rather than constructively responding to it.

Developers are not alone in making better-for-everyone claims. On
September 23, 2005, the *Seattle Times* published an editorial titled "Making
Our Economy Work Better for Everyone."[16] The author, Diane Sosne, was
the president of Service Employees International Union District 1199NW, a
union of more than 18,000 healthcare workers in Washington:

> On Tuesday, representatives of 6 million working Americans will join
> together in St. Louis to launch an ambitious new campaign to make
> our economy work better for everyone. This group of seven major
> unions, called the "Change to Win" coalition, decided to leave the
> national AFL-CIO earlier this summer to find new ways to ensure that
> hard work is again rewarded in America.

The editorial continued by describing decreasing health benefits for some
workers, the growing American income gap, and declining union membership. It then revealed that "the seven 'Change to Win' unions have committed to work together to help millions more workers in today's economy join
the union movement and raise living standards for everyone."

Without being too critical of this editorial, I think that most observers would agree that increasing the membership of these unions will have no effect on many people's living standards and may even decrease them for others (such as whomever pays these workers' salaries and benefits—or people who lose jobs, or fail to get jobs, if an employer has to reduce the size of its workforce in order to afford increased salaries and benefits—or people who have to pay more for the products or services if employers' increased costs are passed on to consumers). The point is not that the union president's appeal is illegitimate or unimportant, the point is that whenever someone in an extended political negotiation (who is also announcing a divorce from a former organization) claims that what they want is better for everyone, then at least one thing they are saying is seen by others in the negotiation, or in the former organization, as untrue.

11E. CONCLUSION

Attention is limited, and issues are often complex. As a result, educators who want to increase knowledge or competence must choose which aspects of an issue to emphasize. To draw attention, educators can choose issue attributes that prospective learners perceive as directly relevant in helping them advance their core concerns. As values often alert people to the link between new information and core concerns, frames that are consistent with a prospective learner's values have a greater chance to succeed.

Values, however, are not the only element that educators should consider. A prospective learner's perception of the net benefit of information will depend on their beliefs about what, if anything, they can do with that information. In previous chapters, we established that information that is necessary or sufficient to increase a valued competence offers more benefits to prospective learners than information that has no such power. A related factor is the opportunities that prospective learners have to use what they learn. It is to this topic that we now turn.

12

Political Roles: *Who* Needs to Know?

Up to this point in the book, we have established that educators' ability to develop and defend claims about the benefits of conveying certain types of information depends on the logic of competence, a prospective learner's values, and framing decisions. For the purpose of this chapter, I proceed as if an educator has developed such a defense and turn attention to an important procedural question. To increase a competence, *who* needs to know *what*?

For example, citizens have opportunities to vote for other people (i.e., candidates) who then make decisions on their behalf. If an educator is seeking to increase a competence using a criterion that produces particular kinds of policy outcomes, then competence depends not only on citizens' direct actions, but also on the subsequent actions of those whom they elect.[1] Suppose, for example, that an educator's goal is to increase math proficiency among second-graders in a given school district. If a citizen votes for a school board candidate who voices the same desire, this vote is not sufficient to produce the desired outcome. That candidate must actually win the election—which requires votes from other voters. If elected, the candidate must work with other school board members to write the desired policies and then must count on others, such as school district employees, to enforce the policies. If we evaluate a citizen's school board voting competence by whether it makes increased math proficiency more likely, many decisions other than her vote affect the evaluation. As a result, the kinds of information that can increase this competence depend on how the voter can use them.

Variations in political roles affect *who* needs to know *what*. By political role, I mean a person's opportunities to affect political outcomes. Some individuals, like a president or governor, have roles with great authority. Their singular actions can change important social outcomes. Other roles carry less political authority—such as being one of several million voters in a two-candidate election whose lone vote is unlikely to affect who wins the election. Information that a president needs to accomplish his or her most important tasks can be meaningless to a working parent, and vice versa.

In this chapter, I describe how educators can use knowledge of political roles to develop more effective and efficient educational strategies. A key insight is that when citizens have different political roles, information that is highly valuable for one person may have no value to another. This can be true even if both citizens' efforts are needed to achieve a desired competence. As a result, effective educational strategies may involve giving different information to different people. For information that increases competence, one size need not fit all.

Note that the point of this chapter is not to argue that people need to understand how their decisions link to outcomes they care about—though such knowledge can increase competence in some cases. The point of the chapter is to demonstrate that *educators can be more effective and efficient if they understand how information becomes competence in settings where people have different political roles*. Educators who understand these relationships can target information more effectively—giving prospective learners information they can actually use.

By way of analogy, for several years I helped to coach the Burns Park Penguins, a boys' soccer team in Ann Arbor. The team won 101 of its 105 games over a five-year period, including 43 straight victories. I worked with the defense and the goaltenders. In that experience, I saw that a coach, whose task is to help very young boys understand how to work together to achieve a common goal, must provide different types of information to the defense and the goaltender than she or he would provide to the forwards. Information that is very valuable for the goaltender is often less valuable to the other players on the team—and young boys are particularly unforgiving in "the attention department" when receiving information whose relevance is not immediately apparent. For the team to achieve its goals, each player needs knowledge that reflects the opportunities they will have during a game. The best use of a coach's time is to focus on giving each player the information that is most valuable for their position. For those of us educators who seek to coach others in a wide range of educational domains, a similar rule applies. We can increase competences more efficiently by understanding what different kinds of people can do with different kinds of information.

The main lessons of this chapter are as follows:

- The consequences of providing information to prospective learners depend on their political roles.
- A common supposition about competent voting is that it requires voters to select candidates whose preferences over policy outcomes are closest to their own. This is not always true. A candidate's ability to serve voters depend not only on the candidate's preferences but also on the candidate's political roles.
- When a voter's competence is judged with respect to policy outcomes, the bargaining power of the candidates from which she can choose, and the behavior of government employees, affect what kind of vote is competent.

The chapter continues as follows. In section 12A, I describe how political roles affect relations between information and competence. In section 12B, I describe how educators can use knowledge of these relationships to make educational strategies more effective. In section 12C, I use this knowledge to more accurately interpret numerous claims about the public's apparent political ignorance. In short, I show that many critics scold citizens for not knowing things that, while important in their own lines of work, have little or no value to those who have different roles. In each section, I show how educators can use knowledge of political roles to correct these errors and increase knowledge and competence more effectively.

12A. THE LONE VOTER: HOW POLITICAL ROLES AFFECT VOTER COMPETENCE

How can educators use knowledge of political roles to improve a voter's competence? I answer this question with an example that starts simply. It begins with a lone voter.[2] The lone voter's role is to cast a single vote that determines which of two political parties will have complete control over all aspects of government for the rest of time. The selected party will be a dictator that implements its preferred policies without delay. To simplify this first version of the example, let's assume that everyone in society agrees that when evaluating the actions of government, only the lone voter's well-being matters. So, with respect to our judgments about the voter's competence, all that matters is what is best for her.

One of the two parties is actually better for the lone voter. The outcomes it will produce if elected are better for the voter than what the other party will do. I call this party "the better party". So, in this initial version of the example, the competent choice always entails the lone voter choosing the better party.[3] In cases like this, where differences between political parties are stark with respect to an agreed-upon set of values, a simple cue (i.e., a candidate's partisan identification) can be sufficient for casting a competent vote.

When we diverge from this ideal situation, more information may be needed to vote competently. To see how, I now change the lone voter's role. Instead of casting a single vote that determines which of two political parties will have complete control over all aspects of government for the rest of time, the lone voter now picks one member of a large legislative assembly. I continue to define competence only with respect to the lone voter's well-being.

In this case, choosing the party with preferences closest to her own may no longer be the lone voter's competent choice. The reason is that in many legislatures, groups of legislators must act together to produce desired policy outcomes. When a voter's competence is judged by whether an action produces policy outcomes of a certain quality, a legislator's negotiating skills vis-à-vis other legislators can be more important than her chosen representative's policy preferences.

Passing new laws, for example, requires legislators to obtain majority or supermajority support in their chamber. Suppose that there are multiple versions of an annual budget that a majority of legislators would support. Perhaps these budgets fund services that a legislative majority considers vital and keeps taxes in a range that is acceptable to the lone voter. If, however, these legislators have different preferences over these potential budgets, then even if a majority agrees that one of the budgets should pass, they may disagree about which one to choose.

Negotiation is how such disagreements are managed. In such cases, the lone voter's elected representative will have to negotiate with other members of the legislature to pass a budget. In negotiations, legislators exchange proposals and offer reasons for particular courses of action. Negotiation outcomes turn not only on the participants' desires, but also on the allocation of negotiating skills and bargaining powers among them.[4] Legislative bargaining skills and negotiating powers derive from several sources. One source is other legislators' preferences.

For example, if the lone voter's representative prefers budget X to budget Y, and if all other legislators prefer budget Y to budget X, the deck will be stacked against the lone voter's preference affecting government actions. In contrast, if all of the other legislators are split over which option is better, the lone voter's elected representative might have more leverage to get the types of outcomes that the lone voter desires. The lone voter's representative would have a lot of bargaining leverage if she can break the tie in the X-Y debate or if she can use that tie-breaking ability to gain advantages on other issues that matter to the lone voter.

In some cases, a legislator can drive the hardest bargain for a cause precisely because he or she is unlike his or her co-partisans. Consider, for example, a legislator who has a history or attribute that makes him less willing to compromise. In some cases, this legislator may be different from the lone voter in some respects and yet better able to pull legislative outcomes in directions that the lone voter prefers.[5]

For example, suppose that the lone voter holds a moderate position on the one policy issue that she cares about most. If this issue is sufficiently important to her, it might seem reasonable to conclude that the voter would best be represented by a moderate who shares her views on this issue. But if moderates compromise in ways that extremists do not, then choosing the moderate candidate may not be the competent choice.

Figure 12.1 depicts such a situation. In it, the lone voter most prefers policy outcome S. To the extent that a policy other than S will be passed, she prefers that the policy be as close to S as possible. Let's say that ~S denotes a different policy outcome that other voters desire.

Suppose that bargaining power is distributed among the legislators in a manner that leads them to split the difference between the preferred policy positions of the lone voter's representative and the policy ~S. If a moderate represents the lone voter in this case, splitting the difference will lead to a policy outcome halfway between S and ~S. This point is labeled Z in

Extreme Left	Moderate	Extreme Right
W------------------------------------S--------------------------------- ~S		
	S-----------------Z-------------- ~S	

FIGURE 12.1. Two Cases of "Splitting the Difference" (outcomes in bold).

figure 12.1. If, however, the lone voter were to choose someone whose preferences are more extreme than her own (i.e., suppose that there exists a legislator whose most preferred outcome is W and that S is halfway between ~S and W), and if this representative agreed to split the difference with supporters of outcome ~S, then this compromise will result in S being chosen. S is the lone voter's most preferred policy. Given that competence in terms of this example is defined as what is best for the lone voter, voting for the extremist is the competent choice in this case. Choosing the candidate who shares the lone voter's preference would be incompetent with respect to the stated criteria.[6]

So, if I am a moderate liberal and I elect a moderate liberal, perhaps she will bargain with a staunch conservative and they will reach a compromise that is moderately conservative. But if I instead elected a staunch liberal, rather than a moderate one, perhaps the compromise outcome would have been moderately liberal, or exactly what I wanted.

Patience is also another source of bargaining leverage that might make the lone voter's competent choice a candidate whose policy preferences differ from her own. For example, a legislator who needs a decision to be made *now* (perhaps because his reelection depends on it) may be more willing to compromise than a legislator who does not need a speedy decision. In legislative bargaining, patience is often power.[7] To see how this aspect of legislative bargaining can affect voter competence, suppose that the lone voter must choose one of two candidates. Suppose that candidate 1 negotiates well but does not share the lone voter's preferences exactly. Candidate 2 shares the lone voter's preferences but is a horrible negotiator because his personal circumstances lead him to compromise too early, too much, and too often. In such cases, choosing the candidate whose preferences most resemble the lone voter's may not be the competent choice using the criteria laid out earlier in this chapter. Choosing the other candidate produces a better policy outcome.

So, when a legislator must bargain with others to influence the actions of government, characteristics of that negotiation can influence which candidate represents a competent choice for the lone voter. To get a desired policy outcome, it is not just the correspondence between the voter's desires and those of her representative that matters. How well her representative negotiates is also consequential.

When understanding how an individual's choices correspond to policy outcomes, legislators' abilities matter. As a consequence, educators who are motivated to achieve particular outcomes can target information more effectively by understanding how citizens' choices relate to the outcomes in question. Similar dynamics affect the choice of an executive, such as a president who alone controls his branch of government. If the executive is effectively a dictator—as is the case in some nations—then the lone voter does best by choosing a candidate for executive office who will implement the outcomes that are better for her. If, however, creating legislation requires the executive to seek the assent of a legislature and other actors, then bargaining dynamics come back into play.

Consider, for example, a voter who has a choice between two presidential candidates, C and D. Candidate C shares the voter's preferences over policy outcomes. However, it is also known that candidate C is all too willing to compromise with those who disagree with him. Candidate D, in contrast, has policy preferences that are somewhat different from those of the voter but has personal abilities to bring other legislators around to his point of view. If the competence criterion entails choosing the candidate who produces policy outcomes that are best for the voter, then voting for C need not always be the competent choice.

Of course, electing someone who is different than the lone voter can produce other outcomes, such as legislative gridlock or the threat that the representative will produce less desirable outcomes on other issues. In such cases, the competence of supporting an extremist depends on the relative weight of these various outcomes in the competence criterion.

In general, to claim that a voter is incompetent because their vote appears to correspond to a particular policy outcome entails at least two assumptions. One assumption is that this policy outcome is so much more important than others that a competence judgment can be based on observing this outcome alone. The other assumption is about the voter's ability to affect the outcome in question. There are many political contexts in which neither assumption is likely to be true. Suppose, for example, that someone wants to base a competence judgment on whether a vote reduces income inequality. Suppose, moreover, that one candidate is less likely than another to bring about laws that reduce income inequality (perhaps because he cares less about the issue or is a lousy negotiator). If that same candidate produces other policy outcomes that are important to the voter, a claim about a voter's competence or incompetence includes not just depend on a theory about a legislator's political role and bargaining power, but also on a subjective judgment about what values or means of weighing the different issue attributes the voter ought to have.

In general, when assessing a voter's competence with respect to the policy outcomes that her vote produces, it is important to remember that policy outcomes are also affected by attributes of legislators who were elected by other people living in other districts and legislative bargaining dynamics over which the voter has no control. These factors can limit, or even eliminate, a voter's ability to affect an outcome with her vote. As a result, outcome-based claims about what vote is competent should be rendered with respect to greater knowledge of how the votes in questions relate to desired outcomes.

12B. HOW LEGISLATORS AND BUREAUCRATS AFFECT THE VALUE OF INFORMATION

In many cases, legislative dynamics affect what information is valuable for educators to convey to prospective learners. Consider, for example, educators whose motives include the US Congress taking certain actions. The House and Senate operate under different rules. The House uses majority rule to make many important decisions. The Senate requires supermajorities and sometimes unanimous consent for many of its key decisions. These rules give members of each chamber different abilities to affect policy outcomes.[8] For example, if 41 senators are dead set against a particular bill being passed, Senate rules (at the time this book was written) give the 41 powers to block the bill. Even if the president and every single member of the House of Representatives want the bill to pass, 41 senators can engage in a filibuster (which prevents the Senate from conducting any other business) as a means of pursuing the outcome they want. This ability to delay other activities gives Senate minorities leverage that similarly sized House minorities do not have.

Now, suppose that an advocate-educator's goal is to provide information that changes a federal policy outcome in a particular way. If two versions of a bill are sufficient to achieve this goal, but only one of the two versions would survive a filibuster, and if all else is constant, an advocate-educator can achieve her goal more efficiently by providing information that advances the viable version. This is true even if the educator prefers the filibustered bill to the non-filibustered bill, as long as she also prefers the non-filibustered version to the status quo. An educator who chooses to ignore this aspect of political roles may waste time providing information about a proposal that has no chance of becoming law. Similar dynamics affect the value of information to citizens at state and local levels.[9] Knowledge of political roles in all such instances can help educators achieve many policy-related goals more effectively.

Educators whose ambitions cross national boundaries can also use knowledge of political roles to increase their effectiveness. For example, many nations have parliamentary governments. In many parliamentary democracies, no single political party obtains a majority of seats after an election.[10] When no party earns a majority, post-electoral negotiations are needed to produce a majority that can govern. This manufactured majority is a negotiated agreement among multiple parties. Across countries, differences in post-election negotiation dynamics affect what kinds of parties end up in the majority. So even if a particular voter casts the decisive vote with respect to a single member of Parliament, differences in post-election bargaining dynamics can change the relationship between such a vote and policy outcomes from country to country. Hence, outcome-based claims about what citizens should know, and what votes are competent, will depend on a country's electoral dynamics and legislative bargaining dynamics as well as on the other components of the politics of competence.

Actions taken outside of legislatures also affect the kinds of information that would be most valuable for educators to convey. For example, whether at the state or local level and whether domestic or international, after a legislature passes a law, it asks bureaucrats (typically employees of administrative agencies) to turn a law's words into actions. Educators whose objectives pertain to achieving specific policy outcomes can use knowledge of relationships between legislatures and bureaucrats to target information more effectively. One thing that is important for such educators to understand is that bureaucrats vary in their expertise and aspirations. Some are driven to carry out laws exactly as they are written. Others seek to implement and enforce laws in accordance with their own objectives, rather than those of the legislature.[11] In some cases, the interpretative discretion available to bureaucrats is a result of vaguely worded legislation. In other cases, bureaucrats purposefully reject legislative mandates. Studies of legislative delegation to bureaucrats find that legislatures that have effective ways of learning about bureaucrats' actions and that have means of sanctioning wayward agents are more likely to find bureaucratic actions aligned with their stated intentions.[12] Means for this kind of legislative inquiry include formal congressional hearings, as well as electronic venues for citizens and interest groups to report on agent activities.[13]

Since bureaucratic actions can affect the correspondence between an election outcome and the manner in which policies are implemented, insight about this correspondence can help educators understand how to target information and increase competence more effectively and efficiently. If, for example, it is best that the actions of government lead to policy outcomes that are as close as possible to what is best for, say, the safety of a particular kind of child, then the types of votes that citizens should cast depend not just on the legislative bargaining dynamics previously described, but also on bureaucratic actions. When bureaucrats faithfully execute legislative instructions, citizens' knowledge of legislative bargaining dynamics can help them cast votes that correspond to the desired outcome. When bureaucrats run amok, however, the question of which votes are competent will depend on just how the bureaucrats run amok.[14]

To make these dynamics more concrete, let's return to a slight variation of the lone voter example. As before, her welfare remains our sole competence criterion. Suppose that the lone voter is a moderate and that it is well known that the bureaucracy is controlled by extremists. In such situations, the voter can be well served by electing those legislators who can best contain the extremists. Echoing the previous section's logic, the lone voter's need to constrain extremist bureaucrats may be best accomplished by electing legislators whose policy preferences are *not* identical to her own.

In sum, educators whose ambitions are related to specific policy outcomes can benefit by understanding whether and how prospective learners can affect that outcome. Such an understanding includes how a prospective learner's vote affects an elected representative's incentives, how elected representatives negotiate with others to pass legislation, and how legislatures monitor and influence bureaucratic behaviors. Educators who have such knowledge can better differentiate information that is necessary or sufficient for achieving an educational goal from information that has no such potential given the roles that prospective learners' actually have. If an educator's goal is to provide information with positive net benefits, knowledge of political roles can help them deliver information to where it can make a real difference.

12C. HOW POLITICAL ROLES AFFECT WHAT
CITIZENS SHOULD KNOW

Many people make claims about what others should know. These claims privilege certain facts and are often associated with calls to give precedence to these privileged ideas in subsequent educational endeavors. Some people who make these claims may even seek to make you feel foolish for questioning the relevance of the facts that they privilege.

If we can agree that it is worthwhile to give people information they need to manage tough challenges competently, then the question for many civic educators becomes, "To whom, and under what conditions, does forcing people to learn things like the names of Supreme Court justices provide positive net benefits?" Given what we know about cues, procedural memory, and the manner in which value diversity, issue complexity, and political roles affect when and to whom particular types of information are valuable, the personal or social benefits of having citizens memorize the justices' names is not self-evident.

Of course, there are tasks and political roles for which it is important to know such facts. I suspect that most of the people reading this book are civic educators, social scientists, journalists, reporters, lawyers, students, or other people with a deep interest in some area of politics, policy, or science communication. In any of these roles, we have responsibilities for which certain types of knowledge are helpful—even essential.

For example, I am a political science professor at a major research university. I am expected to teach classes, conduct research, and mentor graduate students and younger researchers. To accomplish these tasks, I must know certain things. As I occasionally publish in law journals and often give lectures and conduct research on topics for which the US legal system is relevant, the names of Supreme Court justices happen to be among the things that are beneficial for me to know. There are circumstances in which I would be embarrassed *not* to know them. Something similar is probably true for you too, if my impression of this book's audience is correct.

Compared to many citizens, we have unusual roles. It is not necessarily the case that the information that we must know to do our jobs (or impress our colleagues) has the same value for people in different roles. Information that increases competence at our most important tasks may not increase others' competence at their vital tasks. And so it is for the facts highlighted in many "public ignorance" claims. Knowing such things is often essential to tasks that you and I are expected to perform, given our roles. *These roles make us unlike many citizens—particularly citizens who are often criticized for not knowing certain things that our professional or student communities hold dear.*

Other critiques of the public mind base their conclusions about civic incompetence on claims about how citizens should organize their thoughts. Some of these claims are based on findings like those of Philip E. Converse (1964). He found that only 10 percent of the public could define the meanings of "liberal" or "conservative" as public opinion scholars of that era defined the terms. He showed that an even smaller fraction of the public actually used such ideological categories when evaluating candidates and parties.[15] Drawing direct and broad conclusions about incompetence from such evidence, however, requires the assumption that concepts such as liberal and conservative are *necessary* for making competent decisions. For many tasks that citizens face, such as voting for candidates who identify themselves on the ballot as Democratic or Republican, there are alternate ways to know which candidate best aligns with certain facts and values. Voters who understand how the terms Democrat and Republican correspond to outcomes about which they care may learn nothing of value by focusing on, what is from their point of view, redundant and less actionable labels (liberal and conservative).[16] While ideological terms are helpful to people who write about politics for a living, they need not be as valuable to people in other social roles.

One thing to realize about numerous voter ignorance critiques is that many people who write about civic incompetence aspire to, or have already reached, the pinnacles of their respective academic or journalistic fields. Many write for prestigious outlets with national audiences. The lure of a national audience induces some scholars and writers to focus more on presidential elections than on local elections, more on Congress than on state or local legislatures, and more on federal bureaucrats than on their counterparts in states, counties, cities, and special districts. It is very difficult for ambitious journalists and scholars to obtain prestigious positions and large paychecks if they spend time writing about the politics of a small community about which few members of a national audience know or care.

Without minimizing the importance of federal activities, it is important to recognize that they constitute but a handful of all the politically relevant actions that occur on any given day. Suppose, for example, we were to take all of the people involved in some aspect of American government and politics on any given day and toss them into a large hat. Then, without looking, we reached in and grabbed one of these people at random. It is very unlikely that the person would be working on federal government activity. At the same time that there are 435 members of the US House of Representatives, for example, there are 1,191 mayors of cities with populations of 30,000 or more,[17] 7,382 state legislative seats,[18] and more than 90,000 school board members serving in districts across the United States.[19] These numbers do not in any way diminish the important decisions that are made in Washington, DC, but they are strong evidence that when it comes to the politics that influence people's everyday lives and, the actions in which many people other people in government actively engage on a regular basis, DC is not the only game in town.

Yet, when we reexamine the most widely publicized academic and journalistic claims about what citizens "ought" to know, we will rarely if ever find any reference to activities of the nearly 100,000 state and local political decision-makers (or their hardworking administrative staffs). Indeed, if the academic and journalistic literatures of civic competence and voter ignorance were all that we ever read, we might have difficulty believing that state and local politics even exist.

So, should citizens who want to be competent at the tasks that provide the greatest value to themselves and others learn the specific pieces of information about which national academics and columnists write? I suspect that a number of readers, as well as people who are active in state and local governments, would push back on any such suggestion. Getting information to people who will use it can make a big difference in performance at all levels of government.

Moreover, individuals can often have a bigger influence on decisions when the number of voters is small. For example, and all else constant, one member of a five-person school board is more likely to influence the outcome of a majority vote than one member of a 10-million-person electorate. If an educator's goals entail giving information to people who can affect outcomes, then we can make a strong case for the value of informing the board members.

Indeed, many citizens are far more likely to have opportunities to influence political outcomes at the local, parish, or neighborhood levels than they are to influence any of the national-level activities on which scholars and critics who write about political ignorance are often fixated. I know that some people consider this type of argument to be provocative. Indeed, when I make such claims in front of scholarly audiences, it sometimes prompts questions such as "Where would we be if everyone ignored the pieces of information on which many academics and journalists focus?"

This is a good question.

A democracy would be a farce if nobody knew anything at all about politics or policy. In many other cases, however, it requires a grand leap of logic (usually accompanied by a substantial dose of illogic) to go from this possibility to the conclusion that everyone, or even most people, ought to be able to answer a narrow and oddly selected slice of questions about the federal government that a small group of elites has privileged. This is particularly true when no logic or evidence demonstrates that answering these questions is necessary or sufficient for improved performance for other people's high-value tasks.

As I show in greater detail in the chapters on how the concept called "political knowledge" is measured (chapters 15 through 18), many academics and journalists who make claims about voter ignorance are in exactly this situation. They misunderstand or misinterpret much of the data on which the claims are based. The political knowledge literature's lack of attention to data quality, to the accuracy of its empirical claims, and to the logic and politics of competence described in chapters 5 through 13 reduces its relevance to many important educational endeavors.

Perhaps citizens are more competent than critics allege because they realize that investing heavily in the minutiae of many aspects of federal politics is akin to tilting at windmills. Political communication scholar Lee Shaker (2012) provides evidence to this effect. He was one of the first scholars to simultaneously measure citizens' recall of national-level and local-level political phenomena. To be sure, his study identifies clusters of individuals who are more knowledgeable about national than local politics. But he also identifies a significant proportion of the population whose ability to answer local political questions exceeds their recall abilities of national-level phenomena. Many people in his study know more about selected details of politics in their local communities than they do about a narrow and oddly selected slice of questions about the politics of Washington, DC.

Political scientist Lauri Rapeli (2014) reaches a similar conclusion in a study of what Finnish citizens know about local, national, and European Union politics. He asked over 1,000 citizens a short list of questions about government at each level. Among his more noteworthy findings (2014: 438) was that citizens' knowledge of facts about these different levels of government were only "modestly correlated" with one another. This result provides evidence that people differ in their attention to the three levels of politics. He also finds (2014: 440) that "people living in rural communities are more knowledgeable about local politics than urban residents, but not about national or EU politics. Whether a person lives in an urban or a rural location has no relevance for a person's knowledge of national or EU politics, only for local politics." While both Shaker's and Rapeli's results are based on small numbers of questions, they provide evidence that for many citizens, local politics deserves more than a footnote in descriptions of what they know about politics in total.

Anthony Downs anticipated such dynamics years ago. He articulated conditions under which voters will make an effort to become politically well informed. He found (1957: 216) that for phenomena such as federal politics, that "many rational citizens obtain practically no information at all." He contends, for example, that voters who are unlikely to break ties in elections have very little practical incentive to invest in detailed information about those elections.[20] His calculus explains why "rational persons" whose political roles limit their abilities to influence federal actions, and who have greater opportunities to help more local concerns, would spend little or no time learning information that certain journalists and scholars wouldn't be caught dead not knowing.

All of us have varying civic responsibilities. Our roles affect what information is valuable to us. Citizens who run for office, work in governmental agencies, or serve on legislative staff should—of course—have expertise in matters that many of us lack. Citizens who have other important roles in and out of politics can provide benefits to themselves and their communities by knowing very different sets of things. Given that prospective learners are limited in how much attention they can devote to information, understanding what information various learners can actually use is a critical skill for outcome-oriented educators to have.

13

Costs and Benefits

Education is seldom "free" for anyone who participates in it. It requires people to give time, effort, or money in exchange for the possibility of increased knowledge and competence. Educators devote resources to presentations, syllabi, textbooks, websites, videos, and other presentations. Every one of these products takes time and effort to prepare. Students also face costs. Education can require a student to sacrifice alternative opportunities, such as spending time with loved ones and engaging in recreational activities. Are these costs worth paying?

When costs are a concern, educators gain incentives to provide information that produces positive *net benefits*. Once we contemplate net benefits and to whom they accrue, the concept of *paying too much* for an educational outcome becomes a significant concern. If prospective learners believe that an educator is going to ask them to learn information that is of no value to them, they are likely to view the situation as one that imposes time and energy costs in exchange for no tangible benefit. When made such offers, prospective learners tend to opt out. So providing too much (or the wrong) information can be costly, and by reducing others' willingness to participate, it can cause otherwise promising educational endeavors to fail.

In situations when providing information is a way to increase a beneficial competence, another related question arises: *Who should pay?* Answering this question can be difficult. To see how, suppose that we have identified information that is necessary for a particular audience to increase a valuable competence. Suppose, however, that most of the benefits of this increased competence accrue to someone other than the members of that audience. Such situations are not uncommon in politics. In politics, one group's actions often affect others.

For example, suppose that childless voters in a local school board election will cast the decisive votes on a matter that affects the quality of life for other people's children. Suppose that it is costly for the childless voters to learn what they need to know in order to make the best choice for the children. Suppose, moreover, that our competence criterion places great weight on the children's well-being. At the same time, suppose that learning about the issue would prevent a few childless voters from doing as much as they can to get a desired job and would prevent others from spending increasingly scarce time with an ailing relative. Should these individuals be less obligated than others to learn the information needed for the competent choice? Should the community as a whole be obligated to compensate those who are being asked to learn for the sake of the children? Having answers to such questions is important when designing an educational strategy. It can help educators understand who will be motivated to participate as teachers and students and who will need additional incentives to learn. This chapter provides ways to develop such answers. Its main lessons are as follows:

- The net benefit of learning a piece of information is the benefit of such learning minus its costs.
- The net benefits of information can be different for educators and prospective learners.
- Educators who are mistaken about prospective learners' beliefs about how and to whom such benefits accrue become vulnerable to developing failed educational strategies. The strategies fail because prospective learners refuse to participate in ways that educators anticipated.
- If a piece of information can increase multiple kinds of beneficial knowledge and competence, its net benefits are higher than information that increases only a subset of these outcomes.
- If a simple cue and a piece of complex information are sufficient for the same competence, and the cue costs less for a prospective learner to process, the cue provides higher net benefits.

- When an educator's goal requires participants to learn information that does not provide positive net benefits, achieving this goal requires offering additional incentives for learning. This situation is more likely when one person's learning confers benefits to others (e.g., when learning is a "public good").

The chapter reaches these conclusions in the following way. In section 13A, I describe when and for whom learning about politics conveys positive net benefits. In section 13B, I use a variation of chapter 12's lone voter example to demonstrate how knowledge of net benefits can improve attempts to increase competence. In section 13C, I describe why some educators need to provide extra incentives to achieve their educational goals. In section 13D, I explain why seeking to make voters fully informed can yield lower net benefits than attempts to teach them less. In section 13E, I use this chapter's lessons to help educators answer some difficult questions about what people should know. Section 13F concludes the chapter and part I of the book.

13A. IS POLITICAL LEARNING
A GOOD INVESTMENT?

When educators ask others to learn about a topic, the offer is one of investment. In return for a sacrifice of time, money, or effort, the educator offers the prospect of improved knowledge and competence. What returns make such investments worth pursuing?

In financial markets, the logic of investment is that people invest in real estate, stocks, and mutual funds with the hope that their participation in these activities will produce increased value over time relative to other things they can do with their resources. People who are considering a financial investment have an incentive to think about how its return compares to other things that they can do with their investible assets. For example, if a person invests $100 into a stock A that will be worth $105 dollars when she needs to sell, the soundness of the investment depends on what other returns the $100 can produce. If investment opportunities exist that will return $200 when she needs to sell, then her investment in stock A provides a relatively poor return.

So it is with investments in learning. In many political contexts, a great deal of potentially relevant information exists. In modern US presidential elections, for example, more information is now produced in a single election cycle (statements of fact, interpretations of events, statements of opinion, etc.) than any person can digest in a lifetime. Hence, many people have incentives to compare the returns on attempting to learn any particular piece of information with the returns from other things in which they can invest time and effort. Indeed, people who fail to think about their time in this way are vulnerable to spending so much time learning low-value information that they have little time remaining to learn or do more important things.

To motivate thinking about this point in classrooms, I use a passage from the film *Monty Python's The Meaning of Life* (1983). The scene is of a board meeting in which all of the British actors have American accents, all are wearing suits, and the general demeanor leading up to this point is entirely formal and professional.

CHAIRMAN: . . . Item six on the agenda: the meaning of life. Now, uh, Harry, you've had some thoughts on this.

HARRY: That's right. Yeah, I've had a team working on this over the past few weeks, and, uh, what we've come up with can be reduced to two fundamental concepts. One: people are not wearing enough hats. Two: matter is energy. In the universe, there are many energy fields which we cannot normally perceive. Some energies have a spiritual source which act upon a person's soul. However, this soul does not exist *ab initio*, as orthodox Christianity teaches. It has to be brought into existence by a process of guided self-observation. However, this is rarely achieved, owing to man's unique ability to be distracted from spiritual matters by everyday trivia.

[pause]

BERT: What was that about hats, again?

So the question becomes, what kinds of information generate returns high enough to draw a prospective learner's attention? The return on an investment in information depends on what the recipient can do with it. Consider, for example, a consumer in a grocery store's produce section. When he is in the store and thinks about whether or not to buy a loaf of bread, his volition plays a huge part in determining whether or not he ends up owning it. He can cause the bread to be at his dinner table that evening. Hence, there is information about the bread that he can use to cause an outcome about which he cares.

The next day, the same consumer heads to the ballot box. He can cast a vote for US senator. He favors candidate Chang, and he can base his vote on things he has learned about Chang and his opponents. However, he is very unlikely to cause Chang to be elected to the US Senate in the way that he can cause a loaf of bread to be on his table. The consumer is but one of thousands or millions of voters. Unless all other voters in his state split their votes evenly between the top two candidates, his vote will not break a tie in the electorate. If the consumer were to invest in information about the Senate candidates, the information will almost certainly have no effect on the election's outcome. Hence, the return on investing in such information is less direct than that of investing in information about the bread.

What a potential learner can do with information, and hence its investment value, depends on their political role. To see how, consider an individual who can devote a limited amount of time to learning about politics. Recalling a comparison from the previous chapter, which activity provides a better return: learning about candidates for federal office or learning about local school board candidates?

Consider the school board option. A school board acts on behalf of citizens in a school district. These boards make decisions that affect the content of school curricula, the way in which various funds are spent, how disciplinary issues are managed, and so on. Moreover, nearly all school board voting districts are far smaller than the typical US House or Senate voting district.[1] In these relatively small voting districts, single voters or small blocs of voters have a greater chance of breaking a tie in a school board election than they do in a federal election. Add to this the fact that school board elections typically have far lower turnout than senatorial or presidential elections, and the likelihood of making or breaking an electoral tie is further magnified. Seen from this perspective, learning about the school board has some investment advantages.

To stir the pot further, it is also worth noting that the average American citizen has few and limited opportunities to influence federal policy at the ballot box. Americans do not vote on federal policies directly.[2] They can cast one vote for a president and vice president every four years, one vote for a senator every three years, and one vote for a member of the House of Representatives every two years. In other words, the US Constitution offers the average American 13 votes for federal elections every 12 years. This is just over one vote per year—and in almost all of these general elections, at least in the 20th and 21st centuries, there is either a sitting officeholder with significant incumbency advantages or, at most, two candidates (one from each of the major parties) who have any chance of winning.[3]

Of course, Americans also participate in primary elections or caucuses. These elections determine which of several candidates will represent political parties in general elections. There is typically one primary election preceding every federal election. So the average American can also participate in just over one of these elections per year on average. These elections, however, do not determine the identity of a federal officeholder. Moreover, many primary elections are not seriously contested. When a major party has a strong incumbent in a federal office, many potential opponents choose not to challenge the incumbent or are discouraged from doing so by party leaders.[4] Hence, many apparent opportunities to cast a vote in a federal election afford voters no real opportunity to affect who holds federal office. And as we saw in chapter 12, even in the rare case where a person casts the decisive vote for their district's representative, legislative bargaining and delegation dynamics may render that person's elected representative powerless to affect important political outcomes.

Having identified factors that reduce investment returns for learning about federal politics, relative to other important topics, it is also possible to build the opposite case. Consider, for example, this argument by Democratic political consultant Donna Brazile (2012):

> Let's look at some of the accomplishments of the Obama administration: the auto industry bailout, a restructured student loan program, mortgage refinancing, getting U.S. troops out of Iraq, cash-for-clunkers, lower drug costs for seniors, expanded SCHIP for children, putting the U.S. in compliance with the Geneva no-torture policy, using U.S. influence—but not troops—to remove Qaddafi, killing Osama bin Laden and so much more. Let's not forget his executive order allowing immigrant children a path to citizenship. He also held the first Passover Seder at the White House. An informed voter needs to know those facts.

Moreover, the actions of the typical school board have a far more limited impact than many federal actions. It is also true that there are many other ways to try to affect federal policy including making monetary contributions to various candidates and causes and participating in many types of advocacy. Depending on the goal, people who become informed about federal issues can have an influence that extends beyond the ballot box.

For most people and most issues, however, opportunities and abilities to change federal outcomes are quite scarce.

So, if citizens have a limited amount of time to learn about politics and a limited ability to affect federal politics, is it better for them to invest in learning minute details of federal policies, or should they spend their time learning about the candidates and issues associated with their local school board? To the extent that citizens can have a greater impact on school boards than they can on the federal government, it is likely that the individual net benefits of learning school board information are higher than the benefits of studying many federal topics. If an educator's objective is to help others affect a policy outcome, it is arguable that educating people about school board and other local elections yields higher net benefits.

Put another way, the conclusion that every citizen will produce higher net benefits for themselves and others by devoting their civically oriented time to national politics is unlikely to be true. To defend such a conclusion requires the claimant to argue that the potential effect on national policy of every individual learning the federal information is so much greater than the potential effect on local policy of that individual learning the school board information, that it overwhelms the fact that many people's ability to affect many federal outcomes is effectively nil.

I understand that some people will find these claims counterintuitive. Some assert that learning about politics and policy is a civic duty and should be pursued regardless of cost. Others will claim that the costs of learning are not important enough to worry about. Of course, there are circumstances when both assertions can be legitimately made (though I have seen little evidence of people who make these arguments ever actively investigating the costs beforehand). In many cases, however, the costs are real. When the costs are real and significant, they can reduce participation and prevent learning.

13B. CALCULATING THE NET BENEFIT OF LEARNING

When educators fail to recognize that they and their target audiences have different views of the net benefits of information, the consequences can be devastating. Educators who overestimate net benefits—or who are mistaken about prospective learners' and supporters' beliefs about how such benefits accrue—become vulnerable to developing educational strategies that fail because prospective supporters and learners refuse to participate. This possibility is more than theoretical. As is abundantly clear from every investigation ever conducted into civic knowledge, many citizens regularly conclude that most political information is not worth memorizing. So educators who want their information to avoid a similar fate have a strong incentive to understand how their audiences calculate net benefits.

In this section, I offer a way to understand political information's net benefits. An appendix to this chapter offers a mathematical version of the argument for readers who are interested in that type of explanation. I begin this presentation by calling chapter 12's lone voter back into service. Let's return to the example's initial version. There, the lone voter casts a single vote that determines which of two political parties will have complete control over all aspects of government for the rest of time. Let it also be the case that when evaluating any subjective aspect of competence, only the voter's well-being matters. As before, I call this a decision to choose the party that is best for the lone voter the "competent choice."

What is the net benefit of giving a piece of information to the lone voter? It is the benefit of the information minus the cost.

What is the benefit? In this example, the benefit of learning new information depends on whether or not it increases the lone voter's competence and the value of that competence to her. Put another way, the benefits depend on whether or not the information is necessary or sufficient to increase a competence and on the value of that increased competence to her. Think of this part of the net benefit equation as "probability that the information increases competence" *times* "the value of the increased competence to the lone voter."

What is the cost? The cost of learning new information is counted in terms of the time, effort, and money that someone must spend to acquire and process this information. *Opportunity cost* should be part of the equation. Opportunity cost is a concept from economics that prompts us to consider the value of alternate uses of a person's money or time. When learning requires people to miss other events that they enjoy or makes their other obligations more difficult to satisfy, opportunity costs increase. If, for example, the lone voter has a job that provides more value to her when she works for a whole day rather than a half day (e.g., more income, more time with coworkers, the joy of job-related creation or service), then attending a civics class that requires her to miss a full day of work entails a higher opportunity cost than a half-day civics class. Opportunity costs also include effort needed to retrieve relevant information. Suppose, for example, that learning the new information requires significant effort. Such efforts are also reflected in an accounting of costs.

Having laid out costs and benefits, we can now clarify when giving information to the lone voter produces a positive net benefit. For information to confer a positive net benefit, it must be the case that "the probability that the information increases competence" *times* "the value of the competence increase" is greater than the associated costs.

In other words, for information to have a positive net benefit to the lone voter, one of the following statements must be true:

- The information is *sufficient* to cause a decision change, and the change is more beneficial than the learning is costly.
- The information is *necessary* but not sufficient for increasing competence, the change is more beneficial than the learning is costly, the probability that the lone voter will obtain the additional information that competence requires is not too low, and the cost of obtaining that additional information is not too high. In other words, information is likely to be net beneficial when the voter knows enough to convert its content into competence.

With these ideas in hand, we can think of net benefits in more general ways. Consider, for example, information that increases competence at multiple tasks. In this case, calculating net benefits requires us to aggregate the benefit of increased competence at each task. Simply adding the benefits may not be the best approach. If the lone voter cares about some tasks more than others, we need to weight the benefits calculation accordingly. We also need to account for the fact that a piece of information can have different effects on different tasks. That is, knowing a given fact may be necessary for competent performance at some tasks, sufficient for competence at other tasks, and *neither* necessary nor sufficient for others.

One implication of this way of viewing information is that information that can increase multiple beneficial competences can produce higher net benefits than information that increases only one competence. To the extent that prospective learners and supporters must perceive net benefits as a condition for participation, information that prospective participants perceive to have this quality can help an educational endeavor succeed.

The flip side of this implication is also important for educators to understand. Information that is neither necessary nor sufficient for increasing a valued competence, information to which people will not attend, information that people do not find sufficiently credible, and information that people cannot use because of their political roles cannot produce positive net benefits. Moreover, to the extent that prospective learners and supporters must perceive positive net benefits as a condition for their participation, information that appears to have any of these qualities will not help an educational endeavor succeed.

For example, when tangible results are a currency that is valued by needed participants, an educator who demonstrates these benefits is in a stronger position to obtain the participation that she desires. Consider, for example, advice given by former US Senator Bob Graham (2010: 35):

> "I want my community to be a better place to live" is a nice sentiment with which almost everyone can agree, but it is far too broad and vague to be useful. More focused starting points might include the following:
>
> - We don't feel safe because crime has increased in our area.
> - Our neighborhood drinking water looks, smells, and tastes odd.
> - In the past year my property taxes have doubled.
> - My small business is losing workers because I can't afford their health insurance.
> - Our daughter is one of thirty-five children in a single kindergarten class...

This change from abstract desires to concrete concerns can alter prospective participants' perceptions of the potential net benefits of acquiring relevant types of knowledge.

This section's logic also offers a framework for understanding why individuals have different views about what is worth knowing. Such knowledge is important because educators who need the support of people with diverse values or political roles can be more effective if they understand their desired participants' net benefit calculations. People may have different net benefit calculations because some view a type of learning as costly and onerous, whereas others view the same activity as enjoyable. Some may see the benefits of learning about a certain topic as likely to help them accomplish many important things. Others may view the same prospect as useless drudgery.

Seeing net benefits from other points of view can help educators understand what kinds of strategies will elicit the participation that their educational goals require. Suppose, for example, that an educator knows that a particular strategy can provide important concrete benefits to a population. If needed participants do not perceive positive net benefits, and if the educator cannot force them to participate, then he must find a different strategy—one that not only increases the competence but *is also perceived by the needed participants as sufficiently beneficial.*

Of course, some people resist this way of thinking about prospective learners. I have met any number of advocates (and some experts) who resist discussions of education's cost. Some even question the morality of anyone who raises the issue. If, however, these people are seeking to provide valuable information to members of a bigger tent, and if some of the tent's members recognize that their concerns about costs are not being addressed, needed participants may be less likely to participate in an educational endeavor. Indeed, for most people most of the time, the costs of learning about politics are not a theoretical abstraction—they are a tangible reason for opting out. This is why most people choose not to learn most things that could be learned about most topics. Identifying information that offers a shared net benefit to different kinds of people can increase individuals' motives to participate and allow an expanded set of competence-increasing educational outcomes to be achieved. The next section offers constructive ways to think about how to affect others' motives to learn.

13C. COMPENSATING LEARNERS AS A MEANS OF INCREASING COMPETENCE

In politics, many decisions are made collectively. An individual citizen is one of many who vote. An individual legislator or bureaucrat is one of many whose assent produces important policy outcomes. In such instances, the individual net benefit of learning is reduced by the probability that individual actions are not sufficient to affect outcomes of value. For example, a single citizen can rarely make or break an Election Day tie. So, if we ask people to take the time and effort required to learn about outcomes that they are unlikely to affect, should they do it? If, for example, a citizen realizes that the outcome of an election will not depend on his vote, and if he does not find gaining the information to be worthwhile for other reasons, should he do it?

One can argue that citizens in these situations should think about interests other than their own. Suppose, for example, that the citizen's personal net benefit of information is negative, but the *social net benefit* of learning that information is positive. In other words, the citizen's learning provides benefits to others. For the sake of this example, suppose that everyone in a community agrees that learning a certain type of information produces a positive social net benefit. In such cases, another question arises—should the citizens for whom the personal net benefit of learning is low or negative be compensated for the time and effort that they would have to devote to learn things of value to the community? If so, what compensation would be sufficient? When benefits of information do not accrue to those who are asked to pay learning costs, educators may need to consider compensation as part of a strategy to increase desired competences.

To see why compensation may be necessary, when people are asked to pay learning costs that will benefit others, they are being asked to provide what economists call a *public good.* The principal attributes of a public good are that it provides benefits to multiple people and is non-excludable. For example, if one person buys a cup of coffee and consumes all of it, there is nothing left in the cup for anyone else. In this sense, a cup of coffee is not a public good. In contrast, if a streetlight illuminates my way and this does not prevent it from illuminating your way, the streetlight is a public good.

A seminal study of public good provision is Mancur Olson's *The Logic of Collective Action* (1965). Olson argued that we should expect many public goods to be underprovided in the absence of ways to compensate those who are asked to pay their costs. The reasoning is as follows.

When a person makes a decision with only his own circumstances in mind, he will pay the costs of an activity only if he believes that its personal net benefits are positive. In contrast, when a person is asked to contribute to a public good, he has an incentive to pay as little of the bill as possible. After all, if others pay for the streetlight that illuminates his way, he can benefit from the streetlight and use the money that he does not contribute to pursue his other interests. Olson refers to this phenomenon as *free riding.*

Some groups are better situated than others to overcome free riding. In some groups, members can see one another's actions and inactions. If these members can reward and punish one another for inaction, they can mitigate free riding. In other groups—such as large, spatially dispersed groups whose members lack the technological means to track one another—a more likely outcome is that members will free ride, and broadly beneficial public goods will be undersupplied.

Many educators are in situations of asking prospective learners to learn because in order to provide public goods for their community. Research on public good provision provides interesting ideas about how to limit free riding in such cases. Compensation is key: how educators compensate individuals for participating in educational endeavors can be the difference between the endeavor's success and failure.[5] In the rest of this section, I give two suggestions for how to offer needed compensation.

The first suggestion follows from previous chapters. It is to specify the tasks for which the information is valuable, demonstrate the benefit of improved performance of the tasks with respect to the values of those whose participation is needed, and prove that the information being offered is necessary or sufficient for the improved performance. An educator can use these demonstrations to make the benefits of participating in an educational endeavor more concrete.

The second suggestion follows from Olson's *The Logic of Collective Action*. Olson argued that "only a separate and 'selective' incentive will stimulate a rational individual in a latent group to act in a group-oriented way" (Olson, 1965: 51). A *latent group* is one that cannot otherwise overcome free riding and, hence, underprovides a public good. Selective incentives are tangible private goods that are separable from the public good and that can partially compensate individuals for their contributions. Well-known examples of selective incentives include the discounted magazine subscriptions and insurance policies that are offered as side benefits of membership in labor unions, professional associations, and automobile clubs. Public television in the United States, another public good, has often offered selective incentives such as coffee mugs, Sesame Street puppets, concert recordings, and personal copies of popular documentary programs to prospective contributors.

Given the many things that people can do with their time, including spending time with their families or participating in cultural activities as a participant or observer, selective incentives can increase participation in educational endeavors. So, in addition to making the benefits of education more concrete for prospective learners, an educator can pair participation with a lunch, gift card, or other tangible asset to further increase the individual net benefit of participating. If the compensation is sufficiently valuable to elicit participation and sufficiently inexpensive to provide, then offering the incentive can increase competence and hence produce extensive and broadly shared net benefits.

Of course, to some critics, the idea of paying people to learn information is blasphemy (e.g., Why pay people for what they *ought* to be learning anyway?). The difference between such perspectives and this chapter's approach is the difference between an unrealistic and idealized view of human nature and a better understanding of actual human nature. If the value of increased competence is sufficiently high, and if selective incentives can be provided to an audience at a sufficiently low cost, then paying the cost of providing these incentives can help educators provide benefits of high social value.

13D. THE INVESTMENT VALUE OF TEACHING "ALL THE FACTS"

A lesson plan on a popular civic education website offers the following pedagogical goal:

> This lesson focuses on a voter's need to be fully informed prior to casting a vote on Election Day and how to acquire the necessary information.[6]

Many critics, and some educators, are motivated by a similar idea: Voters should be "fully informed" or voters should know "all the facts" before voting. As mentioned in earlier chapters, it is difficult, if not impossible, to define what "all the facts" would constitute for many issues. As political scientist E. E. Schattschneider (1960: 131–132) explained:

> Presidents, senators, governors, judges, professors, doctors of philosophy, editors, and the like are only a little less ignorant than the rest of us. . . . Everybody has to accommodate himself to the fact that he deals daily with an incredible number of matters about which he knows very little. This is true of all aspects of life, not merely politics. The compulsion to know everything is the road to insanity.

Even if it were technically possible to teach people "all the facts," the social net benefit of doing so, especially when compared to other educational strategies, is not at all obvious. In what follows, I will show that the "fully informed voter" is not a useful standard for educators who seek to maximize the net benefits of their educational endeavors. Moreover, the "fully informed" standard is actually harmful when educators use the standard to absolve themselves of actually understanding what kinds of information offer net benefits. Let's begin, however, by making a case *for the opposite* of my conclusion.

One benefit of being broadly informed about politics is that it facilitates convergent expectations. Working from a shared knowledge base is useful for social interactions.[7] When people share knowledge bases, they are more likely to understand one another's frames of reference.[8] Common frames of reference can help people articulate common interests, develop trust, and induce strangers to engage in socially productive activities.[9]

Another way to think of the benefits of broad knowledge is as an insurance policy. Here, educators may seek to prepare prospective learners for circumstances in which information (as insurance) can help them get through potential catastrophes. In this frame, paying the cost of learning (the insurance premium) purchases an opportunity to improve bad outcomes whose occurrences are uncertain. Here, the value of the information depends on the probability of the bad events occurring and the extent to which the insurance improves outcomes when bad events do occur.

For these reasons and more, learning about politics can be beneficial. Perhaps we can also agree that for most tasks, some people must know *some* things. But the logic and evidence of earlier chapters also show that for many tasks, people in different political roles can do different things with information, which brings us to the counterargument of the claim that citizens should be "fully informed."

We know that all information about politics does not provide equal net benefits to everyone. In previous chapters, we have seen that educators can provide greater benefits to others by providing information necessary or sufficient for increasing competences that they value. We have also encountered lots of information that does not have this power. Recall that information can be incorrect, irrelevant, or not usable given a person's political role. In other cases, cues and procedural memories can substitute for knowledge of certain facts as a condition for increasing competence. If it is costly to acquire information, then providing information that is neither necessary nor sufficient to increase a high value competence is inconsistent with a desire to develop and educational strategy that produces net benefits.

To be sure, modern societies need people who have great expertise in a wide range of areas. In reality, however, most people who are considered experts on one topic know very little about most other topics. So, as we contemplate the net benefits of trying to make a voter fully informed, the comparison is not to complete ignorance, but rather to smaller sets of things that a person could know.

With this standard in mind, we can now answer the question, "Is social net benefit ever maximized by trying to require a large group of people to know something approaching 'all the facts' about a political topic?" The short answer is "probably not." Here's why.

First, for many tasks, knowing everything is impossible. Consider, for example, a decision about whether or not to stop a war in progress. What does it mean to have all the facts pertinent to that decision? Does it mean all of the intelligence that the military has gathered? Does it mean comprehensive interviews with every soldier who has seen the conduct of specific operations from a first-person perspective? Does it mean getting all of the opponent's information? If relevant facts include how various people feel about the war, does having "all the facts" mean gathering data on their opinions? And, if a rationale for stopping or continuing a war is to provide a future benefit, how much information is required about the future? Does having all the facts require estimates of future consequences? If it does, whose estimates of these consequences should we choose? After all, there are usually multiple ways to forecast futures. So, when people claim that decision-making should be based on all the facts, there is little to be gained in treating the claim literally.

Second, there are many situations for which knowing something approaching all the facts is not necessary for making a competent decision. Cues and procedural memories allow people to make competent choices while knowing far less than all the facts. This fact implies that concrete progress in improving highly and broadly beneficial civic competences comes from more realistic foundations than the fully informed voter.

So, even if we could convey all the facts to voters, they would have to pay learning costs, process the information, and, in the end, many facts would be irrelevant to their decisions. So, what matters more than trying to give people information that they will not use is trying to understand the conditions under which giving an audience certain kinds of information increases their competence at valuable tasks.

To justify prospective learners' costly participation in competence-increasing endeavors, educators need to develop strategies that participants perceive as compensating them adequately. Although compensation can take many forms (better decisions, better outcomes, entertainment value, cash), it must accrue. Confronting cost-related challenges directly, as opposed to ignoring their existence, can help educators develop stronger arguments about why a particular strategy is worth pursuing. Such forward thinking views can help educators gain the support and attention they will need to increase knowledge and competence.

13E. THE SILVER BULLET REVISITED (OR WHAT SHOULD I EAT?)

Which facts should we teach in a civics class? Which questions should we ask on a citizenship exam? These are questions that I am sometimes asked. I respond that the answers to the questions depend on what you want students or citizens to do. In other words, what kinds of value are you hoping that the students or citizens will create for themselves and others through their actions?

Some people are impatient with this response. They want a list, and preferably a short one. They seek a quick heuristic that they can use to determine who does and does not measure up. They want a silver bullet.

Given the ground that we have covered since chapter 4's "silver bullet" discussion, I want to propose a more advanced way to answer these questions. To motivate this proposal, I introduce an analogy.

What should I eat?

This is an important question. It affects every one of us. The search for sustenance is essential to our quality of life. What is the answer? The answer depends on what you want to do and aspects of your situation.

Beneficial answers to the question "What should I eat?" depend on your answer to questions about the tasks you want to accomplish. Such questions include: Are you running a marathon? Recovering from surgery? Are you breastfeeding a child? Do you want to participate in meals that are an important part of your culture or family history? Do you want to live a long life? Do you need to be especially alert a few minutes from now? If you want to do more than one of the things listed above, what tradeoffs would you want to make if no food allowed you to do all of these things simultaneously? What tradeoffs would you make if foods that helped you accomplish one goal made accomplishing one of the other goals less likely?

Regarding your situation, a beneficial answer to the question "What should I eat?" also depends on your situation. For example, *Do you have teeth?* Many people, including babies, have very few teeth. Some are toothless and, as a result, cannot easily eat many foods that provide nutrition to others. *Do you live in conditions of severe heat or at high altitude?* Such answers would alter the effect of a food's water content on its ability to help you achieve the goals above. *Do you have nut allergies or GERD (acid reflux disease)?* If so, foods that are beneficial to others may be harmful to you. And so on.

Of course, some people are impatient with this response. They want someone to give them a list—and preferably a short one. They seek a quick heuristic that they can use to determine which foods do and do not measure up. They want answers like "eat more vegetables" (which is not always good advice). They want a silver bullet.

In the realm of nutrition, scientific advances can help people choose foods that align with their goals and circumstances. The current science-based advice is not for everyone to eat the same thing. The National Institutes of Health offer many different kinds of recommendations—where the differences reflect circumstantial and physical variations such as those listed above (see http://dnrc.nih.gov/education/education-adults.asp for more information).

In the realm of political decision-making, similar resources can help citizens make choices that do, and do not, align with their goals. For example, in the way that eating concrete is inconsistent with many nutritional goals, learning information that is of no use with respect to people's political roles is inconsistent with many decision-making goals. Understanding how inputs (food/information) become desired outputs can help educators offer more effective and efficient advice about what others should (eat/know) to achieve desired goals.

A difference between the cases of *what to eat* and *what to know* is that issues become political because they are associated with value conflicts that societies do not resolve in less institutionalized means. In contrast, value conflicts tend not to cause a substance to become food. So, while it is possible to imagine something approaching a short list of foods that many people can eat most of the time (see, for example, the US Department of Agriculture's Food Pyramid[10]—though, it should be noted that this advice is not optimal for marathon runners, babies, and others), a broad consensus on what others should know about politics will be more elusive.

So, to answer questions such as "What facts should we teach in a civics class?" "What questions should we ask on a citizenship exam?" "What are the costs of conveying these facts?" and "Who should pay?" it is essential to know what tasks prospective learners are going to attempt after they leave us. With such knowledge in hand, applying the logic and politics of competence can help us identify information that is not only necessary and sufficient for achieving desired goals, but is also perceived by the necessary participants as delivering sufficiently high net benefits.

13F. CONCLUSION OF PART I: THE NET BENEFITS OF A SERVICE ORIENTATION

In part I, we have clarified kinds of information that can and cannot increase valued competences, we have discussed how different types of memory and cues affect the kinds of information that can increase knowledge, and we have examined how value diversity, issue complexity, political roles, and learning costs affect an educational strategy's net benefits. Through these examinations, we have found that, despite the range and depth of our ignorance, we as educators can provide information that causes people to make decisions that more closely align with relevant facts and desired values. These actions can help individuals and communities improve their quality of life. Table 13.1 summarizes the ground we have covered. It states part I's main lessons in the form of practical advice that educators can use to improve the effectiveness and efficiency of their educational endeavors.

TABLE 13.1 **Ten Practical Implications for Educators**

- Attention is scarce and directed toward stimuli that prospective learners perceive to be directly relevant to their core concerns. Therefore, learning requires educators to provide information to which prospective learners are motivated to pay attention. (ch. 7)

- While teachers and professors can hold the specter of grades over students to get attention, and while supervisors can hold out the prospect of promotion or other material incentives, many other educators must find different motivational sources. Specifically, educators must offer information that prospective learners recognize as offering even greater net benefits. (chs. 7 and 13)

- Information offers greater net benefits to prospective learners if it is necessary or sufficient for them to increase a valued competence. (ch. 5)

- If simple cues produce the same competence as more detailed information, and do this at a lower cost to prospective learners, then the cues provide greater net benefits, all else being constant. In such cases, less is more. (ch. 5)

- Prospective learners interpret information from credible sources differently than information from non-credible sources. When source credibility increases information's net benefits, educators can benefit by establishing common interests and relative expertise as seen from the prospective learner's perspective. (ch. 8)

- Information that prospective learners perceive as consistent with their values is more likely to get their attention and reinforce common interest perceptions. (ch. 10)

- Information offers greater net benefits if it emphasizes parts of a complex issue that are directly relevant to a prospective learner's core concerns. (ch. 11)

- Information itself is not inherently valuable or beneficial. The benefit of information depends on what a prospective learner can do with it. (ch. 12)

- Almost everything of interest in the physical story of how people learn happens between the prospective learner's ears. For an educator's information to increase a learner's competence, the learner has to weave the educator's information into their own internal narrative. It is the content of the prospective learner's subsequent memories, and not the educator's words, that give education its tangible value.

- Increasing others' competence requires hitting the "sweet spot." Offer information that is necessary or sufficient to increase a valuable type of knowledge, and that prospective learners perceive as so beneficial that it motivates them to pay sufficient attention.

While striving to increase educators' effectiveness, I sometimes struggled to find a balance between pointing out errors in current strategies and not leading readers to despair that the errors are beyond correction. With criticisms in mind, I feel that it is important to say that I hold most of the educators that I have ever met, both inside and outside the academy, in very high esteem. I admire what they are attempting to accomplish. But I also see very similar mistakes being made over and over again. A 2013 *New York Times* column by Tim Kreider captures my struggle and the manner in which I sought to resolve it:

> It is simply not pleasant to be objectively observed—it's like seeing a candid photo of yourself online, not smiling or posing, but simply looking the way you apparently always do, oblivious and mush-faced with your mouth open. It's proof that we are visible to others, that we are seen, in all our naked silliness and stupidity.... Anyone worth knowing is inevitably also going to be exasperating: making the same obvious mistakes over and over, dating imbeciles,

endlessly relapsing into their dumb addictions and self-defeating habits, blind to their own hilarious flaws and blatant contradictions and fiercely devoted to whatever keeps them miserable. (And those few people about whom there is nothing ridiculous are by far the most preposterous of all.) ... We don't give other people credit for the same interior complexity we take for granted in ourselves, the same capacity for holding contradictory feelings in balance, for complexly alloyed affections, for bottomless generosity of heart and petty, capricious malice. We can't believe that anyone could be unkind to us and still be genuinely fond of us, although we do it all the time. (Kreider, 2013)

So at the same time that this book's criticisms remain valid, it is fortunate that research and practice on topics relevant to increasing knowledge and competence offer a better way forward. These insights reveal advantages of developing educational strategies with a prospective learner's net benefits of information firmly in mind. Taking the time to think about these matters and basing strategy upon them can induce our prospective learners to pay attention to, thoughtfully process, and find credible the information that is valuable to them.

We have choices about how we present information to others. We can choose small tents and make presentations that are pleasing to us and to those who already agree with us. There is nothing wrong with this. Speaking with like-minded persons can remind us of the excitement of our shared experiences and can motivate those who are already on our side to do great things.

When, in contrast, our goal is to expand the set of people who have a particular type of knowledge or competence, adopting another perspective can produce greater educational success. In bigger tents, it can be difficult to get all members of an audience to pay attention to information, to interpret it as credible, to commit it to memory, and to have the audience form such strong beliefs and feelings about what they have learned that they change how they act. This is particularly true when some prospective learners have little patience for presentations that do not get to the point.

To reach broader audiences in such circumstances, it is up to us as educators to base our presentational strategies on a stronger foundation. Prioritizing information that conveys positive net benefits from intersections of prospective learners's various viewpoints is a means for greater educational success. The more that we learn about what our prospective learners want, the greater opportunity we have to convey what we know in ways that are likely to resonate with them. If we take the time to make presentations that build important new memories for our audiences, we can teach them to replace false beliefs with beliefs that improve their competence at important tasks. In so doing, we can provide civic education of great value.

APPENDIX TO SECTION 13B. CALCULATING THE NET BENEFIT OF NEW INFORMATION

In this appendix, I offer a more technical presentation of section 13B's discussion of net benefits. I do so to help readers who want to compare the net benefits of different educational strategies. To retain precision while attempting to maintain accessibility, I accompany every piece of math with substantive descriptions so that readers who are less interested in math can acquire relevant insights.

In section 13B, a lone voter casts a single vote that determines which of two political parties will have complete control over all aspects of government for the rest of time. For the moment, our calculus will focus only on the lone voter's well-being. As a result, a decision to choose the party that is best for the lone voter is the "competent choice."

Here, the net benefit of learning new information depends on whether or not it increases the lone voter's competence and the value of that increase to her. It is:

$$Individual\ Net\ Benefit = P_{IV}(O_I - O_{\sim I}) - C_V$$

In this equation, I represents information that is given to the lone voter V. O_I is the value to the lone voter of the outcome that will occur if she knows I. $O_{\sim I}$ is the value to the lone voter of the outcome that will occur if she does not know I. Hence, $O_I - O_{\sim I}$ is the value to the lone voter of learning I and changing the outcome from $O_{\sim I}$ to O_I. P_{IV} is the probability that giving information I to the lone voter will produce this change. C_V is the opportunity cost to the lone voter in terms of time, effort, and money of acquiring and processing this information.

I now use the equation to clarify when giving information I to the lone voter produces a positive net benefit.

- For information to have a positive net benefit, it must be the case that $P_{IV}(O_I - O_{~I}) > C_V$.
- If O_I represents a competent choice and $O_{~I}$ represents an incompetent choice, then this equation shows when increasing her competence conveys a net benefit. For example, when costs are positive ($C_V > \emptyset$), and information does not increase her competence in a way that she values ($O_I = O_{~I}$), then the information does not offer a positive net benefit.
- If knowing I is a necessary and sufficient condition for changing the outcome, then $P_{IV} = 1$. In this case, the net benefit of information is the difference in the value of the two outcomes to the lone voter minus the cost of learning $((O_I - O_{~I}) - C_V)$.
- If knowing I is *necessary but not sufficient* for increasing competence, then the value of P_{IV} depends on the probability that the lone voter will obtain the information that she needs in addition to I to change the outcome. For the purpose of this example, I represent uncertainty about whether the voter has, or will acquire, such knowledge as part of what determines the value of P_{IV}. So when it is highly likely that a voter has the supplemental knowledge that converts information I into the more competent outcome, then P_{IV} is high. Otherwise, is P_{IV} is low. Thinking about information in this way clarifies the fact that information is likely to be more beneficial to the voter when she knows enough to convert its content into greater competence (as P_{IV} increases when $O_I \neq O_{~I}$, so does $P_{IV}(O_I - O_{~I}) - C_V$).

With these initial ideas in hand, we can describe information's net benefits in broader contexts. I begin by articulating the net benefit of information when the lone voter can use it to increase her competence at multiple tasks.

$$\text{\textit{Individual Net Benefit for information}} \atop \text{\textit{that can affect N issues}} = \sum_{1}^{N} P_{IVn}(O_{In} - O_{~In}) - C_V$$

In this equation, information I can increase competence at N tasks, where tasks are identified individually as $1, \ldots, n$. Here, O_{In} is the value to the lone voter of the outcome of task n that will occur if she has information I. $O_{~In}$

is the value to the lone voter of the outcome regarding task n that will occur if she does not have information I. Tasks that are more important to the lone voter have higher values of O_{In}.

A piece of information need not affect all N tasks equally. Let P_{IVn} be the probability that the lone voter learning information I produces outcome O_{In} rather than $O_{\sim In}$. This probability is now specific to a particular task, $n \in \{1, \ldots, N\}$. In other words, the equation allows us to represent the net benefit of information that is necessary for competent performance at some tasks, sufficient for competence at other tasks, and neither necessary nor sufficient for others. P_{IVn} has higher values when the information in question is necessary or sufficient for increasing competence at increasing numbers of valuable tasks.

Having specified a way to think about the net benefits of information from a lone voter's perspective, I now revise the example a bit to recognize that differences in other aspects of the politics of competence may cause people to see costs and benefits in different ways. Suppose that a population contains J individuals, with a specific individual denoted as $j \in \{1, \ldots, J\}$. Let O_{Inj} be the value to individual j of the outcome of task n that occurs when the lone voter has information I. $O_{\sim Inj}$ is the value to individual j of the outcome regarding task n that will occur if the lone voter does not have information I.

$$\begin{matrix} \textit{Individual } j\textit{'s view of the Net Benefit for} \\ \textit{information that can affect N issues} \end{matrix} = \sum_{1}^{N} P_{IVn}(O_{Inj} - O_{\sim Inj}) - C_{Vj}$$

This equation could be more complicated if we allow individual j to have different beliefs about whether information I is necessary or sufficient for a change in the outcomes. Having said that, the point of introducing these equations is to provide a basic technical representation of why individuals may have different views about the net benefits of information.

Part II

How to Improve "Political Knowledge"

14

What We Know

To offer prospective learners information that yields high net benefits, it is important to understand what they already know. How do educators learn about others' knowledge? Surveys are a common source of information. In part II of this book, I focus on these surveys and how many different kinds of educators use them.

My goal throughout part II is to improve educators' measures and understanding of what people do and do not know about politics. Better measurement and more accurate inferences from data can help educators more effectively diagnose whether individuals have the knowledge they need to achieve desired competences. Where faulty diagnoses can lead educators to offer information that prospective learners neither want nor need, improved diagnoses can help educators identify information that can help others make more competent decisions.

The way that we will achieve the improvements just described is by examining survey-based research and political commentary on a concept that many people call "political knowledge." The best-known academic book on political knowledge defines it as "the range of factual information about politics that is stored in long-term memory."[1]

The survey questions that are most relevant for this purpose are *recall questions*. Recall questions are designed to measure whether or not a person has selected declarative memories. "Who is the Vice President of the United States?" is an example of a commonly asked recall question.

Interpretations of responses to recall questions are the evidentiary basis for thousands of books and articles on political knowledge and ignorance. If these data accurately measure what people know, and if analysts accurately interpret the data, then educators can use the interpretations to compare what an audience knows to necessary and sufficient conditions for competence at a given task.

Part II's main tension is that not all data and interpretations are accurate. Some survey data are inaccurate, as happens when a survey organization records a survey participant's response incorrectly. Similarly, some interpretations of survey data are inaccurate, as happens when an analyst uses a survey to make a claim about ignorance that is inconsistent with the survey's actual content. We will discover that many analysts, in both academia and the public sphere, unintentionally make inaccurate claims about what people do and do not know. We will also discover how to repair many of these inaccuracies.

If an educator wants to use the reports and data described above to improve their effectiveness and efficiency, they have a strong incentive to interpret the materials accurately. Part I of this book provides a foundation for more accurate interpretations. It covers important relationships among information, knowledge, and competence. It also shows how value diversity, issue complexity, political roles, and learning costs affect the net benefits of learning different types of information. These concepts can help educators clarify the types of things perspective learners can benefit from knowing and will want to learn. Many claims about "political knowledge", however, are not consistent with part I's main lessons. As a result, these reports lead many people to make incorrect claims about what people need to know. We can do better.

Throughout part II, I focus on the recall questions that surveys ask, the ways in which people respond to these questions, and the ways in which analysts interpret the responses when making claims about political knowledge and when offering advice about what other people should learn and know. The objective is greater accuracy. The path to that outcome is as follows. In chapter 15, I examine what we can—and cannot—learn about ignorance and knowledge from individual survey questions. In chapter 16, I do the same for "political knowledge scales"—aggregate numerical representations of what others know. In chapter 17, I evaluate survey interviewers' subjective assessments of survey respondents' information levels—a measure that is used in widely cited papers on political ignorance. In each of these chapters,

I identify common problems with current practices and then show how educators can draw more accurate conclusions from existing (or future) data. In chapter 18, I describe how to create new and better practices.

In the remainder of this chapter, I summarize the lessons from previous chapters on which I rely most in the chapters to come. In all cases, the summaries provide a foundation for drawing more accurate conclusions about what people do—and do not—know.

14A. INFORMATION

There are many claims about what others should know. Some claim that more information is always better. These claims are inconsistent with the following facts:

- There is a lot of information available about most topics.
- Some information is false.
- Many kinds of information are neither necessary nor sufficient for increasing a valued knowledge or competence.

Because some information is false and some information is not useful for increasing specific competences, it is not always true that more information is better for prospective learners. Sometimes, more information makes prospective learners worse off—as when the information is false or unhelpful. So when is additional information necessary or sufficient for increasing a valued type of knowledge or competence? If necessity or sufficiency can be clearly demonstrated, then that logical relationship is the basis for establishing the knowledge's value. If the information cannot be shown to be necessary or sufficient for achieving a valuable knowledge or competence outcome, then the net benefits of learning the additional information are more difficult or impossible to defend.

14B. KNOWLEDGE

Knowledge is an attribute of memory. Different kinds of memory constitute knowledge and can affect competence. Declarative memory is memory of specific pieces of information. Non-declarative memories are memories of how to do things. Recall questions attempt to measure whether or not a person has particular declarative memories. When both declarative and non-declarative memories affect knowledge or competence, surveys that measure only small amounts of declarative knowledge can be less useful in assessing knowledge or competence considered more generally. In general, the accuracy of survey-based claims about what people do and do not know depends on what memories the surveys do and do not record.

These facts about knowledge have other important implications for educators:

- All people are ignorant of almost all facts and of almost all value propositions that could be argued as factually relevant to politics. Claims to the contrary are the product of delusion.
- On most political topics, no one is fully informed.
- Competence at many tasks does *not* require the ability to recall "all the facts." Cues and procedural memory can facilitate competence without such abilities.
- The fact that knowledge *can* provide benefits does not mean that it always *does*. There are an infinite number of things that can be known. For many tasks and from many perspectives, attempts to teach or learn many of these things will cost individuals or groups more than the benefits that they perceive from attempting to learn.
- The net benefits of obtaining knowledge, and to whom net benefits accrue, are often unequal across topics and individuals.

If knowing a certain fact, a set of facts, or a procedure is a necessary condition for a given competence, then a questionnaire that seeks to measure attainment of that goal should ask questions that accurately reflect whether prospective learners know those things. If, for example, understanding a particular scientific fact is a sufficient condition for casting a competent vote, then when accurate data reveal a prospective learner's knowledge of the fact, the educator learns that providing further information will not increase that competence. The educator can then redirect their efforts toward information that increases other competences.

14C. WHAT RESPONSES TO SURVEY QUESTIONS IMPLY ABOUT KNOWLEDGE AND COMPETENCE

To get a sense of the challenge facing people who base political knowledge and competence claims on data, consider a parallel argument about

knowledge and competence in mathematics. A *New York Times* editorial by
a prominent mathematician and an educational innovator asks readers to
consider the value of conveying different types of mathematics information:

> Today, American high schools offer a sequence of algebra, geom-
> etry, more algebra, pre-calculus and calculus (or a "reform" version
> in which these topics are interwoven). This has been codified by the
> Common Core State Standards, recently adopted by more than 40
> states. This highly abstract curriculum is simply not the best way to
> prepare a vast majority of high school students for life. For instance,
> how often do most adults encounter a situation in which they need to
> solve a quadratic equation? Do they need to know what constitutes a
> "group of transformations" or a "complex number"? Of course profes-
> sional mathematicians, physicists and engineers need to know all this,
> but most citizens would be better served by studying how mortgages
> are priced, how computers are programmed and how the statistical
> results of a medical trial are to be understood. . . . Traditionalists will
> object that the standard curriculum teaches valuable abstract reason-
> ing, even if the specific skills acquired are not immediately useful
> in later life. A generation ago, traditionalists were also arguing that
> studying Latin, though it had no practical application, helped students
> develop unique linguistic skills. We believe that studying applied
> math, like learning living languages, provides *both* useable knowledge
> and abstract skills. (Garfunkel and Mumford, 2011)

Think, for a moment, about your own mathematics education. Which
aspects of that education have proven valuable to you later in life? I happen
to like math. A particular slice of advanced mathematics has been critical
for parts of my job. At the same time, I know many other very effective
people for whom the math that I know has no use.

With this example in mind, the question becomes "What are the net benefits of correctly answering the kinds of survey questions upon which common critiques of political ignorance depend?" My answer to this question
begins with the proposition that the value of knowledge depends on its effect
on valued competences. As a result, educators who want to use data to evaluate others' knowledge and competence should ask the following questions:

- Is the information necessary or sufficient for competent
  performance as defined by a clearly articulated competence
  criterion?
- If the information is not necessary or sufficient, why is it valuable
  to know?

When answering these questions, note the following:

- When cues or non-declarative knowledge produce the same competence as another piece of information, the latter information is not necessary for competence.
- How audiences process information depends on what they already know. A piece of information that increases one person's competence may have no effect on another person's competence.
- People differ in their physiologies and experiences. As a result, they may have different values and preferences. As a result, people can know many of the same things but support different policies. So, just because other people have reached different conclusions than we have does not imply that they are less informed than we are or that teaching them what we know will change their minds.
- When a group's members have diverse political roles, the effectiveness of attempts to increase competence can depend on what information is given to whom. If so, administering the same quiz to every person may not be the most efficient way to evaluate group competence.
- Competence can be costly to achieve. Costs reduce the net benefits of increasing competence and affect the types of educational investments that people want to make.

There are additional things to consider when using data to measure a group's competence. Educators who seek to increase turnout, for example, often focus on providing information to individual citizens. Their aspirations are achieved every time they persuade an additional person to vote. When educators focus on group tasks—such as getting a majority of a group's members to take an action—a different evaluation is needed. In cases when the competence being measured is of a group, and not all members of a group require the same knowledge for the group to be competent, data documenting some members' lack of such knowledge need not constitute evidence of the group's incompetence.

Finally, in many political situations, people disagree about what actions constitute competence. Physiological variations or differences in life experiences are among the factors that lead people to have different feelings about political phenomena. Since many competence assessments are based on values as well as facts, data-based competence assessments should account for the different ways that knowledge can produce competence.

In the following pages, we will encounter people who claim that citizens are making incompetent decisions because they fail to answer small sets of recall questions in certain ways. Educators who want to improve their effectiveness and efficiency should consider whether they would reach the same conclusions after applying the logic of competence and the politics of competence developed in part I of this book to the topic and after considering the evidence about most such claims that are presented in part II. Educators who have these insights can use the data to draw more accurate conclusions about what kinds of information are most valuable for prospective learners to know.

15

Reading the Questions, Understanding the Answers

Many people comment on the public's political ignorance. Some blame it for the defeat of a favored candidate. Some cite it as the reason for changing civics curricula. Some use evidence of ignorance to exhort others to change their ways. What is the quality of the evidence underlying these criticisms and exhortations?

Surveys provide the evidence cited in many political ignorance claims. Of particular interest are surveys that ask respondents to recall specific facts about certain people, institutions, and events. These recall questions produce responses that are graded as correct or incorrect. An example of such a question is "What is the job or political office held by Barack Obama?"

Scholars use the term "political knowledge" to describe these questions and the data they generate. The best-known academic book on political knowledge by political scientists Michael Delli Carpini and Scott Keeter defines it as "the range of factual information about politics that is stored in long-term memory" (Delli Carpini and Keeter, 1989: 10). Henceforth, I label this concept PK.

Delli Carpini and Keeter (1989: 306) recommend using five questions to measure PK:

1. Do you happen to know what job or office is now held by [insert current vice president]?

2. Whose responsibility is it to determine if a law is constitutional or not . . . is it the president, the Congress, or the Supreme Court?
3. How much of a majority is required for the US Senate and House to override a presidential veto?
4. Do you happen to know which party had the most members in the House of Representatives in Washington before the election this/ last month?
5. Would you say that one of the parties is more conservative than the other at the national level? Which party is more conservative?

While others use different lists of questions, many scholars and writers use responses to short lists of recall questions to make general claims about political knowledge. A common claim is that the public is generally ignorant and incompetent. Writers who make such claims assume that survey respondents' inabilities to answer a small number of recall questions accurately represent greater cognitive inadequacies.

With such claims in mind, the chapter continues as follows: In each section, I introduce widely publicized claims about political knowledge and ignorance. I then examine the recall questions on which each claim is based. If the claim is based on a misinterpretation of the data, I show how to correct the misinterpretation. Educators can use these skills to more accurately interpret what citizens do and do not know.

In the process of these inquiries, we will discover that the most accurate inferences we can draw from existing data are often very different than current claims. In particular, I will show that many analysts' PK measures focus on a highly skewed set of recall questions. Little or no evidence connects the content of these questions to citizens' political roles. Hence, many PK measures are less informative about and less relevant to broadly valuable competences than most writers and critics assume.

Here is a short summary of the chapter's main claims:

- Many claims about political ignorance and civic incompetence are inaccurate because they are based on a misunderstanding of what recall questions actually measure.
- In section 15A, I show that some claims are in error because they are inconsistent with the content of the questions on which they are based.

- In section 15B, I show that other claims are in error because of mistaken beliefs about how grades of correct and incorrect were applied to recall question answers.
- In section 15C, I show that other claims are in error because of a misunderstanding of why people respond "don't know" to recall questions. Experiments show that for certain types of people (e.g., women) and certain types of questions, respondents sometimes respond "don't know" even when they do have relevant knowledge.

A key implication of this chapter is that continuing to use the term "political knowledge" to describe data that measure just a few arbitrary instances of recall is likely to continue confusing the public about what people do and do not know. By reorienting our conversation to the actual content of recall questions, we can improve what educators of all kinds know about the content of others' declarative knowledge.

15A. THE AMERICAN CIVIC LITERACY PROGRAM AND THE CONTENT OF QUESTIONS

The Intercollegiate Studies Institute's (ISI) American Civic Literacy Program assesses the extent to which America's colleges and universities are producing valuable civic knowledge. In 2006, it surveyed over 14,000 randomly selected college freshmen and seniors at 50 colleges and universities, including the Ivy League schools Brown, Yale, and Harvard. ISI's assessments are often critical of the nation's leading universities.

One ISI claim about that study says that "Students Know Less after 4 College Years." One of its press releases was entitled "New Report Reveals Most Expensive Colleges with Highest Paid Presidents and Largest Government Subsidies Score the Worst on Basic US History Test." Universities revealed as particularly retrograde with respect to ISI's measure of civic literacy included the University of Pennsylvania, Cornell, Yale, and Princeton.

ISI's work raises questions about the effectiveness of our nation's educational institutions. It prompted the *Providence Journal*, the largest newspaper serving the city in which Brown University is located, to offer an editorial entitled "Expensive Ignorance." There, the *Journal*'s editors asked,

"Should we be concerned that our best-educated young Americans know so little about civics and history? We should, if we hope to sustain our representative democracy."[1]

Such concerns are consistent with ISI's stated motivation: "Critics have long expressed their concern that the nation's colleges are not teaching what students need to know to *effectively participate in the American political process.*"[2] About the questions that ISI asked, Josiah Bunting, chairman of ISI's National Civic Literacy Board claimed in *USA Today* that "This is useful knowledge we are talking about."[3]

ISI's findings were not universally well received. Some commentators criticized ISI for having substandard research practices. Others criticized it for having a conservative bias. For the purpose of this chapter, these descriptions of ISI are not the main focus. My interest is in evaluating the extent to which the questions ISI asks and the data that it has collected are consistent *with its own stated claims.* Do ISI's questions measure what students "need to know to effectively participate in the American political process?"

To determine what ISI's data really tell us about the civic abilities of college students, there are a number of questions that we should ask about its work:

- Is the content of each question essential to effective participation in the American political process?
- Is the ability to recall the information sought in ISI's questions necessary or sufficient for effective citizenship?
- If a person wants to argue that the answer to either question is "yes," is the claimed connection between the content of the questions and the more valuable forms of participation mentioned based on logic and evidence, or is the claim merely speculative?
- If the ability to answer the questions is a sufficient condition for competence, rather than a necessary condition, is it appropriate to use ISI's data to draw broad conclusions about students' inability to effectively participate in the American political process? If not, how accurate are ISI's conclusions about the educational failures of leading colleges and universities?

In other words, how much worse off is society if college seniors cannot answer ISI's questions correctly?

To determine how ISI selected its questions, I examined the parts of ISI's website where it describes its methodology. Their method of selecting questions is the result of a process in which a group of "specialists sought to capture the essential facts and concepts of history, political science, and economics that contribute most to civic knowledge." ISI says that "Each question included was intended to test important knowledge. . . . The themes consist of basic civic knowledge or concepts, not obscure or arbitrarily selected knowledge." [4] Their description does not include the criteria and data used to evaluate which questions met this standard.

A typical ISI survey features 60 multiple-choice questions. It is well designed in the respect that it would be difficult to argue that the answers are subjective. But what evidence shows that the questions cover knowledge that people need "in order to participate effectively in the American political process?" Consider, for example, the first question on ISI's 2006 survey.

1. Jamestown, Virginia, was first settled by Europeans during which period?
   a) 1301–1400
   b) 1401–1500
   c) 1501–1600
   d) 1601–1700
   e) 1701–1800

For what present-day tasks is the ability to answer this question a necessary or sufficient condition? The same survey includes questions such as these:

5. Which battle brought the American Revolution to an end?
   a) Saratoga
   b) Gettysburg
   c) The Alamo
   d) Yorktown
   e) New Orleans

13. The struggle between President Andrew Johnson and the Radical Republicans was mainly over:
   a) United States alliances with European nations
   b) the nature and control of Reconstruction
   c) the purchase of Alaska

d) whether or not to have a tariff

e) whether slavery should be allowed in the Federal Territories

14. During which period was the American Constitution amended to guarantee women the right to vote?

a) 1850–1875

b) 1876–1900

c) 1901–1925

d) 1926–1950

e) 1951–1975

19. In *The Republic*, Plato points to the desirability of:

a) tyranny

b) democracy

c) philosopher kings

d) commercial republics

e) world government

26. The Declaration of Independence relies most obviously on the political thought of:

a) Plato

b) Niccolo Machiavelli

c) David Hume

d) John Locke

e) Georg Hegel

People who mistakenly believe that The Alamo ended the American Revolution, or that women gained the right to vote in the late nineteenth century rather than in the early twentieth century, but who also know a range of more contemporary facts that are relevant for tasks *that they actually have to perform*, are likely to have greater competence at these tasks. They are also likely to have greater ability to create social value by performing such tasks with greater competence than are people who are very knowledgeable about the end of the revolution but are out of touch with modern reality. Nowhere in ISI's documentation is it demonstrated that knowing answers to the questions that it asks even approximate a necessary or sufficient condition for being able "to participate effectively in the American political process."

Another question is more controversial, in my view:

6. Which of the following are the unalienable rights referred to in the
   Declaration of Independence?
   a) Life, liberty, and property
   b) Honor, liberty, and peace
   c) Liberty, health, and community
   d) Life, respect, and equal protection
   e) Life, liberty, and the pursuit of happiness

If we are going to use answers to this question to judge the value of a university education, it is worth noting that the Declaration of Independence,
historically important though it is, *is not legally binding*. Questions about
key components of the US Constitution (e.g., length of presidential and
congressional terms of office, relationships between the branches of government) are likely to be of greater value to voters seeking to make the
kinds of choices they are offered on Election Day. Though, for many
important tasks that we ask voters to accomplish, not even knowledge of
such constitutional characteristics are necessary or sufficient for competent performance.

While we can criticize ISI's claims, and by extension many media organizations' interpretations of ISI's findings, we can also acknowledge the
potential value of their work. Is a common culture important? Of course
it is. Can a common knowledge of historical facts among members of a
social group provide benefits to that group by serving as a basis of shared
norms, expectations, or values? Of course it can. But these facts do not
imply that every historical fact that can be commonly known is worth
commonly knowing. Absent a competence criterion that differentiates
high-value task performance from low-value performance and absent a
logic that shows recall of ISI's questions to be necessary or sufficient for
increasing such valued competences, broad assertions about the value of
ISI's highlighted facts to broader audiences are difficult to defend—even
with their own data.

ISI does not demonstrate that recalling the items on its survey is a necessary condition for achieving high-value social outcomes. It only specu-
lates about this connection. ISI does not account for the fact that a student's
ability to use cues or recall a different set of facts may also be sufficient to
perform competently at many different tasks using a wide range of criteria
(including criteria that conservatives would endorse). Many colleges, for

example, emphasize training in critical thinking over rote memorization of facts. ISI discounts the role of the latter in their claims despite ample evidence that critical thinking increases competence at many tasks.

ISI's press release claims that the elite universities and their "presidents are simply not doing enough to help preserve our traditions of freedom and representative government. The time has come for higher education's key decision-makers ... to hold the nation's colleges and their presidents accountable for teaching their students America's history and institutions." What is clear is that universities are not emphasizing the kinds of facts that ISI claims to be essential to effective political participation. But ISI has provided no coherent logic or externally validated evidence that universities that emphasize ISI's chosen list of facts would be more competent at preserving freedom in any tangible sense.[5] To the extent that ISI's current demands on colleges and universities have any force, the force is to impinge on universities' freedom to offer knowledge that is of measurable value to contemporary governance.

Indeed, ISI claims that their selection covers areas of important knowledge and is not arbitrary. One underlying assumption is that their questions are important because their panel said so. To be fair, ISI does explain the procedures involved in assembling their survey. However, the connection between their stated criteria and competence at tangible political acts in which citizens can participate effectively or ineffectively is nowhere documented. The value of ISI's efforts *to its own stated causes* would increase if they took the time to offer defensible logic and evidence that recalling the answers to their questions is necessary or sufficient for accomplishing a specific set of socially valuable tasks. It is hard to see how the ability to recall the exact timing of the founding of Jamestown meets such a standard. To advance its own stated causes, ISI's questions or its stated causes need to be revised.

If I were advising ISI, I would tell them that a better way to bolster effective political participation is to identify specific competences that it believes American citizens should have, state those competences transparently (so that others can determine whether they agree on the necessity of such tasks to protect and enhance American democracy), and then develop civic knowledge surveys with content that corresponds to the necessary and sufficient information for accomplishing those tasks. Senator Bob Graham (2010: 25), for example, argues that citizens who want to change policy outcomes do not benefit from traditional approaches to teaching civics. For people who want to accomplish such goals, he encourages schools, colleges, and universities

> to shift civic teaching from a lecture-based approach that focuses on governmental structure to a dynamic experience that emphasizes personal engagement. Imagine if basketball coaches tried to teach the sport by explaining it to their players rather than taking them on the court to play the game. Civics is being taught in just that way, and it is no surprise that many citizens can't play when they step on to the court of democracy.

Harvard professor Jennifer Hochschild (2010: 119) draws a similar conclusion when she says that "democracy is not a graduate seminar." In other words, not all information that is of interest to scholars offers positive net benefits to people outside of the academy.

In general, when people or organizations use surveys as the basis for broad claims about civic ignorance, they should be able to provide logic or evidence showing why teaching and learning the facts on their tests are more important than, say, spending the same time teaching and learning facts included in *The Book of General Ignorance*.[6] This book sold over half a million copies worldwide and was favorably reviewed by trivia buffs in many countries. It provides answers to questions that many people incorrectly believe that they know, such as "What's the name of the tallest mountain in the world?"[7] and "How many penises does a European earwig have?"[8] (The answers to these questions are in the endnotes section of this chapter.) The book also covers topics with greater political relevance, such as "How many prisoners were freed by the storming of the Bastille?"[9] and "Whose official motto is *e pluribus unum*?"[10] I contend that most of my readers would not rank the ability to recall such facts at the top of their lists of important things for citizens to know. The challenge for educators who seek to provide educational outcomes of tangible net benefit to others is to offer information that is necessary or sufficient for increasing valued competences.

15B. THE AMERICAN NATIONAL ELECTION STUDIES AND THE CONTENT OF ANSWERS

The American National Election Studies (ANES) is widely considered the "gold standard" of academic election surveys. Originating in 1948 at the

University of Michigan, the ANES is now funded by the National Science Foundation and is, at the time of this writing, conducted in partnership with Stanford University. The ANES provides data about how thousands of Americans perceive politics, policy, and the nation as a whole.

The ANES develops and asks questions that researchers, students, and the public use to evaluate numerous hypotheses about why Americans vote as they do. ANES data are freely available to the public. They are the basis for thousands of academic and popular articles and books about politics and elections. Many other surveys rely on the ANES' innovative methods to improve their own questionnaire design, sampling, data management, and accuracy. Indeed, dozens of countries base their own national election studies on the ANES model. As Nobel-prize winning economist Paul Krugman (2009) argued in the *New York Times*, the "ANES is a treasure trove of information that can't be found anywhere else."

Recall questions are among those that the ANES asks. ANES recall questions have provided the evidentiary basis for hundreds if not thousands of PK-related claims. A common inference drawn from ANES recall data resembles that of political scientist Robert Luskin (2002: 284): "The verdict is stunningly, depressingly clear: most Americans know very little about politics. . . ."

To understand the relevance of these claims, it is worth examining the content of ANES recall questions. Luskin's dull impression is drawn from responses to questions like this:

> Now we have a set of questions concerning various public figures. We want to see how much information about them gets out to the public from television, newspapers and the like. . . . What about . . . William Rehnquist—What job or political office does he NOW hold?"

In 2004, the ANES reported that fewer than 28 percent of respondents correctly identified Rehnquist as the chief justice.[11]

ANES recall questions have been used in this manner for decades. For most of those years, the data's veracity went unquestioned by the thousands of people who based their claims on it. But the ANES made decisions when producing and releasing the data that obscured what citizens really knew. As I show in the story that follows, a generation of scholars and journalists neglected to check on how these ANES decisions affected the accuracy of their own claims about public ignorance. The consequence of this neglect is that many people over a long period of time came away with a negative impression of the public that did not reflect what ANES respondents really knew. Many scholars and critics who proclaimed public ignorance of a critical political fact were themselves ignorant of a critical fact about the data.

This story begins after the 2004 election. James L. Gibson of Washington University and Gregory Caldeira of Ohio State University conducted a study that did two important things. First, they examined the manner in which the ANES produced its recall data. Second, they ran their own study on public knowledge of the Supreme Court. Their study used the ANES versions of the Rehnquist question described above and then added a few more. From this research, Gibson and Caldeira (2009: 429) concluded that "much of what we know—or think we know—about public knowledge of law and courts is based upon flawed measures and procedures."

One of Gibson and Caldeira's inquiries was into how the ANES assigned grades to its respondents' answers. This was an interesting inquiry because these ANES questions are open-ended. In an open-ended question, a respondent does not choose from answers as on a multiple-choice test. Instead, respondents answer the questions in their own words. Prior to 2008, the ANES did not release transcripts of the respondents' words.[12] From the 1980s through 2004, the ANES hired coders to grade responses as correct or incorrect. The coders' decisions, and not the original responses, were published in the ANES dataset. For decades, scholars and pundits assumed that these codes were valid measures of respondents' political knowledge. *These assumptions were wrong.*

As part of their study, Gibson and Caldeira requested access to the ANES transcripts and examined them. They identified numerous differences between how the ANES assigned correct and incorrect grades and what scholars assumed about how the ANES graded these questions. For example, the ANES counted as correct only responses that included "Chief Justice" and "Supreme Court." A respondent who said that Rehnquist was on the Supreme Court without saying that he was chief justice or a respondent who simply said that he was a federal judge, both of which are correct answers to the question that was asked, were graded as incorrect.

Gibson and Caldeira found many respondents who recognized Rehnquist as a Supreme Court justice or as chief justice and who the ANES had graded as answering the question incorrectly. A subsequent examination brought specific consequences of the ANES' grading practices to light. As a report that I wrote with the ANES leadership team (Krosnick, Lupia,

DeBell, and Donakowski, 2008:4) noted, the ANES graded as incorrect answers such as:

- Supreme Court justice. The main one.
- He's the senior judge on the Supreme Court.
- He is the Supreme Court justice in charge.
- He's the head of the Supreme Court.

Answers like "He's a judge" were also coded as incorrect.[13]

The number of ANES respondents who knew important things about Rehnquist and were graded as incorrect was substantial. As Gibson and Caldeira (2009: 432) report:

> By our analysis of the open-ended ANES data, 71.8% of the respondents coded as giving incorrect replies . . . could be considered to have given "nearly correct" answers. Of these 349 respondents, 91 identified Rehnquist as a Supreme Court justice, 54 as a Supreme Court judge, and for 61 the only recorded reply was "Supreme Court."

They found (2009: 429) that the ANES data contributed to "a serious and substantial underestimation of the extent to which ordinary people know about the nation's highest court."

Gibson and Caldeira complemented their investigative work by examining other ways to assess respondents' recall abilities. In one study, they embedded a wording experiment into a survey. In the experiment, they asked all respondents to identify the current or most recent political office held by William Rehnquist.

A control group was asked these questions in the traditional ANES format. Using the traditional ANES method of scoring open-ended responses as correct or incorrect, 12 percent of respondents correctly identified Rehnquist as chief justice. However, another 30 percent identified him as a Supreme Court justice. Because these latter responses did not explicitly refer to him as chief justice, the traditional ANES measure would have counted these responses as incorrect.

A treatment group received the question in a multiple-choice format. They were asked to recall whether Rehnquist, Lewis F. Powell, or Byron R. White was chief justice (with the order of the response options randomized across respondents). When asked the question in this format, 71 percent correctly selected Rehnquist.

Gibson and Caldeira (2009: 430) showed that "the American people know orders of magnitude more about their Supreme Court than most other studies have documented." The broader implication of their finding is that many critics' ignorance of how the ANES graded recall questions contributed to an overly negative image of the public's knowledge.[14]

Jon Krosnick and I had just become principal investigators of the ANES when Gibson and Caldeira started to circulate their findings. Seeing their work caused us to launch a comprehensive inquiry into potential problems with how ANES recall data was produced. Sadly, we found errors in coding instructions beyond those that Gibson and Caldeira identified. For example, ANES' 2004 grading instructions said that "Prime Minister of the United Kingdom" is not a correct answer for the office held by Tony Blair.[15] The given reason for this instruction was a mistaken assumption about the status of Ireland and a lack of quality control in the ANES data production process.[16]

Krosnick, the ANES staff, and I used these discoveries to change the production, and hence clarify the meaning, of subsequent ANES recall data. We corrected the grading schemes and published a great deal of detailed information about the production process to help scholars and the public better understand the true content of citizen responses to ANES recall questions. We also released transcripts of the respondents' answers to the public. Now, anyone who wants more information about what respondents recalled about a person's job or political office can read the transcripts themselves.[17]

Yet, we encountered some pushback. Many writers and scholars valued the simplicity of ANES' longstanding correct/incorrect grades. So we sought to provide data that would be true to respondents' verbal answers while being in a numerical format that facilitates statistical analysis. The lingering question was which answers to label as correct, incorrect, or something in between.

The challenge for us was that survey respondents gave diverse answers to ANES' office recognition questions (the official name at the ANES for recall questions that ask about Rehnquist and other people's jobs or political offices). Some respondents provided correct information about the political figure named in the question (such as their state of residence or political beliefs) that did not reflect the political figure's job or office. Other responses were colorful (or vulgar), indicative of substantial knowledge about the person, but did not explicitly reference their job or political office.

We decided to provide numerical representations of the responses that were as accurate as possible *with respect to the question that was actually asked.* Hence, ANES data now indicate whether or not respondents correctly identified the named person's job (i.e., the tasks to which they are assigned by virtue of their political office) or political office.

This decision reflects the main lesson of this chapter—when using recall questions to make a claim about someone else's knowledge or ignorance, it is critical to—well—*read the question.* The errors witnessed in this chapter come principally from analysts and critics not taking the time to read the question that was asked. For the ANES questions listed above, the accuracy that comes from reading the question has another implication, as described in a report that I wrote with Matthew A. Berent and Jon A. Krosnick (Berent, Krosnick, and Lupia, 2013: 26–27):

> In the course of our attempts to develop better coding practices for OR [office recognition] responses, we recognized a disconnect between the wording of the OR questions and what many scholars believe the wording to be. Recall that each OR question seeks a respondent's beliefs about the "job" or "political office" held by a particular political figure. The question does not ask a respondent to free associate about the person in question or to convey any thought about the person that comes to mind.
>
> This is an important fact to recognize for any scholar seeking to use the OR questions to evaluate a person's "general knowledge" about a political figure. When, for example, a respondent replies that Nancy Pelosi is a "liberal from California" or that Dick Cheney "shot a friend while on a hunting trip," he or she is conveying factually accurate information about the political figure in question. However, these respondents are not providing a correct answer to the question that was asked. Such non-job or non-political-office responses would be appropriate answers to a different question, such as "Tell me everything that you know about [Nancy Pelosi/Dick Cheney]?"
>
> Now consider the problem that this question wording causes for people who use the ANES OR questions to conclude that a respondent has little or no general knowledge about the person in question. Respondents who pay attention to the question they were asked, follow its instruction, and cannot recall the job or political office held by a particular political figure, will not offer a response that the ANES would have coded as "correct" prior to 2008. These respondents could know hundreds of things about the political figure but would not offer that information in response to the question. The only people who would offer such responses are people who did not understand the

question or who chose to answer a question other than the one that was asked. As the number of people in a sample who [chose not to] follow the question's instructions grows, the accuracy of the claim that OR responses reflect the sample's general ignorance about the figures decreases.

The ANES office recognition questions do not ask respondents to free associate about important political figures. If they did, many respondents would answer differently. Others would reveal that they know things about candidates that current ANES questions do not solicit. For the first time, the new ANES coding system reflects the correctness of an answer with respect to the question that it actually asks.

In retrospect, it was disappointing to learn about the mistakes that had been made in the production of ANES recall data. More surprising to me, however, was the fact that a generation of scholars and writers had based hundreds of books and articles on the data without bothering to check on their accuracy. There is no record of anyone having asked the ANES for information about how they graded responses to office recognition questions prior to Gibson and Caldeira's inquiry—though Mondak (1999: 66n) stated suspicions about the data in an influential article. In other cases, it was apparent that scholars and critics failed to reconcile their broad claims about others' ignorance with what the office recognition questions actually asked.

The irony here is that many scholars and pundits felt free to castigate the public for its ignorance of particular facts without checking their own facts first. Today, analysts who are interested in accuracy can consult not only ANES' transcripts of respondent answers to office recognition questions, but also comprehensive reports about how it produces all of its recall data. These changes are good news for scholars and educators whose educational ambitions depend on accurate interpretations of recall data.

15C. HOW TO INTERPRET "DON'T KNOW" RESPONSES

One controversial topic in attempts to measure recall pertains to the response "don't know." To a recall question, a respondent can give an answer that is correct or incorrect, or they can say that they don't know the answer. The controversy over such responses concerns how to interpret them.

The challenge is that people say "don't know" for different reasons. Some people give the response because no search of their declarative memory would produce the answer (i.e., they really don't know). Other people may have the memory needed to answer the question correctly, but are not motivated to think about the question when asked about it by a survey interviewer.[18] Others may know the answer but hesitate to give it. In fact, a long line of research on survey responses provides many explanations for such hesitancy (Krosnick 1991) including gender, personality traits, and socioeconomic status.

A number of scholars have conducted experiments to examine the extent to which "don't know" answers reflect a lack of knowledge rather than other factors. Jeffrey Mondak and his colleagues inserted experiments into two surveys. The surveys were the 1998 ANES Pilot Study and a Tallahassee-based survey. In each survey, the control group received recall questions that began with the prompt "Do you happen to know. . . ." Interviewers were instructed *not* to probe further after an initial "don't know" response. Treatment groups received questions with identical substantive content, plus a guess-inducing phrase ("even if you're not sure, I'd like you to tell me your best guess"). In the ANES version, the interviewer first recorded any "don't know" responses and then probed to see if respondents who initially said "don't know" actually knew about the concept in question.

In each experiment, respondents were significantly less likely to choose "don't know" when they were encouraged to guess.[19] Moreover, women were significantly more likely than men to respond "don't know" even when encouraged to guess.[20] In this analysis, discouraging "don't knows" reduced the extent to which men outperformed women (in terms of questions answered correctly) by about half.

The experiments also show that ignorance was far from the only reason many respondents chose "don't know." Mondak and Belinda Creel Davis (2001) analyzed the responses offered by respondents who initially claimed not to know the answer. These responses were significantly more likely to be correct than responses that would have emerged from blind guessing. Taken together, Mondak and his colleagues show that many previous PK measures confound what respondents know with how willing they are to answer questions when they are uncertain of themselves.

Building on these findings, political scientists Melissa Miller and Shannon Orr (2008) designed an experiment where the "don't know" option was not just discouraged; it was eliminated altogether. It was run on 965 undergraduates via Internet surveys. Each respondent received eight multiple-choice recall questions. Each question offered three substantive response options. What differed across their experimental groups was question format. The first group's questions encouraged "don't know." The second group's questions discouraged "don't know." For the third group, the "don't know" option was removed. Miller and Orr found that discouraging "don't know" (rather than encouraging it) led to a substantial drop in "don't know" responses. They also found that discouraging "don't know" (rather than encouraging it) corresponded to an increase in the average percentage of correct answers given.

The most interesting thing about their comparison between the "don't know"-encouraged and "don't know"-omitted groups is that the increase in the number of correct answers was greater than the increase in the number of incorrect answers. This is interesting because each question had three response options. If people who respond "don't know" simply guess randomly when the "don't know" option is taken away, they should have only a one-in-three chance of answering correctly. Hence, if respondents were simply guessing when Miller and Orr removed the "don't know" option, there should be two new incorrect answers for every new correct answer. Instead, *the increase in correct responses was actually larger than the increase in incorrect responses.* Miller and Orr's experiment shows that the "don't know" option attracts not just respondents who lack knowledge about the questions' substance, but also some people who possess relevant information but are reticent to offer it for reasons like lack of confidence or risk aversion.

A more recent paper by political scientists Robert Luskin and John Bullock titled "'Don't Know' means 'Don't Know'" takes a different view. It concludes that "[b]y and large . . . those saying don't know really don't know." Its authors reach this conclusion despite the existence of mixed evidence in the studies listed above—and in their own work.

In their main experiment, over 1,500 subjects were asked recall questions about the length of a US Senate term, about how federal judges are nominated, and about the trend in the US deficit. These subjects were randomly assigned to one of three treatments. In one treatment, they were actively encouraged to give a "don't know" answer. Others were actively discouraged from giving such an answer. Others were neither encouraged nor discouraged. Table 15.1 conveys the data from their experiment.[21]

TABLE 15.1 **Data from Table 1 of Luskin and Bullock (2011)**

Dependent Items	Correct	Incorrect	DK
Senate Term			
DK-encouraging	31.2%	47.0%	21.8%
DK-neutral	43.0	53.6	3.4
DK-discouraging	41.9	57.6	0.6
Nominating Judges			
DK-encouraging	44.9	20.2	34.9
DK-neutral	54.8	38.0	7.2
DK-discouraging	54.0	43.0	3.0
Deficit Trend			
DK-encouraging	81.6	9.7	8.7
DK-neutral	88.1	9.9	2.0
DK-discouraging	86.1	13.3	0.6

In their description of what to expect from the experiment, they raise the specter of "lucky guessing." About this they say: "Here the question is of balance—of the extent to which discouraging DKs exposes hidden knowledge more or less than it stimulates lucky guessing. *Our money is on the lucky guessing, and by a wide margin*" (Luskin and Bullock, 2011: 549, emphasis added). If they are correct that subjects who will engage in lucky guessing when moved from being encouraged to say "don't know" to one of the other treatments, and if we can assume—as they do—that the randomization was done correctly so that the three experimental groups are similarly knowledgeable on average, then we should not expect to see correct answers increase at a rate greater than chance. Given that subjects can choose from three multiple-choice options in the deficit and judge questions, and if the authors are correct that "don't know" really means don't know, then lucky guessers should answer correctly only one-third of the time. The Senate question has four options, so lucky guessers should answer correctly 25 percent of the time.

Table 15.2 provides a reanalysis of the data in table 15.1. It shows a pattern very different from the lucky guessing conjecture. For the Senate and deficit questions, correct answers appear at rates far greater than mere chance. For the deficit question, the effect is particularly stark. When moving from encouraging "don't know" responses to a neutral condition, Bullock and Luskin's data show that nearly *all* of the new answers given are correct. Like the studies before it, this experiment shows us that there are combinations

TABLE 15.2 Effect of Luskin-Bullock Experimental Treatment on Correct Answers

Dependent Items	Change in % Correct Compared to DK-encouraging	Change in % Incorrect Compared to DK-encouraging	L-B "lucky guessing" prediction	Percent of "movers" who gave correct answers
Senate Term				
DK-neutral	11.8%	6.6%	25%	64%
DK-discouraging	10.7	10.6	25	50
Nominating Judges				
DK-neutral	9.9	17.8	33	36
DK-discouraging	9.1	22.8	33	29
Deficit Trend				
DK-neutral	6.5	0.2	33	97
DK-discouraging	4.5	3.6	33	56

of question content-incentives-and respondent attributes that lead significant numbers of respondents to say "don't know" when, in fact, they do possess relevant knowledge.

In sum, decades of surveys and experiments provide evidence that "don't know" responses are mixtures of several factors. Ignorance is one such factor. Low motivation, personality, and gender also affect responses. For people who seek the most accurate possible measures of what others know, it is counterproductive to pretend that "don't know" only means "don't know."

15D. CONCLUSION: READ THE QUESTION, UNDERSTAND THE ANSWER

This chapter examines the relationship between claims made about PK and the content of questions that are used to support such claims. The main finding is that broad claims about ignorance and incompetence are inconsistent with the data on which the claims are based. There are numerous instances where claims are based on erroneous interpretations of the questions that were actually asked.[22] For educators whose goals are to provide substantial net benefits effectively and efficiently, accurate interpretations of valid measures are an important asset.

My conclusions in this chapter, however, should not be read to imply that the questions cited in this chapter have no value. They can have value. If well written and accurately interpreted, questions such as these supply valid representations of individuals' abilities to recall specific things. Such evidence is particularly useful when these abilities are necessary or sufficient conditions for increasing high-value competences. A key to success in these and other cases is to interpret the data for what they actually are.

16

Political Knowledge Scales: Something Doesn't Add Up

In 2012, a Fairleigh Dickinson University (FDU) survey made headlines. The headlines questioned Fox News viewers' intelligence. *The Nation*'s headline read: "It's Official: Watching Fox Makes You Stupider." It claimed that "[a]ccording to a new study by Farleigh Dickinson University, Fox viewers are the least knowledgeable audience of any outlet, and they know even less about politics and current events than people who watch no news at all."[1] It concluded that Fox News "fails the fundamental test of journalism: Are you informing your audience?" *The Huffington Post* (2012) claimed that "people who only watch Fox News are less informed than all other news consumers." *The New York Times'* Timothy Egan (2014) repeated the assertion.

Conservative-leaning publications interpreted FDU's findings differently. *The Examiner*'s headline read "Democrats Use Biased 'Study' to Smear Fox News." It claimed that the pollsters "abandoned all integrity to vindictively trash Fox News and peddle the partisan smear that anyone who watches 'right-wing propaganda' (anything that includes multiple sides of the story) is stupid."[2]

FDU's report on its Public Mind Poll (2012) focused not on how respondents answered individual recall questions, but on an aggregate PK scale that FDU manufactured. Like nearly all published PK scales, FDU's scale was formed by adding the number of correct answers respondents gave to a small set of recall questions. Such scales typically range in value from zero-to-five or zero-to-seven, with the high number representing the total number of recall questions included in the scale. If a respondent answers no questions correctly, they get a score of zero. If they answer all questions correctly, they get the highest possible score. PK scales are regularly used to represent "the range of factual information about politics that is stored in long-term memory." FDU's report and the subsequent media reports are based on the finding that Fox News viewers scored lower on FDU's PK scale than did viewers of other networks.

In this chapter, I examine this case and other claims that are based on PK scales. This chapter's main lessons are as follows:

- Inattention to or misunderstanding of several factors has led many writers to misinterpret what PK scales reveal about knowledge and competence. These factors include the content of the questions used to manufacture the scales, how questions for PK scales are chosen, and how a statistical procedure called factor analysis can—and cannot—validate PK scales.
- Claims that existing PK scales represent knowledge generally, or essential knowledge that is necessary for well-defined competences, or are proxies for either of these concepts have never been evaluated directly and are inconsistent with all available evidence.

While chapter 15 showed how to more accurately interpret responses to individual recall questions, this chapter shows how to accurately interpret and more effectively develop claims based on PK scales.

Note that I use the term "PK scale" to reflect the aggregate recall measures used in this chapter's examples. I use a different term, "recall scale," when describing a scale built from a more defensible method for aggregating the same data. I use separate terms for three reasons. First, most scholars who currently cite this variable use the term "political knowledge" to describe it. So, my description of past work reflects theirs.[3] Second, I show that PK is a misleading term when used in this context. Specifically, when the PK term is used in commentary and analysis as if it describes a comprehensive, representative, or essential measure of what people do or should know about politics, it distracts readers from understanding that most PK scales are based on a small set of unrepresentative and arbitrarily selected questions. Third, I use "recall scales" to describe a different method of aggregating the same data. When compared to how the term "PK scales" is used, the term "recall scale", as I define it, offers a more accurate description of what the resulting variable actually measures.

The chapter continues as follows. In section 16A, I examine the FDU example and use it to reveal a broader set of problems associated with common interpretations of PK scales. I then show how to draw more accurate inferences from the same data. In section 16B, I review defenses of existing PK scales that are based on statistical analyses. I show that the most common statistics used to validate PK scales are often interpreted erroneously. I then show how to correct such errors in ways that produce more accurate conclusions about knowledge and competence. In section 16C, I evaluate other common assumptions used to defend PK scales. In section 16D, I apply the chapter's lessons to improve interpretations of some of the best-known PK scales in academia. In section 16E, I offer an alternate method for aggregating recall data. Section 16F offers concluding remarks.

16A. BIAS, IGNORANCE, AND FOX NEWS VIEWERS

FDU's poll was administered in February 2012 on a random sample of nearly 1,200 Americans. The poll asked nine recall questions:

- To the best of your knowledge, have the opposition groups protesting in Egypt been successful in removing Hosni Mubarak?
- How about the opposition groups in Syria? Have they been successful in removing Bashar al-Assad?
- Some countries in Europe are deeply in debt, and have had to be bailed out by other countries. To the best of your knowledge, which country has had to spend the most money to bail out European countries?
- There have been increasing talks about economic sanctions against Iran. What are these sanctions supposed to do?
- Which party has the most seats in the House of Representatives right now?

- In December, House Republicans agreed to a short-term extension of a payroll tax cut, but only if President Obama agreed to do what? (Open-Ended)
- It took a long time to get the final results of the Iowa caucuses for Republican candidates. In the end, who was declared the winner? (Open-Ended)
- How about the New Hampshire Primary? Which Republican won that race? (Open-Ended)
- According to the figures, about what percentage of Americans are currently unemployed? (Open-Ended)

These are interesting questions . . . for some people. As a political scientist, I am interested not just in the answers to these questions, but also in learning about who in America does and does not know each of these things. At the same time, I recognize that these questions *are not* randomly selected from the universe of political facts. They are not a representative sample of the set of facts that many people regard as most relevant to their political roles. Many arguably relevant topics are ignored.

Those details are important to keep in mind as we evaluate claims that are based on FDU's data. For example, FDU's press release opens with a broad claim: "NPR and Sunday morning political talk shows are the most informative news outlets, while exposure to partisan sources, such as Fox News and MSNBC, has a negative impact on current events knowledge." It continues:

> The study concludes that media sources have a significant impact on the number of questions that people were able to answer correctly. The largest effect is that of Fox News: all else being equal, someone who watched only Fox News would be expected to answer just 1.04 domestic questions correctly—a figure which is significantly worse than if they had reported watching no media at all. On the other hand, if they listened only to NPR, they would be expected to answer 1.51 questions correctly; viewers of Sunday morning talk shows fare similarly well. And people watching only The Daily Show with Jon Stewart could answer about 1.42 questions correctly. . . . Results for questions about international current events were similar.

The FDU report (Fairleigh Dickinson University's Public Mind Poll, 2012) draws little attention to the fact that their recall questions cover only a small and, by many criteria, unrepresentative set of current events. Only one paragraph toward the end of the release offers a short description of the topics covered.

Also paying little attention to the content of FDU's survey questions were the media outlets that amplified FDU's claims. *The Nation*, for example, concluded that "[t]his laziness, partisan hackery and lack of regard for basic accuracy is what separates Fox News from [other outlets]. And it is doing their audience a disservice." But what the evidence clearly shows in this case is that publications like *The Nation* made grand claims about Fox News viewers' ignorance without informing their audience about the FDU data's limited and selective issue coverage. If "Are you informing your audience?" is "the fundamental test of journalism," as the *Nation* article proposes, then *The Nation* did not do very well in satisfying its own criteria in this instance.

Conservative critics of FDU's survey fare little better. They judged the FDU survey as "biased" because people with whom they sympathize did less well on the quiz than people with whom they did not sympathize.[4] Given the few questions from which FDU built its PK scale, it leaves out lots of topics and hence cannot help but be viewed as biased from a number of perspectives (e.g., people who are concerned about the environment or religious freedom). But is Fox News viewers' performance on the FDU quiz evidence of a liberal bias? Unless we adopt circular logic of the form "anything that conservatives tend not to know is not worth knowing," the FDU findings need not reflect liberal bias. Indeed, the conservative critics offer no evidence that knowing the answers to FDU's questions is less valuable to conservatives than to liberals.

FDU fueled all of these misinterpretations by phrasing their findings in terms of aggregate numbers of correct answers and referring to those scales as if they represented some kind of general, essential, or comprehensive knowledge of politics. To give readers a more accurate account of its findings, FDU could have presented their data as the Pew Research Center does.[5]

At about the same time as FDU announced its findings, Pew ran a study that evaluated public recall of a set of politically relevant facts. Pew's quiz focused on political parties, rather than politics in general. In a 2012 report entitled "What The Public Knows About the Political Parties" and in Pew's other writings and press releases on the topic, they consistently reference this attribute of their data. They do not fall into the trap of referring to their efforts as measuring general knowledge. More importantly, Pew's writing on this study draws attention to recall of individual items. They do not present a scale of any kind. Where FDU publicized only its aggregate numbers, Pew does just the opposite—all of the statistics it presents are with respect to how various segments of the public answer specific questions. Hence, where FDU's approach contributes to media and public confusion about the content of public knowledge, Pew's approach clarifies what various individuals do and do not know.[6]

A related concern in various interpretations of the FDU report is partisan bias.

This is an important topic for those who seek to use PK scales to assess competence. Recent research has shown how easily bias can infuse a PK scale. For example, political scientists Jennifer Jerit and Jason Barabas (2012), using an examination of recall questions that spans over 20 years, show that self-identified partisans are more likely to recall facts that favor their partisan priorities. An implication of their work is that, by writing recall questions that adhere to a particular ideological or partisan worldview, it is very easy to manufacture scales that make liberals *appear* to be more knowledgeable than conservatives and vice versa.

A noteworthy example of such bias comes from a paper by Zeljka Butrovic and Daniel B. Klein that was featured in *The Wall Street Journal*. It found that

> basic economic enlightenment is not correlated with going to college. We also show economic enlightenment by ideological groups—the "conservatives" and "libertarians" do significantly better than the "liberals," "progressives," and "moderates." (Butrovic and Klein, 2010: 174)

The claim prompted many questions. Some of these questions caused the authors to reevaluate their methods. In their initial survey, the authors asked recall questions that challenged liberal economic orthodoxy. In a second survey, they added questions that also challenged conservative orthodoxy. The second survey led the authors to revise their conclusion.

> It turned out that I needed to retract the conclusions I'd trumpeted in *The Wall Street Journal*. The new results invalidated our original result: under the right circumstances, conservatives and libertarians were as likely as anyone on the left to give wrong answers to economic questions. The proper inference from our work is not that one group is more enlightened, or less. It's that "myside bias"—the tendency to

judge a statement according to how conveniently it fits with one's settled position—is pervasive among all of America's political groups.
The bias is seen in the data, and in my actions." (Klein 2011)

In both the FDU-Fox News case and the Klein-Butrovic case, the authors
and subsequent media paid lots of attention to the aggregate PK scores but
little attention to the questions that generated the scores. In both cases,
problematic interpretations were the result. We can do better.

16B. CAN FACTOR ANALYSIS SHOW
THAT A GENERAL PK SCALE IS VALID?

When I first demonstrated problems with common media and academic
interpretations of PK scales, I was assured that other academic work showed
that the scales were "valid" measures of political knowledge. Indeed, there is
work that claims to do this. It is cited in many academic articles and some
media reports as a reason for taking seriously broad claims about ignorance
that come from PK scales. Delli Carpini and Keeter (1996: 151–152), for example, follow previous researchers by using this work to defend the assumption
that "a scale with a limited number of factual items, if carefully constructed,
can be used to approximate what citizens know more generally about politics."

Factor analysis is a method that is used to defend PK scales in this
manner. Throughout science, scholars use factor analyses to evaluate the
extent to which clusters of individual items relate to a more general concept.[7] For writers who want to use recall data to address broader questions
about knowledge and competence, factor analysis has the potential to show
that people who answer one recall question correctly are also likely to give
correct answers to other recall questions on the same survey. If there is
enough similarity in the kinds of people who give correct answers to the
various questions, then we have a reason to infer that the collection of recall
questions as a whole is measuring a more general knowledge-related factor.

There is nothing wrong with factor analysis as a way to characterize
similarities among certain types of survey responses. But in the context of
PK scales, many people interpret factor analyses erroneously. Specifically,
when PK scales with high factor loadings are interpreted as validating
general political knowledge claims, I will show that the claimant is either
over-interpreting or misinterpreting what the statistic actually shows.

To introduce these errors to broader audiences, I often find it constructive to start with a passage from Stephen Jay Gould's *The Mismeasure of
Man* (1996). Gould argues that general intelligence cannot be meaningfully
abstracted as a single number. While there remains controversy about what
kinds of intelligence can and cannot be so represented, there is little controversy about the accuracy of Gould's description about what factor analysis
can and cannot do to validate the extent to which a "factor" represents general intelligence.[8] His work highlights errors in how factor analysis was used
in attempts to measure intelligence throughout the 20th century.

Gould (1996: 48) finds that "the key error of factor analysis lies in reification, or the conversion of abstractions into putative real entities." To this
end, he describes a common mistake: attributing too much meaning to the
first principal component in a factor analysis (i.e., the main factor):

> The first principal component is a mathematical abstraction that
> can be calculated for any matrix of correlation coefficients; it is not
> a "thing" with physical reality. [Scholars who use factor analysis to
> validate intelligence scales] have often fallen prey to a temptation
> for *reification*—for awarding *physical meaning* to all strong principal
> components. Sometimes this is justified; I believe that I can make a
> good case for interpreting my first pelycosaurian axis as a size fac-
> tor. *But such a claim can never arise from the mathematics alone, only
> from additional knowledge of the physical nature of the measures them-
> selves.* For nonsensical systems of correlation have principal compo-
> nents as well. . . . A factor analysis for a five-by-five correlation matrix
> of my age, the population of Mexico, the price of Swiss cheese, my
> pet turtles' weight, and the average distance between galaxies during
> the past ten years will yield a strong first principal component. This
> component—since all the correlations are so strongly positive—will
> probably resolve as high a percentage of information as the first axis
> in my study of pelycosaurs. It will also have no enlightening physical
> meaning whatsoever. (Gould 1996: 280, emphasis added)

When used on recall data, factor analysis can provide evidence that a set of
questions represents *some* kind of knowledge. But there are infinite kinds of
knowledge—including knowledge about concepts and objects that can be
related to one another in uncountable ways. In politics, moreover, potentially relevant facts pertain not only to the dates of historical events, the
names of officeholders, the content of statutes, constitutions, and regulatory rules; they also pertain to whether and how all such objects relate to

the values and perceptions that people have. All of this content and more can constitute knowledge relevant to a political decision. Factor analysis can show us that one or more dimensions of this knowledge are being well represented. But the statistic itself has no direct means of revealing which dimension(s) of politically relevant knowledge the cluster represents. It is this aspect of factor analysis that is regularly over-interpreted or misinterpreted in claims about PK.

Indeed, many claims about the meaning of PK scales are akin to the general intelligence claims about which Gould wrote. The validity of any such claim, therefore, depends on additional knowledge of the physical nature of the measures themselves. Gould's challenge to contemporary users of PK scales is to locate, in the individual recall questions that constitute their scales, a basis for interpretation that goes beyond reification. This means that it matters how recall questions are chosen for inclusion in PK scales.

So from what theoretical perspective are contemporary PK scales built? The answer is surprising to many people. As mentioned above, the most thorough book on this topic is *What Americans Know about Politics and Why it Matters* by Michael X. Delli Carpini and Scott Keeter (1996). The book reviews the use of recall questions in political surveys up through the time of its writing, and it employs factor analyses to validate PK scales. Even today, it is considered the leading reference on the topic.

Delli Carpini and Keeter provide a very forthright description of how individual recall questions are chosen for inclusion in many PK scales. They say that

> the selection of specific items remains fairly subjective, guided by the goals of the research and influenced by factors not easily quantified. (1996: 299, emphasis added)

For people who want to claim that current PK scales measure general political knowledge or civic competence, this answer should been seen as discouraging—and stunning. The validity of common PK measures now depends on factors that are "fairly subjective" and "not easily quantified." The introduction of subjectivity is not itself an error. The fact that politics often brings together people with different values produces subjective disagreements about what is worth knowing. The error lies in not being aware of, or ignoring, the subjectivity. In other words, the error is in treating the fact that the questions "scale together" as evidence that a PK scale is a valid measure of politics generally considered.[9]

To be sure, factor analysis can detect important data relationships. It can document the extent of similarities in how various variables move. *But factor analysis itself has no power to specify what is being measured.*

What has happened in the academic study of PK is that scholars have assigned to factor analytic results a meaning that they do not deserve. If we review the individual questions that constitute commonly used PK scales; if we review how these questions were chosen out of all the questions that could be asked; if we consider all of the various ways in which different sets of questions could have been combined to create a recall scale, we can achieve a far better understanding of what current PK scales measure. When we do this for any PK scale that is regularly cited in the press or in academic papers, we can see that they are nowhere close to a measure of the full range of information relevant to politics that people hold in long-term memory. Hence, attributing too much meaning to the main factor in factor analysis on popular PK scales is exactly what many researchers, and those who use their work, do when they claim that a factor analysis shows that a PK scale produces a valid measure of general political knowledge.

Factor analysis is not magic. It cannot transform a small, narrow, and skewed set of questions into a comprehensive representation of all that could be known about politics. When PK scales with high factor loadings are interpreted as validating general PK claims, the author is either over-interpreting or misinterpreting what the statistic actually shows.

16C. TWO QUESTIONABLE ASSUMPTIONS

Factor analysis is not the only way that PK scales have been defended. Two other assumptions about the scales' comprehensiveness and essentiality are made to support the validity and meaning of the scales.

The first assumption is that PK scales somehow accurately and proportionately represent all of the aspects of politics that are worth knowing. As Jon Krosnick, Penny Visser, and Joshua Harder argue (2010: 1290, emphasis added), this has never been demonstrated:

[I]mportant new developments in political psychology raise questions about whether this sort of evidence convincingly documented a pervasive lack of essential knowledge among American citizens. To make claims about how knowledgeable Americans are about political matters, one would ideally first specify a universe of knowledge that people "should" possess to be competent at directing a nation. Then, one would randomly select a sample of pieces of information from that corpus and build questions to tap whether members of a representative sample of Americans possess each sampled bit.

This has never been done. Numerous surveys of representative samples of Americans have asked quiz questions to gauge possession of facts. However, no scholarly effort has begun by defining a universe of knowledge that those questions supposedly represent, and scholars have very rarely offered rationales for why they chose the question topics they did rather than others instead.

Indeed, recalling our previous discussion about the possibility and value of knowing "all the facts," it is very unlikely, nigh impossible, that all of the people who have used PK scales to make claims about public ignorance would come to an agreement about what topics or facts such a universe would contain. Value or preference diversity, issue complexity, political roles, and learning costs would lead these people to have massive disagreements about what is important to know. Even if people could begin to converge on a set of issues that would define a "PK universe," they would need to evaluate whether to weight these components equally in a recall scale or give greater weight to selected items.

For example, suppose that we want to measure a population's knowledge of something like economic enlightenment and that we share the ideological commitments of *The Wall Street Journal*. Would it make sense to construct a recall scale by simply *adding* the number of correct answers to a series of ideologically grounded recall questions? The answer is "yes" *only if* the underlying criterion for making claims about such knowledge places equal importance on the answer to every question and if the set of questions covers all of the facts that the criterion requires a person to know. Suppose, however, that within the worldview described above, some tenets are more important than others. In such cases, any aggregate depiction of knowledge needs to consider counting some questions more than others. In the current literature that uses PK scales, there is little to no evidence that scholars have considered these factors. Rarely, if ever, will you see a PK scale that is built from unequal weightings of included questions. Scholars and critics alike treat simple sums as comprehensive knowledge. Most offer no credible basis for this assumption.

The second assumption is that a PK scale's individual components are so fundamentally important that a respondent who cannot answer these questions is necessarily prevented from having more important kinds of knowledge and competence. We will see claims such as this by Ilya Somin (2004: 8) later in this chapter and William Galston (2001: 218–219) in the next.

This claim is logically possible. Consider, for example, someone who is at home on Election Day and is registered to vote. The task that he wants to accomplish is to cast a vote for all local, state, and federal elections for which he is eligible to participate on that date. Suppose that he lives in a state where he is allowed to vote only at a designated polling place. In this case, knowledge of the location of the polling place is necessary to accomplish the task. If someone else knows the location and can transport him to the polling place, then it is not necessary that *he* know the location—but to accomplish the task, it is necessary that someone who can get him to the location knows where it is. More generally, in places where virtual or absentee voting is not allowed, knowing how to get to the voting place and securing a way to get there are among the necessary conditions for voting in that election. So there are certainly facts that are necessary or sufficient for important competences.

However, it is also true that the types of recall questions asked on existing surveys and used in PK scales *have never been demonstrated to be necessary or sufficient conditions for the broader competences or important kinds of knowledge that writers commonly reference.* Claims of necessity or sufficiency would be easy to prove. A writer, for example, could demonstrate that a particular type of broad knowledge or competence is impossible without knowing all or some of the facts on a PK scale. In such a case, however, the writer would have to demonstrate that no cues or other detailed facts could substitute for the facts in question to produce the desired knowledge or competence. To the best of my knowledge, this has never been done.

In the educational assessment literature, this type of analysis is done. The demonstrations offer information that educators can use to evaluate and improve strategies that are designed to increase important competencies.[10] In the literature on PK, this type of analysis is not visible. It is certainly not done in published work. As a result, published work that uses PK scales has comparably little to offer educators who seek to improve important competencies.

If a survey's recall questions don't cover or represent the entire universe of things that could be known, or do not include facts that are a necessary or sufficient condition for a desired type of knowledge or competence, then PK scales provide no basis for making general claims about that knowledge or competence. To put matters another way, if you add two elephants and three shoes, what do you have five of? In the PK literature, scholars have been adding elephants and shoes and hoping that simply adding them together—while ignoring their true content—will produce a scale with meaning that is not present in the individual questions. Without evidence that the collection of objects adequately covers and accurately represents a relevant space, the sums produce only the illusion of knowledge.

16D. PK SCALES AND THE AMERICAN NATIONAL ELECTION STUDIES

To this point, we have seen examples of PK scales that are built from small sets of questions and are misinterpreted by scholars and the media. Collectively, these polls and stories have fed a public narrative about broad public ignorance. Academics also develop and use PK scales. The next example shows that some of the same kinds of error are present in hundreds of the most prominent scholarly works on this topic.

This example focuses on the American National Election Studies (ANES). Nearly all published studies that use ANES recall data to explain voting behavior or other political phenomena use PK scales, rather than individual questions, in their analyses. Given that most analysts use PK scales rather than individual recall questions, an important question arises. If we were to take all of the ANES recall questions in a given year, assign correct and incorrect scores to each response, and then add the number of correct responses per person, what would that scale actually measure?[11]

In chapter 15, we discovered that how the ANES assigned correct and incorrect grades to responses contained errors and were often misinterpreted. While these problems limit the extent to which some ANES PK scales can be considered accurate or valid, suppose for a moment that we have fixed these problems. Even in that case, I will now show that common interpretations of ANES-based PK scales are problematic.

In thinking about the most accurate way to interpret ANES PK scales, it is instructive to understand how the ANES chose its recall questions. Fortunately, the ANES has kept good records of the data and evidence used to make these decisions. Focal points in the decision process are reports and memos written by John Zaller (1986a,b) and Shanto Iyengar (1986) to the ANES' Board of Overseers. The challenge facing the ANES at the time was that it wanted to measure recall in ways that would be useful to the ANES' many users. Since ANES data users also want many other concepts and topics measured, the number of recall questions that the ANES can include on any given survey is limited. In the years between its 1984 and 1988 presidential studies, the ANES ran pilot studies that featured dozens of recall questions. Iyengar's and Zaller's memos provide an articulate and comprehensive discussion of these questions. The memos describe tradeoffs entailed in choosing among different kinds of questions. Thirty years later, they remain among the most informative writings on how to measure what people know about politics.

Ultimately, the ANES decided that it did not have the space to ask, say, six recall questions about foreign policy, six recall questions about national defense, ten recall questions about education policy, and so on. So it looked for a very small set of recall questions that might represent PK generally. Zaller's memo to the ANES Board following its 1986 Pilot Study (1986b) used insights from item response theory and factor analysis to propose a framework for selecting questions. The idea was to include questions that varied in their difficulty—a key principle of item response theory—and a goal was to choose individual questions that, when aggregated, produced an index with a high factor loading and to include questions that correlated with what the ANES Board of Overseers saw as highly desirable behaviors—behaviors like turning out to vote. I review the implications of each of these decisions in turn.

High factor loadings provide evidence that the cluster of recall questions that the ANES ultimately chose represents some dimension of something. But as we saw earlier in the chapter, without a reference to the content of the questions chosen, the factor loadings can't tell us anything about the kind of knowledge that ANES PK scales represent. Given the extraordinarily limited coverage of ANES recall questions—usually no policy questions, no questions about state or local government, no questions about bureaucratic decision-making, no questions about foreign policy, etc.—factor analysis offers no credible basis for referring to such scales as a valid measure of general PK.

Zaller also provided evidence about the extent to which questions being considered for inclusion in ANES PK scales corresponded with turning out to vote and other kinds of political participation. Zaller suggested using these correspondences as a basis for selecting recall questions. All available evidence suggests that the ANES followed Zaller's advice and that these choices influenced the content of ANES PK scales for decades to come.

This fact matters because some scholars in recent years have claimed that the ANES PK scale is externally validated as a general measure of knowledge *because* it correlates with turnout and other forms of political participation. It is true that such correlations persist. However, it is important to remember three things about the correlations:

- First, correlation is not causality. The ANES has never produced evidence that being able to answer its recall questions is a necessary or sufficient condition for competent performance at tasks such as turning out to vote.
- Second, these questions were chosen *because* they correlated with these behaviors. As a result, it is difficult or impossible to use these same variables to demonstrate the scale's "external validity."
- Third, there is no record of the ANES ever evaluating these questions with respect to an alternate externally validated measure of knowledge.

To get a better understanding of the implication of these points for PK scales, let's think a little more about each of them.

First, a person can be ignorant of many things and still turn out to vote. I would argue that all voters fit into this category given the large amount of things that each person does not know. It is also the case that one can be very knowledgeable about many things and fail to vote. So, there is lots of knowledge, including every recall question that is included in ANES PK scales, that is neither necessary nor sufficient for turning out to vote or participating in politics in other ways.

Second, all available evidence suggests that the ANES followed Zaller's advice: Recall questions with answers that correlated with turnout and certain kinds of political participation were more likely to be included in the survey, and recall questions with answers that did not correlate with these behaviors were systematically excluded from the survey. As a result, subsequent relationships between PK scales and turnout should not be surprising to anyone. Put another way, using correlation with turnout and other factors that were an original basis for placing the questions on the survey to externally validate ANES PK scales today is akin to a circular argument—it is very much like trying to defend an argument by simply assuming that its conclusion is true.

Third, these facts about PK scales undermine the argument that even if the scales are not really representative of the facts stored in memory and are not really necessary for valuable competences, combinations of these questions as occur in PK scales can be treated as *proxies* for these kinds of knowledge. Here's the problem with this claim: *No one has validated it.* If anyone had demonstrated the representativeness of current questions, or their necessity or sufficiency for the competences in question, they might be able to provide evidence of the proxy argument. But, as was the case with other common PK scale assumptions, this work has never been done. As a result, the "proxy" argument is a speculation for which no externally valid evidence has ever been presented.

In sum, the recall questions used to produce ANES PK scales have never been shown to be representative of knowledge generally, nor have they ever been shown to be collectively necessary or sufficient for accomplishing any high-value task. Moreover, factor analysis cannot speak to either of these points. Therefore, claims that ANES and similarly constructed PK scales are externally valid measures of general PK are based on speculation, a misunderstanding of the content of the questions, a misunderstanding of factor analysis, or a basic confusion about the relationship between correlation and causality.

16E. IMPROVING CURRENT PRACTICE

[PK] lies at the heart of research on public opinion and voting behavior. And yet, for decades, scholars have operationalized this concept in different ways and with little attention to the variation in the types of knowledge questions.

Barabas, et al. (2014: 851)

My point in this chapter is not to argue that all possible recall scales have no value. But to claim, for example, that existing ANES PK scales measure general knowledge, basic knowledge, basic awareness of politics, or the full range of facts stored in memory is to ignore basic and uncontroversial facts about the actual content of ANES data. Absent a coherent criterion that supports aggregating these questions in a particular way (e.g., perhaps something other than arbitrarily adding the number of correct responses), the most accurate way to interpret ANES' recall questions (and their parallels on other surveys) is individually.

With this outcome in mind, here is a basic rule for future scholars, analysts, and educators: If we are tempted to give a name to a variable, and the new name does not actually describe the data that we have, then avoid the temptation. *Don't give it that name*—particularly if that name is one, like "political knowledge," that misleads others about the limited nature of the data's true content. Accurate interpretation and truthful labeling of survey-based recall variables can help educators more effectively increase valuable competences.

One counterargument that several people have raised after seeing me present this evidence is that they have occasionally tried out more than one version of a PK scale in analyses of voting behavior and public opinion. To the best of my knowledge, the different PK scales that they used did not involve weighting one question, say, three times more than another or following a well-articulated definition of the type of knowledge they wanted to measure—as recommended above. The more common move is to add a question here and drop a question there. These scholars report that changing the scale did not affect their findings. Moreover, they have observed statistically significant relationships between their various PK scales and other variables of interest.

With such "findings" in mind, scholars have asked me about the extent to which my critique of PK questions and scales (represented in this book as chapters 15 and 16) affects the validity and relevance of their work. The questioner's initial belief is always that since their alterations to the scales made little difference to their findings of statistical significance, my critique does not affect the truth-value or relevance of their claims. Unfortunately, they are wrong.

To see why, note that these questioners are always using the term "political knowledge" (or a parallel general-knowledge term like "political sophistication") to describe the scale. In working papers and published articles and books, they refer to the significant statistical relationships found between their PK scales and other variables in their analysis as evidence of a causal relationship between political knowledge generally considered and another variable of interest. As is the case with almost all published PK work of this kind, the questioner's work contains no explicit reference to the limited and unrepresentative nature of the recall questions in their survey.

The typical causal or correlational finding in such work has this form: "An increase in political knowledge causes (is associated with) a change in [dependent variable]." I have shown, however, that these PK scales neither accurately represent "knowledge" generally considered nor do they include knowledge that has been shown—with anything more than speculation and platitudes—to be necessary or sufficient for highly valuable types of knowledge or competence. So, at a minimum, I encourage these people who use these scales to find a more accurate label for their recall variables. If more accurate labels are chosen, clearer and more meaning-ful claims about knowledge can be made. Consider, for example, claims of this form: "A voter's ability to recall the number of justices on the Supreme Court correlates with their views of the Court's legitimacy." Unlike most published claims about the effects of PK, the truth value of this claim can be evaluated without applying a label to existing data that misrepresents their true content.

To this end, in a few cases where analysts produce multiple PK scales, they often do so by using different sets of questions (e.g., building a scale from five recall questions from a survey as opposed to seven). This is a form of weighting—in the sense that "zero weight" is effectively assigned to questions that are dropped from the scale. It is rare, however, to see such alternative indices defended in more than a cursory manner. In many cases, the criterion for selecting or excluding questions for a scale is not appar-ent. No theoretically defensible reason is offered. It is usually impossible to reject the hypothesis that the analyst selected questions because they produced the "knowledge" result that the scholar wanted to see in the first place (this practice is also known as "p-hacking" or "significance fishing"). When questions are selected in this manner, it is difficult to attach a general "knowledge" label to the index that is accurate or meaningful.

Going forward, I encourage the following steps in constructing a recall scale. First, read the individual questions in the survey. One of the most astounding things I encountered while writing this book was how often this step was skipped in published work. This step cannot be skipped. If it is, then it is impossible to know what the scale actually measures. Second, align an appropriate subset of the questions with a theoretically or practically relevant definition of the kind of knowledge one wishes to measure. In so doing, identify necessary or sufficient relationships between individual questions and the measure itself. Third, use the definition to articulate decisions about which recall questions were included in the index and why each one was weighted in the scale as it was.

If these steps are not taken, then there is one more piece of advice that I can offer. Understand that any statistically significant relationship that emerges from an analysis using that scale, and indeed nearly every existing PK scale in published work, reflects a high likelihood of a non-zero correspondence between a misleadingly labeled variable that is called "political knowledge" and variables that are not called political knowledge. In all such cases, even though a statistically significant relationship exists, it is of little value in drawing accurate inferences about how general knowledge affects the analyses' factors.

In other words, my criticism is devastating for the truth value of most existing PK claims because it reveals many existing causal and correlational claims about the causes or consequences of PK to be false—or at least very difficult to support with available evidence. Building a recall scale from more defensible theoretical and measurement foundations would cause a considerable change in what kinds of claims about knowledge can be validated with statistical analyses. Hence, the criticism applies whether analysts use PK scales as independent variables to explain other phenomena or whether they use PK scales as dependent variables to explain levels of knowledge. *The implications of this chapter's main lessons renders as unreliable almost every existing claim that uses existing PK scales to show how "the range of factual information about politics that is stored in long-term memory" affects, or is affected by, anything else.*

Fortunately, there is a better way for educators to interpret recall data. The first step in any such interpretation is for the educator to identify tasks at which they seek greater competence. The second step is to identify types of knowledge that are necessary or sufficient for increasing competence at those tasks. If it is the case that knowing a representative sample of a large set of facts is necessary or sufficient for increased competence at focal tasks, then the question becomes whether a given recall scale accurately represents that knowledge. In such a case, "representativeness" means more than just covering a number of issue areas. We may also need to make a decision about the relative weight of each issue in the measure. Suppose, for example, that our competence criterion requires that knowledge of one topic (say, knowledge of the impact of rising taxes on consumer demand) be treated as much more important than, say, knowledge of which specific firms such taxes might put out of business. In this case, a recall scale would be a valid measure of the relevant knowledge only if it reflects that asymmetry.

In general, a person's ability to recall idiosyncratically selected pieces of information about national-level politics and government has not yet been demonstrated as necessary for competence in performing even common political tasks. At the same time, some scholars use factor analysis to claim that the ability to answer these questions correlates with, and hence accurately represents, political knowledge broadly defined. It may do so. But claimants tend not to provide direct evidence of these relationships. Indeed, the most common demonstration is that the answers correlate to answers of other recall questions, which themselves tend to be of "fairly subjective" origin, or to variables like voter registration and turnout, which are important politically but not widely accepted as valid measures of general knowledge.

So, when critics use PK scales to castigate the public for its inability to answer common recall questions, they are condemning others for not buying into their own questionable assumptions about how information affects knowledge and competence. To claim that a measure represents general knowledge, one must make a decision about the relative importance of many pieces of information about many topics. The fact that critics rarely describe their assumptions does not mean that they have not made them. It means that they don't understand what they have assumed. We can do better.[12]

16F. CONCLUSION: WHAT THE SCALE MEANS

If a person is using survey data to make a general claim about ignorance, knowledge, or competence, then they are making an assumption about the relative importance of different kinds of knowledge. There is no way around this. In such instances, ignorance of this assumption is not bliss. It can lead critics to insist that others know things that are of little or no personal value.

Many current critiques of civic ignorance are based on recall questions that focus only on selected fragments of national politics. Such a focus is understandable for some journalists and scholars. Journalists who work for or aspire to work for the nation's most influential news outlets have incentives to produce stories that are of interest to a national audience. Similarly, scholars who write articles about political knowledge in a small town will have limited opportunities to publish their work. Hence, both types of writers have incentives to focus on the nation and ignore many other types of politics. But few citizens are scholars or journalists. There are substantial differences between the tasks that most people perform on a daily basis and the tasks that journalists and scholars with national or international ambitions are asked to perform.

So when journalists, scholars, or others attempt to defend PK scales as valid representations of general political knowledge, the question to ask them is, "How do you know this?" If the response references a factor analytic finding, then your question should become, "You have evidence that the questions measure something when scaled together, but how do you know what 'that something' is?" "How do you know that your measure is representative of a valuable kind of knowledge or knowledge considered generally?" Recognize that claims about the self-evident importance of the information in question are often attempts to dodge, rather than answer, these questions. Recognize that claims alleging that the importance of the information has been proven in some unnamed location are often the products of wishful thinking. Insist on seeing the logic and evidence that prove the point.

Consider, for example, law scholar Ilya Somin (1999, 2004, 2013), who defends various arguments about civic competence by making numerous references to political ignorance. Recall, for example, the claim that

> [o]verall, close to a third of Americans can be categorized as "know-nothings" who are almost completely ignorant of relevant political information (Bennett 1998)—which is not, by any means, to suggest that the other two-thirds are well informed. . . . Three aspects of voter ignorance deserve particular attention. First, voters are not just ignorant about specific policy issues, but about the basic structure of government and how it operates (Neuman, 1986; Delli Carpini and Keeter, 1991 and 1996, ch. 2; Bennett, 1988). Majorities are ignorant of such basic aspects of the U.S. political system as who has the power to declare war, the respective functions of the three branches of government, and who controls monetary policy (Delli Carpini and Keeter, 1996: 707–771). This suggests that voters not only cannot choose between specific competing policy programs, but also cannot accurately assign credit and blame for visible policy outcomes to the right office-holders.

This argument is a textbook example of ignorance claims that are affected by the errors described in this chapter. His arguments hinge on the assumption that ANES recall questions and others like them "represent very basic political knowledge, without which it is difficult or impossible to place more complex and specific knowledge in useful context" (Somin, 2004:8). He offers no evidence for this claim or the claim that this type of information prevents people from accurately assigning credit or blame for policy outcomes. These claims are speculative at best.

Moreover, and as we have seen, the ANES questions were chosen not because they represent basic knowledge, but because they scale together (i.e., people who answer one of the questions correctly are likely to answer others correctly) and because they correlate with turnout and participation. We also know that these questions have never been shown to be necessary or sufficient for obtaining more complex or specific knowledge of the topics about which Somin speaks. Among a set of over 40 recall questions that the ANES evaluated in the 1980s, the ones chosen for subsequent inclusion were not chosen because they were more "basic" than other questions that could have been asked. This is indisputable.

In sum, many existing claims about "what people should know" depend not on any demonstration that the information in question is necessary or sufficient for a high-value competence, but on untested or untrue assumptions about the logical relationship between information and competence, what values people should have, what parts of an issue matter more than others, what outcomes people of various political roles can accomplish, who should pay the costs of learning, and, in some cases, a fundamental misunderstanding of the data upon which the claims are based. We can do better.

No person is free of ignorance. Most people are ignorant about almost everything that can be known. An important difference among people is that we are ignorant about different things. To achieve individual or collective competence, the key is to effectively convey what we do know to people who can make effective use of the information. This is why it is important for educators of all kinds to interpret existing knowledge-related data as accurately as possible.

17

Assessing Information Assessments

While many analysts use PK scales to make claims about what people know and why it matters, others use subjective interviewer assessments. The ANES is a common source of these assessments. The ANES asks its interviewers to offer "a five-level summary evaluation of each respondent's level of information level." Interviewers rate each respondent as "very high," "high," "average," "fairly low," or "very low."

Data from these assessments appear in widely cited academic articles on political ignorance. In one such article, Bartels (1996: 203) argues that this variable's use is preferable to PK scales. He claims that interviewer assessments are

> no less (and sometimes more) strongly related than factual
> information scales are to relevant criterion values such as
> political interest, education, registration, and turnout (Zaller
> 1985: 4). Given the added difficulty of making comparisons
> from one election year to another using scales based on
> rather different sets of available information items of vari-
> able quality, the simpler interviewer ratings seem preferable
> for my purposes here.

Other scholars have augmented the case for using interviewer assessments in attempts to understand the relationship between knowledge and other factors. As Claassen and Highton (2006: 415) write:

To measure political information, we rely on NES interviewer ratings of respondents' levels of political information. This indicator has two primary virtues. First, it is present in each of the surveys we analyze providing a consistent measure across survey years. Second, it has proven to be a valid measure. Bartels used it to provide important insights into public opinion toward . . . information effects in presidential voting (Bartels, 1996). Given our focus on changing information effects over time, we share the view that because of the "added difficulty of making comparisons from one election year to another using scales based on rather different sets of available information items of variable quality, the simpler interviewer ratings seem preferable."

In a footnote (2006: 415n), they continue the argument:

> For the purposes of this paper, we also prefer the interviewer rating to measures of policy specific information. By design, we track changes in the contours of public opinion about health care during a time when the amount of media attention devoted to health care varied significantly. Because we are interested in determining how general political knowledge shaped citizens' views about health care in eras characterized by dramatically different levels of media attention to health care issues, our interest in policy specific information is primarily limited to variation in the information environment.

Using interviewer assessments, these authors find that "political ignorance has systematic and significant political consequences" (Bartels, 1996: 200; Claasen and Highton, 2006: 420).

In this chapter, I evaluate these interviewer assessments. The main finding is that there are severe problems in the way that existing interviewer assessments have been produced. These problems render existing assessments unreliable as measures of general knowledge. I then show how we can change the production and evaluation of future assessments to increase their relevance to educators and value to analysts.

The chapter continues as follows. In section 17A, I evaluate claims about interviewer assessments' possible virtues as information measures. In section 17B, I examine how interviewer assessments are produced and evaluated. There, I evaluate common assumptions about the quality of these measures. In section 17C, I review prominent articles that have used the assessments to characterize the effect of information on the quality of public decisions, and I call their main findings into question. In section 17D,

I reevaluate my own work and that of others on a broader set of information assessments. In section 17E, I offer ways to improve future outcomes.

17A. ZALLER'S ORIGINAL EVALUATION

The 1986 memo by John Zaller described in chapter 16 evaluated informa-tion measures. It raised important questions about the reliability of ANES PK scales. Some of Zaller's concerns were driven by the fact that scholars use ANES data to track and explain opinions over long periods of time. Anticipating such uses, Zaller warned the ANES Board of Overseers against the scales.

> [A scale] of the other information variables contained in a given survey, has two serious drawbacks. First, the number and quality of information items available for building a [ANES-based recall scale] vary from one survey to another. The *kind* of information item also varies across surveys. In some years, there is a good selection of direct information tests (e.g., what is the term of the U.S. Senator?) and no location items [asking respondents to place political parties on a left-to-right ideological scale], while in other years the situation is reversed. Relying on [ANES-based recall scales] would, in these cir-cumstances, wholly undermine our capacity to evaluate, for example, the comparative merits of direct information tests and location items. (1986: 4)

As a response to these challenges, Zaller argued that what the ANES needed was a measure "that is both valid and independent of the information items contained in a particular survey" (1986: 4). This was a prescient argument. To the extent that a recall measure could be independent of year-to-year changes in the ANES' recall questions, it would facilitate true apples-to-apples comparisons across years. To accomplish this goal, Zaller proposed interviewer assessments.

> I believe that the interviewers' subjective appraisal of their respon-dents' level of political information meet these requirements. (1986: 4)

A question for any person considering using interviewer assessments as a measure of PK is whether they are, in fact, valid and accurate representa-tions of the concept in question. Zaller provided evidence on this topic by examining how the assessments correlated with other ANES variables. He found that (1986: 4)

> the one-item [interviewer assessment] correlated more strongly than did a 15-item information scale with self-reported interest in the campaign, self-reported turnout, and [turnout as validated by government records]. It was also more strongly correlated with each of the criterion variables than was education.

What does this correlation tell us about the validity and accuracy of interviewer assessments as PK measures? To be sure, this finding documents a correlation between the interviewer's assessment and a set of behaviors that many political scientists find desirable. Moreover, it is not controversial that some information is required to perform each of these behaviors. Turning out to vote, for example, requires knowing how to access a ballot. However, this correlation only directly demonstrates that an interviewer's subjective view of what a respondent knows is associated with behaviors that some political scientists find desirable. It does not directly validate the measure as an accurate representation of a well-defined form of knowledge.

Indeed, self-reported interest in a campaign and turning out to vote are not widely considered as valid measures of knowledge. People vote and are interested in politics while being ignorant of many political facts. Other people who have a vast amount of knowledge about a wide range of political topics choose not to vote. So the variable to which Zaller compares interviewer assessments is itself questionable as a means of externally validating a knowledge measure.

The claim that interviewer assessments are independent of the "information items contained in a particular survey" is also problematic. The problem is that the interviewer completes her assessment *after* asking all of the questions on the survey. This means that the assessment comes after the interviewer has asked all of the recall questions, after the interviewer has asked if the respondent turned out to vote, and after the interviewer has asked if the respondent is interested in the campaign.

Is it reasonable to assume that the interviewer's assessment is not influenced by how a respondent answered these questions? If the assessment is so influenced, then the measure is not independent of a survey's recall questions and can vary from year to year just as the ANES' list of recall questions does. Moreover, if the interviewer made the assessment after hearing a respondent describe the extent of her political participation, we should neither be surprised when the interviewer's assessment is correlated with a respondent's self-reported participation levels nor believe that the assessment is independent of the respondent's descriptions of her political participation.

So, over the last few paragraphs, I have asked a number of questions and raised doubts about whether interviewer assessments constitute a valid and accurate measure of general political knowledge. It is possible, however, that when we examine the assessments, we will discover that they have other properties that make them a valid and accurate measure of a certain type of knowledge (where the type of knowledge in question would need to be defined explicitly rather than asserted as a measure of general knowledge or competence). We might discover that

- the interviewers are well trained in making these assessments;
- the assessments accurately convey a respondent's recall of facts that are necessary or sufficient for important competences;
- the assessments are consistent across surveys (which would allow scholars to make claims about recall and more general knowledge changes over time); and
- the assessments are consistent across interviewers within each survey (which would allow scholars to make claims about how increases or decreases in knowledge affect or are affected by other factors).

The main problem with existing interviewer assessments is that *there is no evidence that they have any of these attributes.*

17B. THE QUALITY OF EXISTING INTERVIEWER ASSESSMENTS

I was a principal investigator of the ANES when James Gibson and Gregory Caldeira identified problems with the office recognition questions described in chapter 15. To respond to Gibson and Caldeira's findings in the most constructive way, Jon Krosnick and I led an extensive investigation of how the ANES produced its recall data. As part of that investigation, I interviewed all available members of the staff of the ANES and the other organizations that were involved in collecting data for the

ANES over the years. We searched extensively for the instructions that the ANES, and the survey organization it worked with, gave to interviewers about how to assess a respondent's information level. To ensure that all interviewers are using the same criteria to evaluate respondents, it would be important that all of them receive the same instructions stating specific rules about what types of recall would qualify a respondent as "very high" in information as opposed to "average" or "low." It would also be important to evaluate and document interviewers' understanding of these instructions to make sure that some interviewers were not grading respondents more harshly than others.

As available training materials show, ANES interviewers are highly trained in many aspects of survey administration. Before a survey begins, interviewers receive extensive instructions on topics such as how to approach potential respondents, how to persuade potential respondents to participate (if persuasion is necessary), how to pace an interview, how to read questions from a computer screen, how to enter responses into a laptop, how to answer respondent queries during an interview, and so on. Uniform interviewer practices of this kind are essential components in making a survey credible. Nearly all statistical claims derived from surveys depend on the assumption that all interviews were conducted in a comparable way. If interviewers are conducting interviews in very different ways, the reliability of a survey becomes imperiled.

After years of searching and dozens of interviews with staff, no one was able to produce any written instructions given to any ANES interviewers about how to assess any respondent's information level—other than a single line of text that reads "use your best judgment." No current or former staff member that I interviewed could remember written instructions ever having been given during a training seminar. No one could recall conducting or recording evaluations of interviewer understanding of any instructions that had been given. Even staff members who were present for training sessions could only remember interviewers being told to use their own judgment. If such instructions ever existed, no one who is or was involved with the ANES remembers them or could produce any evidence of them over the multiple years of my investigation.

With this finding in mind, it is important to say that I have had many encounters with the people who conduct interviews for the ANES. They are professional and effective in many ways. But these interviewers are not well trained in how to assess the range of knowledge that others have about politics—particularly after administering surveys that have very few factual questions. As we have seen in previous chapters, making accurate assessments of others' knowledge is difficult even for scholars and organizations with more recall data and extensive training. Therefore, assuming that interviewer assessments are accurate, independent of questions asked during a survey, or unaffected by different understandings of the assessment instructions is just not a smart thing to do.

Zaller's initial proposal foreshadowed potential problems. Toward the end of his analysis of interviewer assessments (1986: 6), he said: "All this said, an important caveat must be entered. There appears to be some variability in the quality of the rated information variable from one survey to another" (1985: 6).

At this point, it is reasonable to ask the following questions about how ANES interviewers assess respondents' information levels.

- Do interviewers use identical criteria from respondent-to-respondent and from year-to-year, or are they inconsistent across respondents and years when rating respondents? For example, do all interviewers weight each component of an interview equally when assessing a respondent's information level, or are interviewers differently influenced by different segments of an interview?
- Are interviewers trained to recognize how their own biases might influence their judgments of others? Might an interviewer give the benefit of the doubt to someone who is very knowledgeable about their shared theology but less knowledgeable about other topics?

While the ANES has not analyzed these issues, other scholars have. Political scientists Matthew Levendusky and Simon Jackman (2008), for example, found in a conference paper that interviewers varied significantly in their assessments. They found that because categories such as "very high" and "average" lack any sort of absolute meaning, interviewers struggle to categorize respondents in a uniform manner. Indeed they found that a given individual will be scored higher or lower depending on who interviews them and that these differences can have important consequences.

Other work finds significant bias in interviewer ratings. Political scientists Carl Palmer and Rolfe Peterson (2013) examine assessment data on an ANES survey from the 1970s in which interviewers were not only asked to assess respondent intelligence, but also their physical attractiveness. As Palmer and Peterson (2013: 5) describe, "Much like the other assessments, these were made on a five-point scale, from 1 (homely) to 5 (strikingly handsome or beautiful)." While the ANES has produced intelligence assessments for decades, it asked the attractiveness question only once. Using this data, the authors find a strong correlation between perceived attractiveness and perceived intelligence. This relationship holds even after controlling for a large number of potentially confounding factors. In other words, a respondent whom an interviewer rates as highly attractive is far more likely to be rated as highly intelligent. This is true even for people who are rated as attractive but do not answer other ANES questions in a way that scholars have claimed to be correlated with knowledge. Here again, interviewer assessments appear to be affected by factors having no direct relationship to knowledge.[1]

Levendusky and Jackman conclude (2008: 25–26) their paper by stating that

> scholars should accept, once and for all, that the interviewer rating is a flawed measure of political knowledge. There is considerable cross-interviewer heterogeneity, and using this measure risks contaminating the entire model with large amounts of measurement error.

Although I agree with this view of interviewer assessments, this outcome need not persist.

Interviewers who are trained to evaluate respondents according to well-defined criteria and in a consistent manner may be able to provide information about important aspects of a respondent's recall ability. Such judgments would require: instructions that are clearly related to well-defined assessment criteria, evaluations of the extent to which interviewers understand the instructions after training sessions, and evaluations of the extent to which interviewers execute the instructions as directed during the interview process. Well-executed assessments can provide a standardized reflection of some things that respondents appear to know.[2] Such assessments can satisfy Zaller's goal of producing valid apples-to-apples comparisons across interviewers and over time. As of now, however, all existing ANES interviewer assessments are very far from meeting such standards. As a result, there are many reasons to doubt all claims about knowledge and competence that are based on them.

17C. IMPLICATIONS FOR GENERAL IGNORANCE CLAIMS
BASED ON INTERVIEWER ASSESSMENTS

Interviewer assessments have been used to make general claims about political ignorance in two widely cited papers by Larry Bartels. In both papers, the claim is that voters would have acted in a different way if they were more knowledgeable. As has been the case in previous chapters, we can evaluate these claims with respect to the actual content of Bartels's data and his statistical assumptions.

In one paper, Bartels (1996: 195) seeks to "use the observed relationship between information and voting behavior in recent elections to simulate the behavior of a hypothetical 'fully informed' electorate. . . ." He concludes (1996: 220) that

> [w]hatever the sources of the aggregate discrepancies between actual vote choice and hypothetical "fully informed" vote choices may be however, they suggest very clearly that political ignorance has systematic and significant political consequences.

Bartels's approach is to consider variables that might affect voting behavior and then estimate how interviewer assessments of respondent information levels change how each of these variables corresponds to vote choice. He uses the estimates to simulate the difference between actual voting behavior and the choices that a "fully informed" electorate would make.

This is an important kind of claim to evaluate. If it is correct, it can help us identify types of knowledge that correspond to highly valuable competences and information that is necessary or sufficient for obtaining the knowledge or competence in question. With such insight in hand, we could improve the designs of educational strategies that produce broad and substantial net benefits. We saw examples of this type of work in previous chapters.

Suppose, in contrast, that the claims are based on data that are known to be invalid. Suppose that the claims come from statistical models that are difficult to reconcile with known attributes of the manner in which people actually convert information into knowledge and competence. In such cases, the same claims can be misleading and even counterproductive for educators who are seeking to convey information of greater value to citizens who need it.

With these criteria in mind, important questions have been raised about Bartels's work. His conclusions come from a statistical regression model that includes a long list of variables (age, age squared, education, income, race, gender, marital status, whether you own your home, whether you are a housewife, whether you work or are retired) that could also affect voting behavior. The article does not provide a coherent explanation of why variables like "age squared" are included while many of the other thousands of variables in the ANES studies are excluded. This matters because the meaning of any claim that is drawn from a statistical model depends on the assumptions on which the model was built, including why the model was chosen over many others that could have been used.[3] A model that was chosen because it appears to support a particular hypothesis does not produce results as credible as a model that was chosen with respect to a clearly stated and well-defined theoretical framework.[4] Bartels's paper offers no clear justification for which variables are included and excluded in the estimation. The choices do not correspond to any easily identifiable psychological model.

The statistical procedure also assumes that the effects of factors like age, education, income, race, and religion are independent of one another. Yet it is likely that certain combinations of these factors correspond to different life experiences and correspondingly different value orientations. Possible interactions among these factors are assumed not to be relevant to his attempt to understand how information affects behavior (e.g., would a poor black woman respond to new information about a candidate in the same way as a wealthy black woman or a poor white woman). No apparent psychological theory supports the assumption that information's effects— were they to exist—would be independent of any such interactions. These modeling choices make the meaning of Bartels's findings difficult to interpret at best.

Other questions have been raised about the way the paper's information effects are identified. Levendusky (2011), for example, proposes a more accurate means of identifying the effects of information on factors such as vote choice. The ideal method is to identify persons who are similar in every way except in their information levels. When this is done, information effects are more straightforward to detect. When this is not done, as is the case in Bartels (1996), such differences in voting behavior can be due to many factors that are correlated with information differences but are not actually a product of what individuals do or do not know. Levendusky demonstrates that when people are matched in ways that get as close as possible to the ideal method, the kinds of information effects found by Bartels

> shrink considerably after matching. In general, the effects in the matched data are approximately one-half to one-quarter the size of the effects in the unmatched data. These results strongly support my argument: Once the effect of other factors is removed, the effect of information is quite modest. (Levendusky, 2011: 49)[5]

Levendusky's argument is important for educators who wish to interpret academic claims based on existing interviewer assessments. If our goal is to identify whether knowing or not knowing certain facts is necessary or sufficient for accomplishing a certain task in a certain way, it is critical to understand whether studies that are presented as identifying the effect of a specific type of knowledge are actually confounding any knowledge effects with effects of other factors.

That said, even if there was a more theoretically defensible statistical model, a final challenge to Bartels's claim would remain—he uses interviewer assessments as his measure of political information. He defends their use by saying that they are

> no less (and sometimes more) strongly related than factual information scales are to relevant criterion values such as political interest, education, registration, and turnout (Zaller, 1985: 4). Given the added difficulty of making comparisons from one election year to another using scales based on rather different sets of available information items of variable quality, the simpler interviewer ratings seem preferable for my purposes here.

In light of what we know about the actual means by which the interviewer assessments were produced, what we know about the lack of training and quality control associated with the process, and the fact that the assessments occurred after the respondent completed the survey means that the interviewer assessments were unlikely to be consistent across interviewers, independent of respondent answers, or consistent across election years. In other words, it is difficult to defend existing interviewer assessments as having the attributes that Bartels claims for them.

Why does this matter? It matters because, as was the case in chapters 15 and 16's examples, many others cited Bartels's work and used it to support broad claims about civic ignorance. As was the case before, there is no evidence that those who cited the work checked the quality of the assumptions about the data upon which their claims were based. Therefore, the validity of all such claims is now in question.

The same attributes are present in "Homer Gets a Tax Cut: Inequality and Public Policy in the American Mind," an article that we evaluated in chapter 10. In the article (2004: 4), Bartels used interviewer assessments to characterize the opinions of "ordinary people" as "unenlightened" and further argued (2005: 24) that public support for "the Bush tax cuts" was "entirely attributable to simple ignorance." In a response to that paper, my research team found that a relatively simple change to the statistical model dramatically changed the result (Lupia et al., 2007). Having completed an investigation of the information measure that Bartels used, another challenge to its conclusion arose: The ANES study that Bartels used did not ask fact-based questions about that policy. It relied exclusively on interviewer assessments.[6] Hence, for reasons explained in chapter 10 or for reasons explained in this chapter, readers cannot treat that work as having offered reliable evidence of Bartels' main claims.

The main lesson of this chapter is that existing research that uses interviewer assessments as a measure of general political knowledge tells us very little about how conveying various kinds of information to an audience would affect their votes. These assessments are not the products of practices that are likely to provide accurate and consistent evidence from interviewer to interviewer or from year to year. Existing interviewer assessments are unreliable.

17D. USING WHAT WE HAVE LEARNED TO BETTER INTERPRET THE PAST

In the last three chapters, we saw multiple instances of claims about voter ignorance and civic incompetence that were based on erroneous assumptions about the quality of knowledge-related data. In these instances, we saw that if we ask about the individual questions that constitute PK scales, and about why simply summing answers to these questions is meaningful, we can achieve a more accurate understanding of what such data actually measure. Such pursuits are vitally important to drawing accurate conclusions about what people know.

To advance science and improve educational practices, it can be instructive not just to examine what others have done, but also to reexamine your own actions. Knowing what I learned in the process of writing this book, there are two actions that I would like to reevaluate.

First, I have used interviewer assessments as a knowledge measure in a published article. The 2007 article that critiques Bartels's "Homer Gets a Tax Cut" used the same ANES interviewer assessments that he used. It evaluates the assumption that Republicans and Democrats, liberals and conservatives would use additional information in identical ways when evaluating the Bush tax cuts. The article focused on replication. It was built around an attempt to first reproduce Bartels's result and then evaluate whether it would survive a statistical treatment that allowed a more psychologically defensible relationship among party, ideology, and knowledge. I focused on replication rather than the accuracy of the underlying measures. Since that paper was written, I found the problems with the assessments described in this chapter. So, while the finding that Bartels's original result rests on an unsustainable assumption stands, I cannot say that I know what the information measure used in either paper truly measures. I recommend that this variable not be used to draw general judgments about the effect of information or knowledge.

Second, there were several things that I did not know about how interviewer assessments were produced in 2007 and 2008. This timing matters because I was a principal investigator (PI) at the ANES at that time. Knowing what I now know, I would have eliminated the variable from the 2008 data collection or instituted a new set of instructions and evaluations to produce the assessments. I now recommend these practices to everyone who is considering including the variable in their surveys.

Which choice I would have supported during my time as PI depends on when we discovered the measure's problems. Had we discovered them in the middle of 2007 but before the time when the survey was to be fielded, it would have been too late to develop and evaluate an entirely new process for conducting the assessments (it would have to be a process similar in detail and rigor to the one that I described in chapters 15 and 16 for the recoding of the ANES office recognition questions; see Berent, Krosnick, and Lupia [2013]). Knowing what I know now, I would have dropped the questions from the survey. If we discovered the problems earlier than the middle of 2007, my belief is that we would have looked for a way to fix them.

As it happens, I did not understand the scope and magnitude of these errors until well after the 2008 study was fielded. Going forward, I advise people running surveys today and in the future to either develop a credible assessment process or drop interviewer assessments altogether. To continue the assessments in their current form will only add to current confusion about the relationship among information, knowledge, and competence.

Correcting errors in measurement and interpretation is important—and not just for scholars. While part II has focused much of its attention on academic work, the challenges associated with measuring what others know are more than a scholarly matter. PK-based claims are used in broader claims about what others should know.

Political theorist William Galston (2001: 218–219), for example, makes the following claim about what people need to know to be "good" citizens:

> [T]here are signs of an emerging consensus. Competent democratic citizens need not be policy experts, but there is a level of basic knowledge below which the ability to make a full range of reasoned civic judgments is impaired. Moreover, a broad-based discussion during the 1990s has yielded substantial agreement on the content of this knowledge, which in turn has served as the basis for constructing the Civics Assessment of the National Assessment of Educational Progress.

Galston offers an appealing vision. It is one that many educators would want to support. And it is certainly true that there is knowledge that helps people perform important tasks competently. My belief is that Galston and other scholars and writers whom we have discussed are concerned about the effects of ignorance. But their success in improving civic competence depends on reconciling their claims about what people should know with the true properties of existing data and a coherent understanding of how information and knowledge affect competence.

For example, the consensus Galston discusses is important. The "consensus" is also very limited and, more importantly, it is misunderstood by many people who have used Galston's article as a call for reforming civic education. The NAEP is an effort to measure a particular set of educational outputs. The NAEP's consensus reflects the views of about 40 elementary and secondary school teachers and about 20 members of the public.[7] The consensus applies to a civics exam that is given to fourth, eighth, and twelfth graders. While the NAEP is committed to providing a high-quality education for students, its provides no evidence about the extent to which the topics covered on the civics exam actually cause people to perform important tasks competently when they are legally old enough to do so. So, to say that there is a broad consensus on the types of information that people need to "make a full range of reasoned civic judgments" overstates what the NAEP's data and analysis actually show.

Galston (2001: 223) later claims that "the more knowledge we have, the better we can understand the impact of public policies on our interests and the more effectively we can promote our interests in the political process." Of course, there are plenty of kinds of knowledge that can reduce our understanding of public policies—such as when greater knowledge of one aspect of a policy leads a person to falsely characterize other aspects of it.[8] The key, however, is to determine what types of knowledge are necessary or sufficient for beneficial forms of competence. The topics or facts that seem important to one group may have no value for people with other political roles. To design and implement high net-benefit civic education programs is to deliver the kinds of information described in part I—information with factual content that not only corresponds to improved performance at important tasks with respect to well-defined competence criteria, but that is also perceived by prospective learners as helping them advance their core concerns.

In important ways, Galston's claims echo those of literary critic E. D. Hirsch. Hirsch's argument was made 14 years earlier; it referenced the NAEP as part of its argument, and it received substantial attention when it was published. In the book *Cultural Literacy: What Every American Needs to Know*, Hirsch argued that "[o]nly by piling up specific, communally shared information can children learn to participate in complex cooperative activities with other members of their community" (1987: xv).

To be sure, there are many social endeavors for which shared knowledge of cause-and-effect, culture (particularly as it influences the likely responses of others to a range of our own behaviors), and history (as a way of explaining why certain things do or do not exist) allows certain outcomes to be achieved effectively and efficiently. But not all historical, cultural, or causal information has this effect. In fact, it would be more accurate to say that most information fails to have any such effect most of the time. There are many socially valuable tasks for which most historical facts are neither necessary nor sufficient for competent performance.

Hirsch defines *cultural literacy* as "the network of information that all competent readers possess" (1987: 2). Similarly, "To be culturally literate is to possess the basic information needed to thrive in the modern world" (1987: xiii). However, he never explicitly defines what a "competent" reader is nor does he demonstrate that the items on his list are necessary to thrive in the modern world. While the information he lists is pertinent to certain tasks, he does not do the work of showing how the items on this list have the effects he claims for them.

Other writers who examined Hirsch's list raised serious questions about the net benefits of teaching its content. Philosopher Brian Hendley (1989: 57) described Hirsch's list as reading like "an upper-middle class primer for cultural respectability to be used by academic missionaries who must toil among the uneducated masses." Stanley Aronowitz and Henry Giroux (1988) found that Hirsch's list "marginalizes the voices, languages, and cultures of subordinate groups." Hendley (1989: 57) concluded that "[t]here is an elitism to Hirsch's proposals . . . [he] sees the problem of education to be that of bringing the have-nots up to the level of the haves by teaching them what *we* know. Little recognition is paid to the possible contributions of ordinary people to the common good or the value of their experiences and means of communication."

When explaining how items were selected for inclusion on the list, Hirsch (1987: 135–136) argued that

> agreement about literate culture should, in theory, enable a random group of literate Americans to compile a list of its core contents. . . . In 1983 I persuaded two of my colleagues at the University of Virginia, Joseph Kett, chairman of the department of history, and James Trefil, professor of physics, to help me compile such a list. . . . When we finished the first version of our list, we submitted it to more than a hundred consultants outside the academic world. . . . In consulting others about our initial list we did in fact discover a strong consensus about the significant elements in our core literate vocabulary.

It is worth noting that neither of these lists of participants appears to have been randomly selected from a cross-section of experts who represent the wide variety of value orientations that are present in American politics. Without a sense of the range of expertise and values covered by the 100 persons—or how disagreements within the group were negotiated—it is difficult to understand when, and to whom, this manufactured consensus is actually relevant.

About the list that was ultimately produced, Hendley (1989: 56) comments:

> Hirsch and two of his colleagues at the University of Virginia have taken the first step toward attaining this goal by providing a 60-plus page Appendix to the book listing those items that culturally liter-ate Americans know.... Surely such a listing cannot be taken very seriously.... His list brings to mind Dewey's comment in *Schools of Tomorrow* that those who would teach children lists of facts often forget that "it is not their naming that is useful, but the ability to understand them and see their relation and application to each other." (1989: 56)

There is a better way to convey information to help people achieve a wide range of valuable social goals. It begins by naming a set of tasks that are valuable for a society to accomplish and then gathering credible evidence and transparent logic about the types of information and knowledge that produce net beneficial outcomes. For educators who want to achieve their competence-increasing goals efficiently and effectively, there is no good substitute for this.

Other commentators promote the icon of a "fully informed voter". In most political contexts, the icon is a fiction. It is a complete fantasy. But it is not a harmless fantasy. The harm comes from the fact that some people are hesitant to vote because they don't know "all the facts." In an essay entitled "Most People Shouldn't Vote," philosopher Jason Brennan (2012) argued for just such an outcome:

> There's nothing morally wrong with being ignorant about politics, or with forming your political beliefs though an irrational thought process—so long as you don't vote. As soon as you step in the vot-ing booth, you acquire a duty to know what you're doing. It's fine to be ignorant, misinformed, or irrational about politics, so long as you don't impose your political preferences upon others using the coercive power of government.

To be fair, Brennan does not argue that citizens need to know everything. Yet his standards for what disqualifies one for voting are unclear at best. In 2009, when discussing the same problem, he argued (2009: 547) that "[t]he point of the paper is to identify that there is a problem, but it would take much more work to determine how to solve the problem. I argue that people should not vote badly, but I do not explain how to prevent them from voting badly."

In sum, my critiques of Bartels, Galston, Hirsch, and Brennan are not about their aspirations. All express normatively desirable goals. All care about the democracy in which they live. All are concerned about the manner in which certain types of ignorance can reduce quality of life within a democratic system. The critiques are of the stark claims that each makes about the kinds of knowledge that are necessary or sufficient to achieve the normative competences to which they aspire. The critique is of the quality of their advice to others. Even when measured against their own stated aspirations, erroneous assumptions about the relationships among information, knowledge, and competence, and erroneous assumptions about the content of recall data and PK scales reduce or eliminate the potential value of their advice.

Would we be better off if the public spent significant time memorizing the facts on which academics and journalists who write about civic incompetence dote? Would we be much better off if every American could answer such questions as "Which political party is more conservative?" or "How long is the term of office for a US senator?" during a survey interview? Once we realize that teaching and learning impose real costs in terms of time, effort, and money, and once we realize that some information is more valuable to convey to particular audiences, then the net benefits of conveying various kinds of information become relevant.

When critics who are unfamiliar with the logic and politics of competence, and who misunderstand the true content of the surveys and statistical models on which they base their conclusions, adopt the rhetorical strategy of naming one, two, or perhaps even 10 things that an audience does not know and then claim that this evidence is sufficient to draw broad conclusions about others' ignorance and incompetence, they are from the perspective of their own rhetorical strategy, *caught in a catch-22*. In other words, the same critics who call citizens incompetent because citizens cannot recall a small and perhaps basic set of facts about politics would fare no better if asked to answer a small and perhaps basic set of questions about how the information they ask others to learn actually affects valuable types of knowledge or competence. Critics should be able to provide correct answers to questions about why recalling a specific small set of facts is necessary or sufficient for achieving a high-value out-come—particularly when cues and procedural memories can produce the same outcome. Critics who choose not to acknowledge these factors will continue to make demands of citizens that provide little or no discernable net benefit to the normative causes that usually motivate the critiques. Until such critics offer a transparent, credible, and replicable explanation of why a particular list of facts is necessary for a particular set of socially valuable outcomes, they should remain humble when assessing others' competence.

In sum, educators who wish to make credible and defensible claims about knowledge and competence should focus less on PK, a concept that causes confusion, and should ignore existing interviewer assessments alto-gether. A better way forward is to interpret existing data for what they are and create new data that offer better measures of what citizens do and do not know.

17E. CONCLUSION

In this chapter, we reviewed two ways of assessing knowledge and com-petence. First, we reviewed survey interviewers' subjective assessments of respondents' "information levels." Then we reviewed other assessments of what citizens should know. In each case, we discovered that if certain assumptions are true, then such assessments can help citizens improve their competence. We then found that commonly made assumptions about many of these assessments were untested or just untrue.

As was the case with claims made about individual recall questions in chapter 15 and PK scales in chapter 16, this chapter also saw scholarly and journalistic communities demonstrating a great deal of confidence in a measure that did not deserve that confidence. Existing interviewer assessments are not the product of well-trained interviewers following well-defined standards or even a minimal degree of quality control. Many lists of facts that have been claimed as necessary for good citizenship have never been shown to be necessary or sufficient for these outcomes. In many cases, supporting arguments were based on a misunderstanding of factor analysis along with circular logic (e.g., "these facts are necessary for com-petence because a group that I have assembled says they are. We need no other evidence").

People who want to tell others what they ought to know should first understand whether and how information creates knowledge that matters. As we have seen throughout the preceding chapters, speculation and wishful thinking about information, knowledge, and competence are poor substitutes for clear logic and accurate data interpretations. Before making claims about others' ignorance, critics should have their own houses in order. Addressing this point, an anonymous reviewer offered the following reaction to an earlier draft of this chapter (emphasis added):

> As I read, I was repeatedly struck by the fact that there is so little research (at least in political science) about the important questions raised in this book: the conditions under which citizens can learn; the conditions under which information improves competence (however defined); which types of cues/heuristics promote competence in which types of tasks (from ch. 5). *I'd suggest [the author] make this explicit at some point in the book* ... and the obvious opportunities for more systematic research to support the arguments put forth in the book.

I agree.

Critics of civic ignorance and those who want to improve civic competence need a better knowledge base from which to work. My hope is that part I of this book offered a stronger foundation for such efforts than existed before. The reviewer also asked that scholars and other writers learn how to accurately interpret the kinds of data that are brought forward in arguments about what citizens know or need to know. I agree with the reviewer that as a whole, and over the span of several decades, political science and other fields have put the cart way ahead of the horse when it comes to measuring and making claims about what citizens know and why it matters. My hope is that the advice in part II offers an improved foundation for such efforts.

Indeed, one positive outcome of basing claims about what others should know on the logic of competence, the politics of competence, and valid measures of recall is the potential for greater benefits to individuals at less expense to society. This benefit arises because erroneous claims about the benefits of learning certain types of things impose potentially great costs. On society, erroneous claims lead to investments in ineffective civic education programs. On individuals, erroneous claims lead them to be asked to learn information that is of limited value to them or their communities. They also impose the psychic cost of inadequacy and the social cost of withdrawal when people falsely believe that they have nothing to contribute to civic life because they are told to compare themselves to the unrealistic icon of the perfectly informed citizen. We can do better.

Bringing this line of argument back to the main themes of the preceding chapters, we can now reach the following conclusion. Educational strategies can be more effective and valuable to participants and communities when they are based on

- greater attention to tasks that provide substantial positive net benefits if accomplished competently;
- greater attention to the relationship between the ability to accomplish such tasks, the kinds of knowledge that are necessary and sufficient to accomplish the tasks with increased competence, and the kinds of information that can draw attention sufficient to create such knowledge; and
- greater attention to the measurement of whether or not people know the kinds of things that meet these criteria.

Looking forward, another valuable skill is to create new data that more effectively capture what people do and do not know. Part II's final chapter turns to that task.

18

All in Good Measure

This chapter is about how to word recall questions effectively. An example of why this topic matters occurred just days before the opening of the United States Holocaust Memorial Museum. At that time, a *New York Times* headline proclaimed that "1 of 5 in New Survey Express Some Doubt About the Holocaust." The *Times* article's lead paragraph described the finding in greater detail (emphasis added):

> A poll released yesterday [sic] found that 22 percent of adults and 20 percent of high school students who were surveyed said they thought it was possible that Nazi Germany's extermination of six million Jews never happened. In addition to the 22 percent of adult respondents to the survey by the Roper Organization who said it seemed possible that the Holocaust never happened, 12 percent more said they did not know if it was possible or impossible, according to the survey's sponsor, the American Jewish Committee.[1]

Reactions to this finding were swift. Benjamin Mead, president of the American Gathering of Jewish Holocaust Survivors, called the findings "a Jewish tragedy."[2] Elie Wiesel, a Nobel Laureate and concentration camp survivor, conveyed shock and disappointment: "What have we done? We have been working for years and years . . . I am shocked. I am shocked that 22 percent . . . oh, my God."[3] Similar headlines appeared across the country.[4]

In the months that followed these reports, many struggled to explain the finding. Some blamed education, as a *Denver Post* editorial described:

> It's hardly surprising that some Americans have swallowed the myth that the Holocaust never happened. . . . [E]ither these Americans have suffered a tragic lapse of memory, or they have failed to grasp even the rudiments of modern history. . . . Such widespread ignorance could lull future generations into dropping their guard against the continuing menace of ethnic intolerance, with potentially devastating consequences. . . . To this end, the public schools must obviously do a better job of teaching 20th century history, even if it means giving shorter shrift to the Civil War or the Revolution. Today's students, the grandchildren of World War II veterans, shouldn't be graduating if they can't recognize the names Auschwitz and Dachau as readily as Pearl Harbor and Hiroshima.[5]

Others looked at the poll itself. There were many reasons to give credence to Roper's numbers. It was one of the nation's leading polling organizations. Its techniques for sampling the population were consistent with the day's best practices. There was no evidence that Roper's respondents were more likely than other Americans to deny the Holocaust.

Over time, however, people started to raise questions about what memories Roper's survey really measured. The Holocaust question's exact wording was "Does it seem possible to you, or does it seem impossible to you that the Nazi extermination of the Jews never happened?" A "yes" or "no" answer was sought.

Burns W. "Bud" Roper, chairman of the Roper Center for Public Opinion Research, was one of the first people to suggest that the question's wording may have confused respondents.[6] Table 18.1 depicts the question's potential for causing confusion. It shows how a survey respondent with different views about the Holocaust could answer Roper's original question.

Suppose you are certain that the Holocaust happened. From such certainty, it would seem impossible to you that the Holocaust never happened and it would seem possible that it did happen. If you have this belief, then the darkly shaded boxes in table 18.1 represent your feelings.

Suppose, in contrast, you are certain that the Holocaust never happened. In that case, it follows that you believe that it is possible that the extermination never happened and that its occurrence is impossible. If you have this belief, then your feelings are represented by the lightly shaded boxes in table 18.1.

TABLE 18.1 **Multiple Interpretations of a Response**

	Seems Possible	Seems Impossible
Happened	NO	NO
Never Happened	YES	YES

Now reread the question.

If you have a belief that can be characterized by either cell in the bottom row of this table, then "yes" is an accurate answer to the Roper question *as it was asked.* In other words, if it seems possible to you that the Holocaust never happened, or if it seems possible to you that it did happen, then "yes" is the answer that reflects your views.

"Yes" was also the answer that 22% of respondents gave to the Roper question. "Yes" was the answer that produced the headlines.

After several months of speculation, the Gallup organization conducted a survey-based experiment to examine whether the question's wording produced the surprising result (Ladd, 1994: 4). Gallup randomly selected half of respondents to hear Roper's original question. The other half were asked, "Do you doubt that the Holocaust actually happened, or not?" As was the case in the original poll, about a third of respondents who heard the original Roper question appeared to respond that it was possible that the Holocaust never happened. In contrast, when asked the alternate version, fewer than one-in-ten persons appeared to doubt the Holocaust. This is a significant difference. Gallup then asked all respondents a second question: "Just to clarify, in your opinion, did the Holocaust definitely happen, probably happen, probably not happen, or definitely not happen?" To this question, 96 percent of respondents replied that the Holocaust definitely or probably happened.

Two months after the Gallup survey, Roper reran its original survey. This time, it asked the Holocaust question in a more direct way:

Does it seem possible to you that the Nazi extermination of the Jews never happened or do you feel certain that it happened?

To this question, only 1% of respondents replied that it was possible that the Holocaust never happened.[7]

This is a case in which an awkwardly worded question produced a public outcry about civic ignorance. What at first seemed like dramatic evidence of the public's unwillingness or inability to acknowledge the Holocaust was later revealed to be the product of bad question wording. This example, though noteworthy for its public impact, it is not unique. Many surveys ask confusing recall questions. When critics use these questions to judge others' ignorance, false and misleading claims about knowledge and competence tend to follow. We can do better.

In this chapter, I review research on how to word questions in ways that provide more accurate information about what people do and do not know. The chapter draws from research on questionnaire design.[8] Educators who have the ability to develop and administer their own questionnaires (whether through surveys, focus groups, or less formal means) can use this information to learn more about what people know. For educators and analysts who are not in a position to collect new data, this chapter offers guidance on how to more effectively interpret existing recall questions. Educators and analysts who can distinguish between well-worded and badly worded questions are less likely to draw the kinds of false conclusions described above.

This is a short summary of the chapter's main claims:

- For a recall question to measure what a person knows, the person must be able to understand what the question is asking. Many existing recall questions confuse subjects because they use jargon or because they mention multiple concepts while intending to ask about only one. Every question should have a clear purpose.
- For a recall question to measure what a population knows, every person in the population should understand the question in the same way. Some existing recall questions are so vague that people interpret them in different ways. Every question should strive for a universally accessible meaning.
- Responses to recall questions depend on respondents' motivation to reveal what they know. Most surveys provide little or no motivation to answer recall questions correctly. Experiments show that compensating respondents yields more correct answers. An implication is that most existing surveys misrepresent what citizens know.

The chapter continues as follows. In section 18A, I offer basic advice about how to improve recall questions. Key insights include ensuring that each question pertains to a single topic and writing broadly understandable questions. While such advice may seem like common sense, many existing recall questions lack these attributes. In section 18B, I describe the role of incentives. If the point of an interview is to produce accurate measures of a person's knowledge of specific concepts, the measure's accuracy depends on that person's motivation to state what they know. I describe techniques for improving data quality by increasing respondent motivation. In section 18C, I integrate this chapter's findings with the book's main lessons.

18A. QUESTION WORDING

> When I was 5 years old, my mother always told me that happiness was the key to life. When I went to school, they asked me what I wanted to be when I grew up. I wrote down "happy." They told me I didn't understand the assignment, and I told them they didn't understand life.
>
> —quote widely attributed to John Lennon[9]

As surveys have become more numerous and influential, greater attention has been paid to question wording. Survey researchers have developed best practices that are influenced by studies of what people are thinking when they read, hear, or answer survey questions.[10] I call two important themes from this literature "clarity of purpose" and "universality of meaning."

By clarity of purpose, I mean the practices that, to the greatest extent possible, make the meaning of a question clear to the respondent. A common violation of clarity of purpose comes from survey questions that are "double-barreled." A double-barreled question is one that mentions multiple issues in a single question. Herbert Weisberg, Jon Krosnick, and Bruce Bowen (1996: 87–88) describe one such question ("Do you favor reducing American use of gasoline by increasing our taxes on foreign oil?") and how to reword it to obtain better measures of recall.

> There are two issues here: One is whether to reduce gasoline consumption, and the other is whether to use taxes on foreign oil as a means of accomplishing that end. Some respondents may say no to the question because they do not believe consumption should be reduced; others might say no because they believe some other means of reducing consumption should be used. Asking two questions would be better: (a) "Do you think that American use of gasoline should be

reduced?" If the person answers yes, ask, (b) "Do you favor or oppose a tax on foreign oil as a way to cut gasoline use?"

By revising double-barreled questions so that each question pertains to one and only one issue, we can obtain more valid measures of what people recall.

The Holocaust question that opened this chapter was double-barreled in the sense that it asked for a single "yes" or "no" response to a question about two non-identical concepts.

"Does it seem possible to you that the Nazi extermination of the Jews never happened?"
"Does seem impossible to you that the Nazi extermination of the Jews never happened?"

The subsequent Gallup and Roper corrections (especially "Does it seem possible to you that the Nazi extermination of the Jews never happened or do you feel certain that it happened?") clarified the question's purpose by aligning the response options with single and distinguishable thoughts that a person could have about this topic.

By universality of meaning, I mean that all respondents share, to the greatest extent possible, identical conceptions of what they are being asked to do. Examples of questions that violate universality are those that employ scholarly jargon or other words that are likely to be understood differently by different parts of the population. As Allyson Holbrook, Jon Krosnick, David Moore, and Roger Tourangeau (2007: 341) argue:

> Questions are often laden with social science jargon. . . . Because survey researchers are usually well educated, they may find such questions to be easily understandable. It is rare indeed to hear of a questionnaire designer calculating the reading difficulty level of a question or using a dictionary or thesaurus to find synonyms that are simpler and easier to understand.

For example, when analysts use a specific question to generate a statistical claim about recall, they commonly assume that all people who answered the question were asked exactly the same question and understood it in the same way. Analysts do not base estimates of peoples' ability to recall the political office held by Barack Obama by asking some respondents to identify the office held by Obama and asking other respondents to identify the winner of the last FIFA World Cup.

Violations of universality matter for several reasons. Reductions in inter-respondent comparability can reduce measurement validity. Comparability is important because most analysts use statistical methods to characterize a survey's findings, and the most common statistics assume that the underlying units are comparable. For example, surveys are often used to describe the percentage of a population that supports a particular candidate or policy proposal. When survey respondents read a question in different ways, their responses are less comparable, and the resulting statistics tell us less about what the population actually knows.

Similar violations are visible in jargon-laden recall questions. If some respondents know the jargon and others do not, non-identical interpretations of a question can arise. A question from ISI's American Civic Literacy assessment (first discussed in chapter 15) shows how jargon can produce misleading conclusions about knowledge.

53. National defense is considered a public good because:
   a) majority of citizens value it.
   b) resident can benefit from it without directly paying for it.
   c) military contracts increase employment opportunities.
   d) majority of citizens support the military during war.
   e) airport security personnel are members of the Federal civil service.

Here the answer to the question depends on knowing how economists define the term "public good." This definition leads to response B being labeled as correct. As a professor in a discipline that has close intellectual relationships with economics, knowing the economists' definition of a public good is a fundamental skill. Given my job, I would be embarrassed not to know it.

But the survey was administered to a general population that commonly uses words like "public" and "good" in other ways. If we define what makes national defense "good" for the "public" in ways that people commonly use these words, then other responses are not incorrect. Indeed, defining B as the question's only correct answer changes the question from an inquiry about how government provides services of value to its citizens to a question about recall of economic jargon. If people understand that tax dollars fund national defense and that national defense confers public benefits, then whether or not citizens know the economists' definition of the public good reveals little about ISI's stated goal of evaluating students' abilities to "effectively participate in the American political process." Hence, this question impedes rather than advances ISI's ability to use the data to achieve its own stated mission.

When a question is asked in a way that makes its meaning unclear, it tells us less about what people know. The same outcome occurs when a recall question's response options are not sufficiently distinguishable. Jon Krosnick, Penny Visser, and Joshua Harder (2010: 1291–1292) describe such a question.

Which of the following are the inalienable rights referred to in the Declaration of Independence?
A. life, liberty, and property
B. honor, liberty, and peace
C. liberty, health, and community
D. life, respect, and equal protection
E. life, liberty, and the pursuit of happiness

With respect to this question and what it tells us about people's knowledge of the Declaration of Independence, Krosnick et al. offer a provocative alternative:

Which of the following are the inalienable rights referred to in the Declaration of Independence?
A. to own a boat, to laugh occasionally, and to have a good meal daily
B. to have a pet, to sleep in a bed every night, and to breathe air daily
C. to live, to learn, and to love
D. to vacation in a country away from home, to chop vegetables with a knife, and to get regular haircuts
E. life, liberty, and the pursuit of happiness

This question might bring smiles to the faces of all survey respondents, or worse, might lead respondents to wonder about the researchers' competence or seriousness or both. Yet answers to such a question would also most likely indicate that the vast majority of Americans possess this piece of knowledge.

In this example, we see that a question's apparent difficulty depends not just on the content of the question but also on the content of the alternative responses that are offered.[11]

Wording questions that have a clear purpose and a commonly understood meaning can help educators gain important insights about what citizens do and do not know. If an analyst has reason to believe that the distinctions in the first version of the Declaration of Independence question are necessary or sufficient for a highly valued competence, then they can produce a logical argument for the superiority of that version. If an analyst is more interested in knowing whether the respondent can simply identify the Declaration of Independence as a document about governing principles, rather than the other options in the second version of the question, then the second version of the question is better than the first. Wording matters.

Another example of this kind involves the IEA Civic Education Study. This study is an international project that seeks to "measure knowledge and understanding of key principles that are universal across democracies." Its surveys are given to 14- to 19-year- olds in over two dozen countries. It is a major undertaking. IEA questionnaires are developed by a panel that includes teachers, educational staff, and members of the public.[12]

IEA studies produce global headlines about civic education. About one IEA study, education professor Carole Hahn (2003: 639) reported that "[o]n the overall test of civic knowledge, U.S. students did exceptionally well on items that measured skills needed by citizens in a democracy, such as the abilities to comprehend political messages, interpret political cartoons, and distinguish fact from opinion." The National Center for Education Statistics said that "U.S. ninth-graders scored significantly above the international average on the total civic knowledge scale. Furthermore, in no other country did students significantly outperform U.S. students."[13] Another headline read "Study of young teens finds civics ranks low; 28-nation survey bodes ill for citizenship."[14]

As in earlier chapters, the meaning of these claims and their relevance to the net benefits of civic education depend on what questions the IEA asked. Figure 18.1 shows one of their questions. In the United States, 79 percent of the study's ninth-graders answered the question correctly. Internationally, the percentage correct was 57 percent. Please read it now.

What is the correct answer to this question? According to the IEA, this question has only one correct answer, A. So if a 14-year old sees this image and concludes from it that history textbooks for children must be shorter than adults or are not interesting or should be written with a computer, they

What is the message or main point of this cartoon? History textbooks...

A. are sometimes changed to avoid mentioning problematic events from the past.

B. for children must be shorter than books written for adults.

C. are full of information that is not interesting.

D. should be written using a computer and not a pencil.

FIGURE 18.1. A Question from the IEA Civic Education Study. *Source: Judith Torney-Purta, Rainer Lehmann, Hans Oswald and Wolfram Schulz. 2001. Citizenship and Education in Twenty-Eight Countries: Civic Knowledge and Engagement at Age Fourteen. Amsterdam: International Association for the Evaluation of Educational Achievement. Image used by permission.*

are marked "incorrect". They grade the question in this manner despite the following facts:

- Many people might agree that history textbooks for children should be shorter than adults. They might agree that eliminating words from a textbook is a valid way to reduce its length. They might agree that the cartoon could be interpreted as a person eliminating words from a long textbook. The cartoon falsifies none of these inferences.

- We might also find wide agreement among 14-year-olds, and many adults, that history textbooks are full of information that is not interesting. Among such people, we could also find agreement that one thing a person could do with non-interesting text is attempt to erase some of its words, and that the cartoon shows a person doing just that.

- We might also find wide agreement that textbooks should be written with a computer rather than a pencil. Among the reasons why writing a textbook with a pencil is problematic is that the words can be easily erased—just as the cartoon depicts.

I also agree with the premise that the picture could be interpreted as showing that people sometimes try to eliminate problematic events from textbooks. To be frank, however, I see nothing problematic in the text that is being erased in the image. In fact, the text being erased *does not include any real words*, so I have no basis for finding its content objectionable or problematic.

So, is it really incorrect for 14-year-olds to choose a response other than A? IEA's own executive summary treated A as the only correct response. It then offered the following conclusion:

> Their understanding of some democratic values and institutions, however, was not strongly demonstrated. For example, only 57 percent of the students could identify the main message of a political cartoon about a country's wish to de-emphasize problematic aspects of its history. (ERIC Development Team, 2001: 3)

I have shown this image to thousands of people in lectures and classes. Nearly everyone quickly sees that the image is too vague to produce a single correct answer. The lack of difference between correct and incorrect responses renders it a poor measure of civic knowledge—its meaning is not universal.

Another IEA question has related difficulties:

In democratic countries, what is the function of having more than one
  political party?
  A. To represent different opinions in the legislature
  B. To limit political corruption
  C. To prevent political demonstrations
  D. To encourage economic competition

In the United States, 72 percent of the study's ninth-graders answered the question correctly. Internationally, the percentage correct was 75 percent. *Which answers would you grade as correct?*

The answer that IEA graded as correct is A, but an important point about this grading scheme should be made. First, widely cited research in economics[15] and political science[16] shows that various forms of competition—including among political parties—correspond to large and significant decreases in many kinds of corruption. So, limiting political corruption is, both empirically and theoretically, a function of having political competition. Hence, B is also a defensible answer. Students who selected this answer are not necessarily incorrect.

The IEA Civic Education Study is a valuable endeavor. However, our ability to draw conclusions about educational effectiveness from its studies depends on the content of their questions—and on how respondents interpret these questions. For the data to be considered part of a valid "measure of knowledge and understanding of key principles that are universal across democracies," it is important that the questions have as clear a purpose and as universal a meaning as possible. At present, not all of the IEA questions meet this standard. Future iterations of the study could benefit from greater attention to question wording. Particular attention should be paid not just to item response theory but also to "cognitive interviewing"—a practice where questionnaire designers conduct thorough inquiries during and after survey interviews to verify that respondents understood the question and response options in the way that the researcher intended.[17] Such practices would help the IEA develop questions that allow for more apples-to-apples cross-country comparisons of the concepts they have identified.

The IEA also produces knowledge scales. Some claim that the IEA scales are valid because they produce high factor loadings. These claims, however, are subject to chapter 16's criticisms of PK scales. The IEA's reported scales are simple sums of correct answers to the questions that they asked. A description of their methods suggests that their questions are chosen for inclusion on the survey, in part, *because* their aggregation produces high factor loadings—just like the ANES. As we saw in chapter 16, neither simple sums of small numbers of questions nor high factor loadings are necessary or sufficient to generate an externally valid general knowledge measure.

Chapter 16's proposed methods for offering more meaningful scales apply to IEA's efforts—greater attention to question content, greater attention to how answers are aggregated, and—absent evidence that the questions are necessary or sufficient for well-articulated competences—"truth in labeling." That is, IES users should refrain from giving the knowledge scale index a misleading name (i.e., one that suggests that the scale represents comprehensive knowledge or knowledge that at some point was shown as necessary or sufficient to increase competence at voting or similar tasks).

One implication of this chapter up to this point is that if the goal of a recall question is to accurately assess a given type of knowledge or competence, the question better serves the goal if it clearly differentiates people who have the knowledge in question from those who do not. Factors other than the words used also affect what we can learn about what citizens know from recall questions. Political scientist Markus Prior (2013) describes an experiment in which some subjects are asked recall questions while viewing a picture of the person named in the question. In the experiment, a control group is asked a recall question in the typical way (e.g., "What position is currently held by Nicholas Sarkozy?"). One treatment group is asked the question "What position is currently held by this person?" next to a picture of Sarkozy. A second group is asked the question "What position is currently held by Nicholas Sarkozy?" next to the picture. The treatment effects are not large for the sample as a whole, but for certain types of people, the effects are substantial. From this work, Prior (2013: 14) concludes:

> As political scientists have shown over and over again, when knowledge is measured using words alone, the less educated do worse than the more educated, and women do worse than men. People with a visual cognitive style also score lower on verbal knowledge than people with a verbal style. All of these individual differences are significantly attenuated or disappear entirely for visual recall.

Work like this shows that what we can learn about a person's knowledge from a survey question depends on how the question is asked. Questions can be asked in ways that allow accurate insights about what others know or they can be asked in confusing ways. Educators who take the time to ensure that a question is well suited to document a specific type of recall can use this information to make more valuable claims about what others know.

We had these goals in mind when, as principal investigators of the American National Election Studies, we had an opportunity to develop a new survey for the 2008 presidential election. Its goal was to measure how that year's presidential election campaign and result affected citizens. For that purpose, we interviewed many of the same people for ten months before and eight months after that year's presidential election.

ANES' users wanted recall questions as part of the design. We worked with many scholars to develop recall questions that would fit the study's purpose. Our emphasis was on clarity of purpose and universality of meaning. Moreover, as we were still in the process of learning about problems with the ANES' open-ended coding practices at the time we had to put the survey into the field (see chapter 15), and as our priority was to produce recall data that analysts could interpret accurately, we stayed away from those types of questions and selected a multiple-choice format. With these priorities in mind, we asked the following questions:

What state does US Senator John McCain represent in Congress?
Arizona [1]
Colorado [2]
New Hampshire [3]
New Mexico [4]

What state does US Senator Barack Obama represent in Congress?
Illinois [1]
Michigan [2]
Indiana [3]
New Jersey [4]

What is Barack Obama's religion? Is he Christian, Jewish, Muslim, Buddhist, or not religious?
Christian [1]
Jewish [2]
Muslim [3]
Buddhist [4]
not religious [5]

What is John McCain's religion? Is he Christian, Jewish, Muslim, Buddhist, or not religious?
Christian [1]
Jewish [2]
Muslim [3]
Buddhist [4]
not religious [5]

Before he was elected to the US Congress, where did Barack Obama work?
A state legislature [1]
The US military [2]
An oil company [3]
A television station [4]

Before he was elected to the US Congress, where did John McCain
  work?
A state legislature [1]
The US military [2]
An oil company [3]
A television station [4]

To be clear, these questions do not represent a comprehensive measure of general knowledge. They have not been shown to be building blocks for other competences. They were not chosen with respect to any factor loading that they do or do not produce. Instead, our responsibility was to produce questions that scholars and other analysts can use for a range of purposes. So, we designed questions to measure whether respondents could recall certain types of facts that scholars might want to use when explaining voting behavior. Compared to existing ANES questions, these new questions (taken individually or perhaps with one or more questions grouped in a scale developed as chapter 16 recommends) provide an improved means for analysts to learn about whether citizens knew a few basic facts about the presidential candidates.

In sum, more accurate survey-based recall measures can come from greater attention to how respondent interpretations of recall question content relate to the types of knowledge in which educators and analysts are interested. Educators can learn much more about what kinds of information they should provide if they write and use surveys that feature clear and broadly understandable questions in which connections to relevant competence criteria are clear.

18B. MOTIVATION TO ANSWER CORRECTLY

On June 25, 2007, an essay by pollster Gary Langer appeared on the ABC News website. It was called "If the Dunce Cap Fits, Wear It." The essay responded to a *Newsweek* report that used survey data as evidence of the public's ignorance.

The latest Newsweek poll, purporting to show how dim most Americans are, puts the dunce cap on the wrong head.

The magazine is following a well-worn path—sneaking up on a bunch of well-intentioned survey respondents, springing a bunch of unrelated factual questions on them and then gleefully reporting that they don't know jack. As a cheap polling trick, it works every time. As an exercise in meaningful measurement, it makes Paris Hilton look sage. . . .

Imagine another approach: Say we ask our respondents to come to a testing center where we engage them in discussion of an issue of the day. Then we hand them sharpened No. 2 pencils and ask them to fill out answer sheets testing both facts and knowledge relating to that issue—with the promise, for good measure, of $10 for every right answer, and $20 for every well-argued concept. I'll bet that simple change in measurement would make our "dunce-cap nation," as Newsweek would have it, suddenly look a lot sharper.

When asked to recall a particular fact about a person, people canvass their declarative memories for the knowledge in question. The means and extensiveness of such memory-based canvassing are the subjects of continuing scientific debate.[18] One factor that affects whether a respondent will answer a recall question correctly is the content of what they know. Another factor is their motivation to retrieve what they know from memory.

For decades, survey researchers gave no incentive to respondents for answering recall questions correctly. They simply expected respondents to do so. But survey respondents have many things to do, and some have interests in topics other than politics. Putting effort into thinking about the answer to a political quiz question asked by an anonymous survey interviewer may not be every respondent's idea of a worthwhile activity.

Markus Prior and I started discussing this issue. We knew that surveys occur in an unusual circumstance. Interviewers have incentives to complete interviews quickly. They are often paid for completing interviews, rather than being paid by the hour or for the quality of the responses. Respondents have their own reasons for not wanting to prolong a survey interview—particularly for surveys that last a half hour or more. As a result, recall questions are asked and answers are expected in quick succession. The typical survey provides no incentive for respondents to think hard about the answers to recall questions.

To determine the extent to which a lack of motivation contributed to poor performance on survey-based recall inquiries, Prior and I (2008) assigned over 1,200 randomly selected members of a national survey to one of four experimental groups.

The control group was asked 14 recall questions in a typical online survey interview environment. They were given only 60 seconds from the moment that a question first appeared on their screens to provide an answer. They were given no financial motivation to answer correctly.

Treatment groups received money and/or a longer period of time to answer (or perhaps use procedural memories to find the answers). One treatment group was offered one dollar for every correct answer. Another group was given 24 hours to respond to the 14 questions. The third treatment group was offered both extra time and the money.

For this study, we selected questions that were more difficult than typical survey recall questions. We did this to reduce guessing's potential impact on our study. Despite the added difficulty, providing a dollar for each correct answer or giving extra time produced significant increases in questions that were answered correctly. Compared to the control group, simply offering a dollar for correct answers increased the average number of them by 11 percent. Giving extra time produced an 18 percent increase in correct answers over the control group. Time and money together increased the average number of questions answered correctly by 24 percent relative to the control group.[19]

The effect of money alone is noteworthy. The only difference between the control and treatment groups is that the latter was paid a small amount for each correct answer. Respondents in the treatment group did not have time to look up correct answers. Hence, the treatment group's performance gain is evidence that low motivation reduces the extent to which respondents in a typical survey convey what they know.

We made further inquiries into the kinds of people who are most affected by the financial incentive. We found that the incentive most affects people with moderate levels of interest in politics. In other words, people who are very interested in politics need less motivation to retrieve items from memory. People with no interest in politics either lack the memory or need an even bigger incentive to seek it out. We (Prior and Lupia, 2008: 169) concluded that existing attempts to measure declarative memories

> confound respondents' recall of political facts with variation in their motivation to exert effort during survey interviews [and, hence,] provide unreliable assessments of what many citizens know when they make political decisions.

Other scholars have subsequently used this method to make additional discoveries.

For example, a survey by Harris Interactive showed that 45 percent of Republicans in 2010 reported believing that Barack Obama was born outside of the United States, compared to only 8% of Democrats (Bullock et al., 2013: 3). Many surveys in which respondents are not given financial motives to offer correct answers to recall questions produce similar results: Partisans give different answers to some recall questions, with the differences reflecting what partisans would like to believe about their parties. Political scientists John Bullock, Alan Gerber, Seth Hill, and Gregory Huber (2013) examined how paying respondents affects these partisan differences. In their experiment, a control group was asked a series of recall questions. Following the practice of nearly all surveys, they offered no monetary incentive for answering correctly. In a treatment group, they paid subjects a small amount for answering correctly or for admitting that they did not know the correct response. They found that paying respondents reduced the partisan differences in answers by over half. In another treatment group where they also paid people to admit that they were uncertain about their answers, the partisan differences were reduced by 80 percent. This work shows that, *without a motive to answer correctly, many people respond to recall questions by giving the answer they want to be true*. However, when given even a small incentive to convey their true knowledge, significant numbers of respondents change their answers.

Markus Prior, Gaurav Sood, and Kabir Khanna (2013) found a similar pattern for questions about the economy. When not paid for giving correct answers to fact-based questions about the state of the economy, Republicans and Democrats gave very different answers. When paid a small amount for each correct answer, the partisan differences diminished. In other words, when given a small incentive to answer correctly, respondents offer more realistic answers. As Prior, Sood, and Khanna (2013) concluded:

> Many partisans interpret knowledge questions about economic conditions as opinion questions, unless motivated otherwise. Typical survey questions thus reveal a mix of what partisans know about the economy and what they would like to be true about it.

These studies reveal that factors other than declarative knowledge affect how people answer recall questions about politics. Law and psychology professor Dan Kahan (2015) describes similar dynamics in attempts to measure public knowledge of science:

> About once a year, Gallup or another commercial survey firm releases a poll showing that approximately 45% of the U.S. public rejects the proposition that human beings evolved from another species of animal. The news is invariably greeted by widespread expressions of dismay from media commentators, who lament what this finding says about the state of science education in our country. (Kahan, 2015: 2)

Kahan then reviews the underlying questions and data. He identifies many questions that force people to make a choice between responding in a way that reflects their deep cultural commitments and responding in a way that reflects the true content of their knowledge. Kahan (2015:2) concludes that

> [n]umerous studies have found that profession of "belief" in evolution has no correlation with understanding of basic evolutionary science. Individuals who say they "believe" are no more likely than those who say they "don't" to give the correct responses to questions pertaining to natural selection, random mutation, and genetic variance—the core elements of the modern synthesis.

In other words, many people who say that they do not believe in the theory of evolution can nevertheless answer questions about its properties. Kahan identifies similar dynamics in the domain of climate change. When viewed in light of the experimental studies described above, we see the following pattern: When survey respondents have little or no motivation to do otherwise, some use recall questions as opportunities to state their political and cultural aspirations, rather than the true content of what they know.

Collectively, these studies show the importance of motivation in attempts to measure recall. Today, most surveys provide little or no incentive for respondents to put effort into thinking about what they know.[20] As a consequence, these surveys tend to misrepresent the true content of some respondents' memories.

Two countermeasures can mitigate problems caused by survey respondents' low motivation. First, pay respondents for giving correct answers. Even small payments can increase respondents' efforts to convey what they know. Second, when a survey offers no incentive for correctly conveying one's memories, analysts should recognize that reports of what percentage of the public "knows" the answer to a particular question likely underestimate knowledge of the question's topic. Hence, the percentage of people who cannot answer a question in such a survey should be treated as an upper estimate of the true rate of ignorance in the population. As research in this area continues, we will learn more about the conditions under which people do and do not report what they know. With such knowledge, we can increase the accuracy of our inferences by adjusting our data interpretations accordingly.

18C. CONCLUSION

As a society comes to understand how the actions of certain groups and individuals affect its desired goals, concerns about citizens' competence at achieving these goals emerge. When such concerns arise and it can be demonstrated that an audience's ignorance of a particular set of facts is preventing a valuable social outcome from occurring, the potential for educators to provide substantial net benefits arises. At these moments, educators who have valid and reliable measures of what people know are empowered to develop with logic, and to defend with respect to clearly stated competence criteria, claims about what kinds of information are most valuable for a given set of citizens to learn.

This book seeks to help educators provide information that is of high net benefit to others. Table 18.2 summarizes lessons from parts I and II that educators can use for this purpose. The left column is a list of erroneous claims about information, knowledge, and competence. The right column lists ways to correct such claims. Moving from left to right in the table shows how to ask better questions, produce better measures, and draw more accurate inferences about what people do and do not know. In such moves are multiple ways for educators to deliver information of far greater net benefit to more people in more circumstances.

TABLE 18.2 **Improving Knowledge and Competence**

Problem	Solution
Inattention to tasks in claims about others' competence.	Define a specific task or tasks for which competence evaluation and improvement are sought. (ch. 3)

TABLE 18.2 **Continued**

Problem	Solution
Undocumented claim that recall of a particular fact or set of facts is necessary for achieving a desired outcome.	Are there other facts or cues that can increase the audience's competence? • If not, then the claim is true. See chapters 6–13 for advice about how to convey the information effectively. • If so, then the claim is false. Use chapter 5 to seek a different and more accurate claim.
Undocumented claim that recall of a particular fact or set of facts is sufficient for achieving a desired outcome.	What else would a person need to know to use the information to make a competent choice? • If there are other things and the person has such knowledge, see chapters 6–13 for advice about how to convey the information effectively. • If there are other things and the person does not already know them, then the claim is false. Use chapter 5 to seek a different and more accurate claim.
Claim that the value of certain types of information for certain audiences is an objective fact rather than a partially subjective assertion.	Are value diversity and issue complexity irrelevant to how people could connect certain pieces of information to desired outcomes? • If not, then subjectivity is present. See chapters 9–13 for a different and more accurate interpretation. • If so, then the claim is true. See chapters 6–13 for advice about how to convey the information effectively.
Claim that political roles need not be considered when making claims about what others should know.	Examine what outcomes prospective learners can affect. • If there is sufficient variation in roles, then different information can offer unequal net benefits to different individuals. In such cases, tailoring information to meet the needs of different political roles can increase an educator's effectiveness and efficiency. (ch. 12)
Claim that learning costs need not be considered when making claims about what others should know.	Examine who benefits from the desired outcome. Compare these benefits to the costs of achieving such an outcome and who pays them. (ch. 13) • If there are one or more groups for whom the net benefit is negative—or if there are large differentials in the net benefits that accrue to particular groups—then learning costs are relevant to determinations of net benefits for the audience as a whole. • If there are some needed participants who perceive an educational endeavor's net benefits as negative, the endeavor's content must be changed, or incentives increased, to accomplish the endeavor's goals.

(*continued*)

TABLE 18.2 Continued

Problem	Solution
Inattention to question wording and survey dynamics.	Inferences about competence and knowledge come not just from the content of a survey respondent's memory, but also from the way that they read the question.
	• Ensure that survey-based claims about knowledge and competence are consistent with the actual content of the questions asked. (chs. 15–18)
	• Factor analysis is not magic. In some cases, it offers evidence that individual items are tapping a certain kind of knowledge, but factor analysis does not reveal the kind of knowledge. The kind of knowledge is determined by question content and how it was interpreted. (ch. 16)
	• Follow question wording best practices, including clarity of purpose and universality of meaning. (ch. 18)

19

The Silver Lining

> The more I read and the more I listen, the more apparent it is that our society suffers from an alarming degree of public ignorance. . . . We have to ensure that our citizens are well informed and prepared to face tough challenges.
>
> Sandra Day O'Connor (as reported in Terhune, 2013)

There are many things that people do not know about politics, policy, and government. In some cases, this ignorance prevents them from making competent choices. It prevents them from making decisions that they would have made had they known certain facts *and* sought to act consistently with certain values. Such circumstances are why effective education is so important.

Educators of all kinds are this book's protagonists. Educators seek to help people make better decisions—where better refers to the decisions that people would have made had they known certain facts *and* sought to act consistently with certain values. All educators, however, face important constraints. There are limits on their time and energy. Money can be scarce, as can the labor of coworkers or volunteers. Also limited are prospective learners' motivation to pay attention to new information. If educators seek to develop effective and efficient informational strategies in the face of such constraints, what information should they provide?

Standing between many educators and the educational successes to which they aspire are their perceptions of learning's net benefits. Over the years, I have met educators, or aspiring educators, who energetically imagine the benefits of conveying their expertise to others. They have strong beliefs that teaching certain facts will improve important outcomes. Many, however, have a difficult time articulating the costs that their educational endeavors will impose. Over the same period, I have met many citizens who are asked to participate in these endeavors. They have a different perspective about these endeavors. For citizens, the costs of becoming informed (e.g., money paid for tuition, the struggle to reconcile new information with old beliefs, time spent away from other activities) are real and tangible—while learning's benefits are often perceived as uncertain. Many citizens as a result tend to be less enthusiastic about learning than educators imagine (and want) them to be.

A key to increasing socially beneficial types of knowledge and competence is to become more knowledgeable about these perceptions. Politics is but one aspect of life to which citizens can devote time and energy. Even for those who are interested in politics, there are many kinds of political information available. So educators should anticipate questions about whether and for whom the information they offer is beneficial. This book provides tools for answering these questions and for basing more effective strategies on their answers. These strategies emphasize information that is necessary or sufficient for desired competence and information levels. They also emphasize information to which prospective learners will pay attention. Hence, the strategies emphasize information that prospective learners will perceive as offering positive net benefits with respect to their values, political roles, and learning costs.

Although some people who are concerned about civic competence seek a silver bullet—a short list of universally acceptable facts that assures "rational voting" or "effective citizenship"—this book offers something more realistic. This book describes a framework for providing information about politics that is more valuable and more relevant to more people. Instead of a silver bullet, it offers a silver lining. It offers a set of insights and tools that can help educators be more effective. The book's main lessons are listed below and also captured in table 19.1.

- Chapter 1: Everyone is ignorant about many aspects of politics. Yet we can learn to make decisions that are more consistent with particular facts and values.
- Chapter 2: Educators want to help others make better decisions. But only so much information can be given. This situation leads to our main question: Which information is valuable to give?

- Chapter 3: The value of information depends on how it can be used. Different competences require different kinds of information.
- Chapter 4: Politics produces disagreements about what others should know.
- Chapter 5: Information is valuable if it increases knowledge or competences that people value. Cues can help people make competent decisions. Critics and scholars who fail to consider this fact make erroneous claims about what others need to know. These errors are correctable.
- Chapter 6: Understanding how audiences process information can improve educational effectiveness.
- Chapter 7: Information that speaks directly to an audience's core concerns attracts the attention that learning requires.
- Chapter 8: Educators can gain needed attention and boost their credibility by demonstrating common interests and relative expertise.
- Chapter 9: A set of factors called the *politics of competence* affects educational outcomes by influencing prospective learners' choices about whether or not to participate in an educational endeavor, whether or not to pay attention to information, and whether or not to find that information credible.
- Chapter 10: Value diversity produces divergent conclusions about what is worth knowing. In "big tents," educators can increase their effectiveness by identifying information that diverse audiences perceive as offering positive net benefits to them.
- Chapter 11: When issues are complex, choices about how to prioritize parts of an issue (i.e., framing) become necessary. Such choices often have substantial subjective components.
- Chapter 12: Requiring that everyone know the same things is often ineffective and inefficient. Understanding political roles can help educators target information effectively.
- Chapter 13: Knowing how, and to whom, the net benefits of an educational endeavor accrue can help educators solicit needed participation and allow them to achieve desired learning outcomes more effectively and efficiently.
- Chapter 14: Surveys are the basis for many claims about what citizens do and do not know. Many of these claims, in turn, are based on misunderstandings of what the surveys measure. By

understanding how researchers collect and analyze recall data, educators can make more accurate inferences about what people do and do not know.

- Chapter 15: Many claims about citizen ignorance are based on mistaken assumptions about the content of survey questions. More accurate inferences come from basing conclusions on the actual wording of survey questions.
- Chapter 16: Many claims about citizen ignorance are based on "political knowledge scales"—simple sums of answers to individual recall questions. Most claims that are based on these scales depend on mistaken assumptions about what the sums mean. These errors are correctable.
- Chapter 17: Some claims about citizen ignorance are based on interviewers' assessments of survey respondents. When interviewers are not well trained to make such assessments, or when training quality is undocumented, the data become difficult or impossible to interpret accurately. Better training and documentation can fix this problem.
- Chapter 18: Question wording can improve. Focusing on a single topic and using commonly understood language can provide better measures.

While I have devoted my attention in this book to helping educators, the main lessons of the book have implications for the broader set of people who are concerned about civic competence and want to respond constructively.

For example, some critics of public ignorance have not taken the time to understand how information, knowledge, and competence are related. As a result, they make claims about what others should know that do little to benefit the affected population. The tragedy of such outcomes is that some critics do possess information that, if understood by others, could lead important audiences to make better choices. For such critics, this book offers an approach to increasing competence that can provide greater net benefits to impacted populations.

A core element of this book's approach is that prospective learners are more likely to respond to information that they perceive as speaking to their deepest and most important aspirations. As a result, educators can accomplish many of their goals more effectively and efficiently by focusing on prospective learners' perceptions of what is worth knowing. With these

TABLE 19.1 A Summary of the Argument

	Clarifying Relationships	Improving Measures	Increasing Competence
Challenges for Citizens	There are many things that many citizens do not know about politics and policy.	Citizens hear data-based claims about what they should know that are not helpful to them. Citizens hear data-based claims about public ignorance and its political consequences that are difficult to reconcile with logic or the data.	Sometimes, what people do not know prevents them from successfully accomplishing tasks.
Challenges for Educators	There are many things that educators do not know about citizens. Some do not name the tasks for which they want citizens to be competent, in many cases assuming that the value of certain types of information is universal and self-evident. Some educators rely on unrealistic theories of the relationship among information, knowledge, and competence. Some educators do not think about value diversity, issue complexity, political roles, and learning costs when developing arguments about who should learn what.	Many educators draw the wrong conclusions from existing data. Some educators use responses to individual questions to draw inappropriate inferences about general competences. Many educators misunderstand factor analysis and its limited ability to validate knowledge scales. Some educators mistakenly believe that interviewer assessments are well-developed and rigorously validated general knowledge measures. Some educators fail to understand how incentives affect survey responses. Hence, many existing "political knowledge" measures are widely misinterpreted and provide little or no information about citizens' political competence at many important tasks.	Many educators work from folk theories of learning that have little to no empirical support. Many educators confound "important to me" and "valuable for you."
How to Help Educators Help Citizens	Name tasks. Choose a defensible competence criterion. In many political contexts, criteria are built from facts and values. Inventory what facts are necessary and/or sufficient for a competent choice. Integrate these facts with knowledge of information's net benefits to find the "sweet spot"—information that attracts needed attention *and* is necessary or sufficient to improve task performance.	Understand relationships between how people respond to surveys and the tasks that those responses are claimed to measure. Understand that the meaning of a recall index depends on the content of its components. Understand incentives of survey environments. Use lessons from optimal question design literature to write more effective measures of recall. Know that badly worded questions yield invalid measures of what citizens know.	See the situation from an audience's point of view. Learn the conditions under which prospective learners see information as conferring positive net benefits to causes about which they care.

insights in mind, I offer supplementary advice to people who are trying to decide whether or not to support an educational endeavor.

Advice for prospective funders. If you are approached by prospective educators for financial support or other valuable assets such as your time, and if you care about your resources increasing a valuable civic competence, please follow this rule:

- If the prospective educator cannot name the tasks for which they seek to improve competence;
- if they cannot demonstrate how the information they propose to distribute is necessary or sufficient to improve competence on the task;
- if they assume but have not actually examined whether the prospective learners perceive the information they propose to convey as having a high net benefit; and
- if they do not commit to accurate interpretations of data to evaluate what prospective learners do and do not know;
- then *don't write the check.*

Instead, require a business plan from prospective educators that shows you

- that they are aware of the special challenges they face;
- that they have developed strategies and measures that reflect these challenges; and
- that their plan of action can deliver the tangible educational or persuasive outcomes that you really want.

Following these two rules will help you support educational strategies that can make a real difference.

Advice for educators who seek support from others. People and organizations that have the capacity to support you are more likely to be persuaded by a presentation that gives them a concrete sense of what you will accomplish. Develop credible measures of the extent to which a well-defined target audience is competent or incompetent at relevant tasks, is (or is not) in possession of particular kinds of knowledge, and has (or has not) been exposed to certain kinds of information. Then provide logic and evidence that your prospective learners will perceive your information as so beneficial that they will give it the attention and thought that increased competence requires. Explain how you will evaluate your strategy with respect to valid measures. Assess costs and benefits of alternative strategies. Commit to practices that will allow you to document, or lead you to improve, the net benefits of your work.

In closing, there are many things about politics that people do not know. We have discovered, however, that people do not need to know "all the facts" to make competent choices. The same is true for educators who seek to improve the quality of life for communities and constituencies about which they care.

Educators can use the logic of competence to make better decisions about what information is most valuable to convey. But factual information is not enough. Prospective learners must see it as valuable. Educators can use the politics of competence to understand how and to whom such value accrues. This skill can empower educators of all kinds to convey information of real value to those who receive it. I offer my gratitude to and remain in admiration of all educators who devote themselves to these pursuits.

Notes

CHAPTER 1

1. Tauberer (2011).
2. Tauberer (2011).
3. Source: http://www.legislature.mi.gov/(S(voijnl21vthayz554grrcnfh))/ mileg.aspx?page=Daily. I downloaded a record of all activity for the dates January 1, 2011, to December 31, 2011. Information downloaded on December 18, 2012.
4. Source: http://www.legislature.mi.gov/documents/2011-2012/publicact-table/pdf/2011-PAT.pdf. Downloaded on December 18, 2012.
5. Potter (2012).
6. Potter (2012: 2).
7. The source for the number of cases is page 9 of the *2011 Annual Report of the Director: Judicial Business of the United States Courts*. The source for a claim about the general content of these cases is on page 11 of the same document.
8. Also see the reviews on attention-related limitations in Baddeley (2012) and in Peterson and Posner (2012).
9. See, e.g., Berridge (2004).
10. See, e.g., Tilly (2006) and Kahneman (2011).
11. See, e.g., Sinclair and Kunda (1999), Kahan and Braman (2006), Druckman and Bolsen (2011).
12. Petty and Cacioppo (1986).

CHAPTER 2

1. Pew Research Center for the People and the Press (2014).
2. Gibson and Caldeira (2009).
3. Annenberg Public Policy Center (2011).
4. Carlson (2003).
5. See, e.g., Jedwab (2011) and Roper Public Affairs (2006).

6. Tyrangiel (2012).

7. Edsall (2012).

8. Terhune (2013).

9. Conversations with Ted Miller about Thomas Hobbes's rhetorical style and manner of conveying mathematical findings to broader political debates influenced how I wrote this book. These views are articulated in Miller (2011).

10. Of course, people who seek to manipulate others for their own benefit, and to the detriment of learners, can also use these insights. I cannot be prevent that. My sense, however, particularly from my work in areas at the intersection of science and policy, is that many schemers of this kind are more adept at knowing how to get attention than are many people whose aims are more public-spirited. Part of my ambition for part I is to level this playing field. I seek to offer greater abilities to educators who seek to improve others' lives.

CHAPTER 3

1. Downloaded from http://www.merriam-webster.com/dictionary/knowledge on May 6, 2015.

2. See, e.g., National Research Council (1994) for a comprehensive and accessible review of basic facts about this type of memory.

3. Squire and Wixted (2015).

4. Kandel, Schwartz, and Jessell (1995: 658); also see Hastie and Park (1986); Lodge, McGraw, and Stroh (1989).

5. Other scholars use different terms to distinguish between kinds of memory. For example, Kandel et al. (1995: 656) refer to declarative memory as "explicit" and non-declarative memory as "implicit." My choice of terms is a result of trying out various descriptions with diverse scholarly and lay audiences. I find that "declarative" and "non-declarative" describe the attributes of each type of memory that are more relevant to my audiences and, hence, more memorable for them. With the same audiences in mind, my examples of non-declarative memory often focus on procedural memories. Although procedural memories are not the only kind of non-declarative memory, I have found that they allow me to convey the general concept in ways that educators find relatively concrete and actionable.

6. Bohannon (2011: 277).

7. Brooks (2007) has written a similarly themed column on how tools like global positioning devices have changed the kinds of information that are valuable for people to memorize.

8. Bohannon (2011: 277).

9. Graber (1994: 343).

10. Also see Gilens (2001).

11. *The Compact Edition of the Oxford English Dictionary* (Oxford University Press, 1971: 1432).

12. See, e.g., Glazer, Steckel, and Winer (1992).

13. Steele and Aronson (1996).

14. Stone and McWhinnie (2008) provide more recent evidence of the phenomenon.

15. Rosenbaum and Hansen (1998: 381).

16. Zernike (2001).

17. Downloaded from http://www.merriam-webster.com/dictionary/competent on May 6, 2015.

18. Downloaded from http://www.merriam-webster.com/dictionary/able on May 6, 2015.

19. Downloaded from http://www.merriam-webster.com/dictionary/competent on May 6, 2015.

CHAPTER 4

1. See Lupia, Krupnikov, and Levine (2013) for a more comprehensive examination of how these changes affect attempts to find consensus on what societies should do.

2. In this respect, my project shares important goals with Habermas (1996).

3. Kuklinski and Quirk (2001: 287).

4. Kuklinski and Quirk (2001: 289)

CHAPTER 5

1. Somin (2001: 289).

2. Langer (2007). Also see Graber (1994); Gilens (2001); and Elo and Rapeli (2010).

3. "Heuristic" is another label for the concept. When discussing this topic with certain types of academics, I find heuristic to be the term that best expresses the idea. In many other cases, people find the term confusing. For that reason, I use "cues" here.

4. See Popkin (1991); Sniderman, Brody, and Tetlock (1991); and Lupia (1994a) for foundational studies of this topic.

5. Graber (1984); Sniderman and Theriault (2004).

6. Gigerenzer et al. (1999); Jussim (2012).

7. Clark (1997: 25).

8. See, e.g., Brady and Sniderman (1985); Popkin (1991); Lupia (1994a,b); Lupia and McCubbins (1998); Boudreau (2009) for examples of these effects.

9. Kingdon (1989).

10. See, e.g., McCubbins and Schwartz (1984); Krehbiel (1998).

11. Lupia and McCubbins (1994).

12. This experiment is described in Hirsch (1984: 3–4) and in Krauss and Glucksberg (1977).

13. Lupia and McCubbins (1998); Lau and Redlawsk (2006: 240–242).

14. Binary choices are common in mass politics. Nearly all ballot initiatives and referendums, for example, allow only "yes" or "no" votes on a specific policy proposal. Similarly, people who have served on juries know that their ability to comment on a case is often limited to answering "yes" or "no" to questions given by a judge. Juries are rarely allowed to state their views in their own words. In many elections for federal office in the United States, moreover, it is widely known that only the major party nominees have any shot of winning. To the extent that a voter cares about casting a vote for a candidate who has any shot of winning, their choice is effectively binary as well.

15. Also see Sniderman and Stiglitz (2012) on this point.

16. Also see Lau and Redlawsk (2006).

17. McKelvey and Ordeshook (1985, 1990).

18. Palfrey (2007: 923).

19. Lupia and McCubbins (1998); Druckman (2001a,b); Boudreau (2009).
20. Also see Lau and Redlawsk (2006).
21. Sniderman and Bullock (2004: 338).
22. Cox (1997).
23. Cox and McCubbins (2004).
24. See, e.g., Bowler, Farrell, and Katz (1999); McCarty, Poole, and Rosenthal (2001).
25. Bowler, Farrell, and Katz (1999).
26. Sniderman and Bullock (2004: 306).
27. Sniderman (2000: 74).
28. Dancey and Sheagly (2012:1); also see Gilens (2001).
29. Shenkman (2008a,b).
30. Gigerenzer et al. (1999); Kelman (2011).
31. In Lupia and McCubbins (1998), we develop a number of learning models, and we conduct a large set of experiments. Our learning models detail conditions under which cues are—and are not—expected to increase competence. Our experiments reveal that the models generate accurate predictions about learning and competence in many circumstances. Chapter 8 offers more information about this research.
32. I developed an earlier version of this example in Lupia (2001a).
33. Grofman and Feld (1988).

CHAPTER 6

1. In 2012, Michelle Arduengo, a science blogger from Promega Connections, reproduced a version of this story as a comic. It appears at http://www.promegaconnections.com/a-walk-in-the-woods-a-short-story-about-persuasion/. Downloaded May 13, 2014.

CHAPTER 7

1. See, e.g., Fishbein and Ajzen (1975) for foundational work on this topic.
2. Collins and Loftus (1975).
3. Shanks (2010).
4. See accessible reviews of this topic in Bjork (1999); Becker and Morris (1999).
5. See, e.g., Pessoa, Kastner, and Ungerleider (2002).
6. See Bjork (1999) for a review.
7. Miller (1956).
8. See the review in Baddeley (2012).
9. See, e.g., Larkin, McDermott, Simon, and Simon (1980).
10. Crookes and Schmidt (1991).
11. Shanks (2010).
12. See, e.g., Andreasen (1995); Ohman, Flykt and Esteves (2001); Berridge (2004); and Kahan, Jenkins-Smith, and Braman (2010).
13. See, e.g., Matthews and Wells (1999).
14. Petersen and Posner (2012).
15. See, e.g., Maddox (1993); Wynne (2006); Oreskes and Conway (2008); and Ward (2011).
16. See, e.g., Pew Research Center (2009); Horst (2011).

17. Crookes and Schmidt (1991).

18. See, e.g., Sinclair and Kunda (1999); Druckman and Bolsen (2011).

19. Westen et al. (2006).

20. Fauconnier and Turner (2002).

21. Spence and Pidgeon (2010); Tebaldi, Strauss, and Zervas (2012).

22. Also see Canham and Hegarty (2010).

23. Freedman (2012).

24. See, e.g., Gillis (2012).

25. Andreasen (1995).

26. Andreasen (1995: 67).

27. Andreasen (1995: 40–41).

28. Andreasen (1995: 49).

29. Fortini-Campbell (2001) uses the term "sweet spot" to describe a similar concept. Her focus is marketing. Her sweet spot is marketing that conveys information about a product and also an insight about the consumer. The idea echoes that of Andreasen (1995): Marketing that does not adopt a consumer focus is less likely to succeed.

30. Miller and Buschman (2015: 113)

31. Shenkman (2008b: 178)

32. Frischen, Bayliss, and Tipper (2007).

33. Klein, Shephard, and Platt (2009).

34. On mistaking attention for inattention, see van Boven, Kruger, Savitsky, and Gilovitch (2000); and Keysar and Henly (2002). On communicative overconfidence, see van Boven, Kruger, Savitsky, and Gilovitch (2000); Keysar and Henly (2002).

35. See Pronin, Gilovich, and Ross (2004) for a review of literature on biases in perceptions of self relative to perceptions of others.

CHAPTER 8

1. Lupia and McCubbins (1998).

2. Jastrow (1899); Wittgenstein (1953).

3. See, e.g., Craik and Lockhart (1972).

4. Krohne (1993).

5. See, e.g., Posner and Rothbart (2002).

6. Green and Brock (2000).

7. Krohne (2011); Green and Brock (2010).

8. Lupia (2000).

9. Basu (1999).

10. Lupia and McCubbins (1998).

11. See, e.g., Lupia and McCubbins (1998); and Pornpitakpan (2004).

12. Lupia and McCubbins (1998, chapters 1, 3, 6, and 7, including appendices).

13. See Pornpitakpan (2004); and Sobel (2009) for reviews.

14. Lupia and McCubbins (1998).

15. See, e.g., the review in Boudreau and Lupia (2011).

16. Variations of this experiment are described in Lupia and McCubbins (1998) and in Lupia (2002).

17. http://earththeoperatorsmanual.com/main-video/earth-the-operators-manual (quote from "Tease and Titles" at 1:22–1:53).

18. Abbasi (2006) offers a description of this event and important narratives and understandings that emerged from it.

19. But for reasons mentioned in chapter 7, a number would present themselves as paying more attention to that part of the sermon than they actually were.

20. Social scientists have examined this topic in many different ways. See, e.g., Kreps and Wilson (1982); Cialdini (2009); and Cialdini and Goldstein (2004).

CHAPTER 9

1. See, e.g., Wedeen (2010).
2. Badash (2012).
3. Huizenga (2012).
4. See, e.g., Wyer, Shen, and Xu (2013).

CHAPTER 10

1. See, e.g., Bruer (1999); Gopnik, Meltzoff, and Kuhl (1999).
2. LeDoux (2003); Iacoboni (2009).
3. See, e.g., Bruer (1999); Gopnik, Meltzoff, and Kuhl (1999).
4. See, e.g., Lakoff and Johnson (1999).
5. Gopnik, Meltzoff, and Kuhl (1999).
6. Clark (1997); Fauconnier and Turner (2002).
7. Fauconnier and Turner (2002); Shanks (2010).
8. National Scientific Council on the Developing Child (2010).
9. Schwartz and Boehnke (2004).
10. Ryan (2014).
11. See, e.g., the theoretical conception of this relationship and its implications for group decision-making in Milgrom and Roberts (1986).
12. Brown and Hewstone (2005: 266) describe research on the contact hypothesis that sometimes produces stirring examples of such changes.
13. When making this argument, I am always reminded of the language in Peart (1980).
14. My thinking in this chapter is influenced by work in social choice theory, particularly Sen (1998).
15. Jones and Harris (1967).
16. See, e.g., Miller and Ross (1975); Bradley (1978).
17. See, e.g., Bobo and Hutchings (1996).
18. See, e.g., Kinder (1998: 169–174).
19. See, e.g., Judd and Park (1988).
20. On mandates, see Hershey (1994).
21. Hurst (2012).
22. Ballasy (2012).
23. Stern, West, and Schmitt (2014) make a related argument.
24. See, e.g., Diermeier (1995); and Aldrich, Alt, and Lupia (2007) in relation to Pious (2004).
25. The authority figure is presented as nearby but in a different location. He communicates with the subjects via video. A common video is used across subjects within an

experimental group, which allows an identical presentation of the stimulus within and across experimental groups.

26. Taber and Lodge (2006); Nyhan and Reifler (2010).

27. Jacoby (2008: xx).

28. Gould (1996).

29. Downloaded on May 8, 2015, from http://www.slate.com/id/2109218/.

30. Downloaded on May 8, 2015, from http://www.sodahead.com/united-states/zogby-poll-almost-no-obama-voters-ace-election-test/question-192808/. Originally on http://www.zogby.com/news/2008/11/18/zogby-poll-almost-no-obama-voters-ace-election-test/.

31. See Bullock (2009) for an excellent treatment of how people can use a common pool of information to reach very different conclusions about a candidate or policy.

32. Lupia (2000).

CHAPTER 11

1. This definition of complexity follows that of Page (2010: 26–27). His treatment of this concept is exceptionally detailed and actionable.

2. Read it in its entirety at http://www.gpo.gov/fdsys/pkg/BILLS-111hr3590enr/pdf/BILLS-111hr3590enr.pdf; downloaded 8/20/11.

3. Bizer et al. (2006).

4. In theory, educators can draw distinctions between the concepts in two ways. First, we can narrow our focus to issues with only one attribute. In such cases, any resulting preference differences cannot be due to issue complexity. Second, if we expand our focus to issues with multiple attributes, then the distinction can be most clearly seen by holding the relevant values of a group of individuals constant, assuming that each individual has a limited number of attributes that they can think about at any one time; assuming that circumstances cause different people to encounter these attributes at different times; and assuming that this sequence affects which attributes come to mind when they think about the issue. In practice, these exercises are difficult or even impossible to conduct.

5. See, e.g., Rahmstorf (2007); Pfeffer, Harper, and O'Neel (2008); and many others.

6. See, e.g., the different points of view offered by Koonin (2014) and Pierrehumbert (2014).

7. Frank (2004).

8. See, e.g., Iyengar and Kinder (1989); Lakoff and Wehling (2012).

9. Political scientists Donald Haider-Markel and Mark Joslyn (2001) find a similar pattern in public attitudes about gun control. They ran experiments seeking subjects' opinions of concealed handgun laws. Subjects were randomly assigned to hear a "self-protection" frame or a "safety threat" frame. Republicans and Independents were less likely to support concealed handgun laws when "threat" was emphasized. The self-protection frame, in contrast, had no significant effect on Democrats. Also see Lau and Schlesinger (2005); Bechtel et al. (2014).

10. See, e.g., Hull (2001).

11. Also see Harrison and Michelson (2013).

12. World Health Organization and UNICEF (2014).

13. Roeder (2015).

14. See www.healthcommcore.org.

15. See, e.g., National Vaccine Advisory Committee (2014).

16. Downloaded from http://seattletimes.nwsource.com/html/opinion/2002514085_sosne23.html on May 8, 2015. Originally published on September 23, 2005.

CHAPTER 12

1. Ashworth and Bueno de Mesquita (2014).

2. This example builds on an earlier version that I developed in Lupia (2011).

3. For empirical studies that characterize correct voting, see Lupia (1994b); Lupia and McCubbins (1998); and Lau and Redlawsk (2006).

4. For reviews and theoretical foundations, see Laver and Schofield (1998); Bergman, Strom, and Mueller (2008) on coalescence; and Bergman, Strom, and Mueller (2003) on delegation.

5. See, e.g., Sin and Lupia (2014); Ryan (2014).

6. If the idea of voting against a candidate with the most similar policy preferences seems counterintuitive and perhaps beyond the capability of most citizens, it is worth noting that studies of voting patterns in several countries suggest that many voters actually take such dynamics into account when choosing representatives. As Kedar (2005, 2010) shows, in electoral systems where voters can use extreme candidates or parties to bring policy outcomes closer to ones they prefer, many voters support extremists even though they themselves are not extreme.

Studies of the US Congress reveal professional legislators making similar calculations. At the beginning of each Congress, members of each chamber decide to give leadership positions to certain members. Particularly in the House, some of these positions are associated with great influence over what kinds of bills become laws. While it may seem logical that each congressperson would always seek to choose leaders who share their policy interests, research in this area shows that members of Congress regularly delegate power to people whose interests are *not* closest to their own. Instead, and for reasons similar to those described in the example, members often allocate special power to people who can gain leverage in important negotiations and produce outcomes that are closer to what many legislators would have been able to negotiate for themselves (Krehbiel, 1998; Cox and McCubbins, 2004; Magleby, 2011; Sin and Lupia, 2014).

7. See, e.g., the review in Lupia and Strom (2008).

8. See, e.g., Gailmard and Jenkins (2007).

9. Consider, for example, educators who have limited resources and are attempting to change laws that appear in a number of US state-level constitutions. In the early 21st century, the legal status of same-sex marriage was such an issue. What information should outcome-oriented educators supply to whom?

An important consideration is the fact that US states differ in the percentages of voters and types of legislative action they require to change state constitutions. Understanding these percentages can help educators identify places where providing information to relatively small numbers of voters and legislators is sufficient to change the desired policy outcome. In states where a simple majority of voters is sufficient to change the constitution, providing information to swing voters can be particularly effective. In other states, constitutions change requires significant supermajorities of the electorate or the legislature. My research team and I (Lupia, Krupnikov, Levine, Piston, and Von Hagen-Jamar 2010) examined these variations in rules identified several instances where changing the votes of just a few members of one political party would be sufficient to change several states' constitutional language on important issues. Advocate-educators who understand state and local variations in policymaking procedures can use this knowledge to develop more effective and efficient educational strategies.

10. Strom, Mueller, and Smith (2010).

11. See, e.g., Gerber et al. (2001).

12. See, e.g., Bergman, Muller, and Strom (2000); and Lupia (2001b).

13. Consider, e.g., the "fire alarm oversight" approach described in McCubbins and Schwartz (1984). Also see Mendelson (2012).

14. See, e.g., Michels (1915); Kiewiet and McCubbins (1991); Carpenter (2001); Gerber, Kiewiet, Lupia, and McCubbins (2001).

15. Campbell, Converse, Miller, and Stokes (1960).

16. This dynamic is different in cases where there are many viable left and right parties. When none of these parties is expected to win a majority of legislative seats, voters who want to understand the likely policy consequences of different electoral outcomes need to know more.

17. Source: http://www.usmayors.org/about/overview.asp. Downloaded August 15, 2011.

18. Source: http://www.ncsl.org/default.aspx?tabid=14781.

19. Source: http://www.nsba.org/; downloaded August 15, 2011.

20. Also see Caplan (2007).

CHAPTER 13

1. I say "nearly all" to reflect the fact Wyoming, which elects one member of the US House of Representatives, is less populated than cities like Los Angeles, home of the largest school district that is governed by a school board. In almost all cases, however, school board district populations are much smaller than state populations. Information about Los Angeles's school district downloaded August 18, 2012, from http://notebook.lausd.net/portal/page?_pageid=33,48254&_dad=ptl&_schema=PTL_EP.

2. Unlike most democratic nations, the United States has never held even an advisory vote on any national constitutional or policy question. Most democratic nations have held at least one such vote (Butler and Ranney, 1994).

3. Abramson, Aldrich, Gomez, and Rohde (2014).

4. Banks and Kiewiet (1989); Krasno and Green (1988).

5. Ostrom (1990).

6. http://new.civiced.org/cns-teachers/lesson-plans/fall-high-school-lesson-plans/1118-lesson-3-the-ballot-and-questions.

7. See, e.g., Stein (1982); Oye (1985).

8. See, e.g., Brown, Collins, and Duguid (1989).

9. See, e.g., Jackson and Watts (2002).

10. http://www.cnpp.usda.gov/publications/mypyramid/originalfoodguidepyramids/fgp/fgppamphlet.pdf

CHAPTER 14

1. Delli Carpini and Keeter (1989: 10).

CHAPTER 15

1. "Expensive Ignorance," editorial, *Providence Journal*, November 7, 2006, B4.

2. Downloaded July 1, 2013, from http://www.americancivicliteracy.org/resources/content/failing_america_9-18-07.pdf.

3. Reported in Briggs (2007).

4. http://www.americancivicliteracy.org/2007/survey_methods.html.

5. In the social sciences, there are different ways of assessing validity. In this book, I refer to content validity and, in particular, whether a set of questions accurately reflects a component of a person's declarative memory (see, e.g., Kane, 2001: 327–328). Here, accuracy depends on the correspondence between how an analyst interprets a respondent's answers to specific questions and the respondent's actual knowledge of the topic that the questions seek to measure.

6. Lloyd and Mitchenson (2006).

7. Mauna Kea is the tallest when measured from the bottom of the mountain to the top. Mount Everest rises the highest above sea level, but it is not the tallest when measured from bottom to top (Lloyd and Mitchenson, 2006: 1–2).

8. Two (Lloyd and Mitchenson, 2006: 60–61).

9. Bastille Day is a French holiday that serves a function similar to that of Independence Day in the United States. Famous paintings of the scene show many liberated revolutionaries as a result of the Bastille being stormed. At the time of the insurgency, however, the Bastille held only seven prisoners. All were freed. The answer is seven (Lloyd and Mitchenson, 2006: 29–30).

10. *E pluribus unum* is the motto of the Portuguese football club Sport Lisboa e Benfica. It used to be the official motto of the United States, but was replaced by "In God We Trust" in 1956 (Lloyd and Mitchenson, 2006: 98–99).

11. Gibson and Caldeira (2009: 431).

12. Berent, Krosnick, and Lupia (2013).

13. Coding instructions sent by ANES staff to Gibson and Caldeira read as follows: "We are strict regarding acceptable answers: We will accept ONLY 'Chief Justice'—'Justice' alone is definitely *NOT* acceptable. (The court must be 'the Supreme Court'—'Chief Justice of the Court' won't do. Note: applies only if R would specifically say 'the Court,' a rare phrasing, rather than 'the Supreme Court')."

14. Political communication scholars Kathleen Hall Jamieson and Michael Hennessy (2007) find a strong correlation between people who misunderstand the Supreme Court's powers and those who question its legitimacy. If we could subsequently show that such beliefs could damage the Court, people who value the court's legitimacy would want to pursue educational strategies that correct the misperceptions. What is less clear is whether, or under what conditions, information deemed essential by journalists and others would really make a difference for improving these and other valuable competences.

15. Krosnick, Lupia, DeBell, and Donakowski (2008: 5).

16. The written instructions given to ANES coders in 2004 were as follows: "The reference must be specifically to 'Great Britain' or 'England'—United Kingdom is *NOT* acceptable (Blair is not the head of Ireland), nor is reference to any other political/geographic unit (e.g. British Isles, Europe, etc.)" (Krosnick, Lupia, DeBell, and Donakowski, 2008: 5).

17. Although we were not able to go back and obtain the consent of previous survey respondents to release these transcripts, we obtained permission from subsequent

respondents. To protect their privacy, these responses are redacted in the sense that they remove words that could identify respondents (e.g., a personally identifying response such as "Barack Obama, he's my uncle").

18. Prior and Lupia (2008).

19. Mondak (2001).

20. Mondak and Anderson (2004).

21. Luskin and Bullock (2011: table 1).

22. An ancillary claim of this kind is that the public's knowledge of politics is less than knowledge needed for other important decisions. As is the case with many such claims, they are almost never based on data or direct comparisons. A notable exception is Burnett and McCubbins (2010), whose survey asked recall questions on politics and recall questions on a number of common consumer decisions. They found that respondents' ability to answer political recall questions correctly was often better than their ability to give correct answers to questions about common consumer products.

CHAPTER 16

1. Adler (2012).

2. Moon (2012); also see Ruiz (2012).

3. Other scholars use this data to develop "political sophistication" and "political awareness" scales. In some cases, the scales are composed only of recall questions. In other cases, self-reports of interest in politics and similar variables are included. In all uses of these terms that I have seen, the terms are used to signal a measure of the named phenomena generally considered. For reasons given throughout this chapter, I demonstrate that such general claims depend on assumptions about the data that are typically untested or untrue. Hence, my critiques of current practices and advice on how to improve measurement and inference apply to most existing sophistication and awareness scales. For simplicity, I use PK scales to refer to all such variables.

4. To be fair, Moon (2012) and Ruiz (2012) also criticize the poll's methodology. But these forays into statistical criticism prove unfortunate. The authors claim that because FDU oversampled Republicans (the poll was conducted during an active GOP primary season), the margin of error for Republicans in the poll would be larger than that for Democrats. If, however, the polling firm did the sampling correctly—and all available evidence supports this proposition—then *The Examiner*'s and *The Blaze*'s claims are the opposite of correct.

5. Pew Research Center for the People and the Press (2012).

6. Also see Jerit (2009).

7. Child (1973).

8. Also see Mondak (1999).

9. Also see Pietryka and MacIntosh (2013).

10. See, e.g., Pellegrino, Chudowsky, and Glaser (2001) for a review.

11. Another question pertains to whether the content of ANES recall questions is the same from year to year. This matters because many analysts use ANES data to make claims about the effects of PK on politically relevant opinions and behaviors at different points in time. The answer to this question is that the ANES changes the recall questions it asks from year to year (Zaller, 1986b: 5; Berent, Krosnick, and Lupia, 2013: 3–4).

This practice reduces analysts' abilities to make apples-to-apples comparisons of PK over time.

12. I thank Jay Goodliffe for comprehensive advice about how to word this section effectively.

CHAPTER 17

1. Also see Whitaker and Fulwider (2012).

2. Healy and Malhotra (2014) describe a promising approach. They begin by noting that only one nationally representative survey has ever asked interviewers to report their party identifications. The survey in question was a small pilot study run in 2006 by the ANES when I was a principal investigator. Healy and Malhotra find that an interviewer's partisanship significantly affects their enjoyment of the interview, but it does not affect other attributes of their experience. The survey did not include interviewer assessments of respondent information levels. People who are concerned about partisan bias in interviewer assessments would benefit from a survey that both conducts competently executed interviewer assessments of respondent information levels and collects information about interviewers' partisanship.

3. White (1996); Ho, Imai, King, and Stuart (2007); Lupia (2008).

4. See, e.g., Simmons, Nelson, and Simonsohn (2011, 2014).

5. Also see Sekhon (2005).

6. In Bartels's 2008 book *Unequal Democracy: The Political Economy of the New Gilded Age*, he repeats the argument made in "Homer Gets a Tax Cut." Following our critique of the methods used in that paper, Bartels presents a changed analysis of the relationship between a variable called "political information" and support for the Bush tax cuts. Like us, Bartels conducts separate analyses for Republicans and Democrats but obtains a different result. He finds that increasing information levels corresponded to reduced support for the tax cuts for both Republicans and Democrats—though only the Democratic effect is statistically significant. Recall that we used Bartels's original data to find that increasing information levels corresponded to greater Republican support for the tax cut. The main reason for the differences between Bartels's original 2004 finding, our 2007 finding, and Bartels's changed 2008 finding is that in 2008, Bartels used different data. In his second attempt, he used data from two ANES surveys (2002 and 2004), rather than just the 2002 study on which his 2004 study was based. For 2002, he measured information using interviewer assessments—as before. For 2004, interviewer assessments were available, but Bartels did not use them. Instead, and contrary to his argument in 1996, he used "an information scale . . . based on respondents' answers to a series of factual questions about politics" (Bartels, 2008: 182n). The book offers no theoretical or substantive justification for the change.

7. "The process of developing achievement levels involves the judgments of informed, well-qualified people from throughout the nation and its territories. Approximately 20 persons served on each of three grade-level panels to develop NAEP civics achievement levels. These 60 people included teachers (about 55 percent), others employed in education (about 15 percent), and members of the general public (about 30 percent). To the extent possible, the panels were proportionally representative of the nation's population with respect to region, race/ethnicity, and gender. The panels for civics were convened in August 1992, and the *National Assessment Governing Board* set

the civics NAEP achievement levels in May 1993. The achievement levels set for the civics assessment were used in reporting results for the 1992 assessment and subsequent assessments. They will be used until the Governing Board determines that a new framework is needed to guide the development of the assessment. At that time, new achievement levels may be developed and set. The Board's complete report on *achievement levels for civics* includes descriptions of achievement levels and cutscores, sample items illustrating achievement levels, and performance data." An achievement level is defined as providing "a context for interpreting student performance on NAEP, based on recommendations from panels of educators and members of the public. The levels, *Basic, Proficient,* and *Advanced,* measure what students should know and be able to do at each grade assessed." Downloaded on August 25, 2013, from http://nces.ed.gov/nationsreportcard/tdw/analysis/2000_2001/describing_achiev_civics.aspx.

8. See, e.g., Dancey and Sheagley (2012); Arceneaux (2008).

CHAPTER 18

1. "1 in 5 in New Survey Express Some Doubt About the Holocaust *New York Times,* April 20, 1993, http://www.nytimes.com/1993/04/20/us/1-of-5-in-new-survey-express-some-doubt-about-the-holocaust.html. Downloaded June 10, 2013.

2. http://www.nytimes.com/1993/04/20/us/1-of-5-in-new-survey-express-some-doubt-about-the-holocaust.html. Downloaded June 10, 2013.

3. http://news.google.com/newspapers?nid=110&dat=19930419&id=9bcLAAAAIBAJ&sjid=3lUDAAAAIBAJ&pg=7313,1495218. Downloaded June 10, 2013.

4. Howard Libit, "Poll Finds 1 out of 3 Americans Open to Doubt There Was a Holocaust," *Los Angeles Times,* April 20, 1993, http://articles.latimes.com/1993-04-20/news/mn-25057_1_holocaust-museum. Downloaded June 10, 2013. Also see Doneson (1999: 212).

5. "In 50 More Years, Will Holocaust Be Just a Footnote?"*Denver Post,* April 25, 1993, 2D. Accessed from *Denver Post* archive on June 10, 2013.

6. Roper's realization of the potential error is reported in footnote 1 of Ladd (1994).

7. Kifner (1994).

8. See, e.g., Krosnick and Presser (2009); Schaeffer and Dykema (2011).

9. I am aware of this quote because students bring it to my attention. The quote is meaningful to them, and I include it here because its relevance to this chapter does not depend on Lennon having spoken the words. I mention this because there is no definitive evidence that he did. For the debate, see http://en.wikipedia.org/wiki/Wikipedia:Reference_desk/Archives/Humanities/2011_October_30#Is_this_a_real_quote_from_John_Lennon.3F. Downloaded July 1, 2013.

10. See, e.g., Krosnick and Presser (2009); Tourangeau, Rips, and Rasinski (2000).

11. Also see, e.g., Hambleton et al. (1991); Embretson and Reise (2000).

12. Schulz and Sibberns (2004) offer a comprehensive description of how the IEA chooses its questions.

13. Baldi et al. (2001).

14. Warner (2001).

15. See, e.g., Ades and DiTella (1999).

16. See, e.g., Montinola and Jackman (2002).

17. See, e.g., Sudman, Bradburn, and Schwarz (1996); Drennan (2003).

18. Lodge et al. (1990); Zaller (1992); Zaller and Feldman (1992).

19. Prior and Lupia (2008) use multiple statistics to show how increasing motivation and time causes statistically significant changes in the kinds and numbers of questions answered correctly. The meaning of any such statistic for general claims about recall depends on experimental design factors like incentive size and question content. For example, an increase of one correct answer on a 14-item survey could be considered substantively significant if answering the question correctly is necessary or sufficient for competence at a high-value task. At the same time, an increase of 13 correct answers on a 14-item survey can mean far less if the answers are irrelevant to valuable competences. For these reasons, and unlike Luskin and Bullock (2011: 555), Prior and Lupia (2008) are careful not to draw general conclusions about effect size beyond documenting statistically significant experimental effects for a range of questions and situations.

20. Singer, Groves, and Corning (1999).

References

Abbasi, Daniel R. 2006. *Americans and Climate Change: Closing the Gap between Science and Action*. New Haven, CT: Yale School of Forestry and Environmental Studies.

Abramson, Paul R., John H. Aldrich, Brad T. Gomez, and David W. Rohde. 2014. *Change and Continuity in the 2012 Elections*. Washington, DC: Congressional Quarterly Press.

Ades, Alberto, and Rafael DiTella. 1999. "Rents, Competition, and Corruption." *American Economic Review* 89: 982–993.

Adler, Ben. 2012. "It's Official: Watching Fox Makes You Stupider." *Nation*, May 12. http://www.thenation.com/blog/167999/its-official-watching-fox-makes-you-stupider#ax82XErjACu0. Accessed July 11, 2013.

Albright, Thomas D. 2015. "Perceiving." *Daedalus: Journal of the American Academy of Arts and Sciences* 144: 22–41.

Aldrich, John H., James E. Alt, and Arthur Lupia. 2007. *Positive Changes in Political Science: The Legacy of Richard D. McKelvey's Most Influential Writings*. Ann Arbor, MI: University of Michigan Press.

Althaus, Scott. 2003. *Collective Preferences in Democratic Politics: Opinion Surveys and the Will of the People*. New York: Cambridge University Press.

Andreasen, Alan R. 1995. *Marketing Social Change: Changing Behavior to Promote Health, Social Development, and the Environment*. New York: Jossey-Bass.

Annenberg Public Policy Center. 2011. "New Annenberg Survey Asks: How Well Do Americans Understand the Constitution?" September 16. http://www.annenbergpublicpolicycenter.org/new-annenberg-survey-asks-how-well-do-americans-understand-the-constitution/. Accessed July 23, 2014,

Arceneaux, Kevin. 2008. "Can Partisan Cues Diminish Democratic Accountability?" *Political Behavior* 30: 139–160.

Aronowitz, Stanley, and Henry A. Giroux. 1988. "Essay Reviews: The Closing of the American Mind/Cultural Literacy." *Harvard Educational Review* 58: 172–195.

Ashworth, Scott, and Ethan Bueno de Mesquita. 2014. "Is Voter Competence Good for Voters: Information, Rationality, and Democratic Performance." *American Political Science Review* 108: 565–587.

Badash, David. 2012. "Yes, Brendan O'Neill, Anti-Gay Voters Are 'Ill-Informed,' And So Are You." May 13. http://thenewcivilrightsmovement.com/yes-brendan-oneill-a nti-gay-voters-are-ill-informed-and-so-are-you/politics/2012/05/13/39460. Accessed August 10, 2012.

Baddeley, Alan. 2012. "Working Memory: Theories, Models, and Controversies." *Annual Review of Psychology* 63: 1–29.

Baldi, Stephane, Marianne Perle, Dan Skidmore, Elizabeth Greenberg, Carole Hahn, and Dawn Nelson. 2001. *What Democracy Means to Ninth-Graders: U.S. Results From the International IEA Civic Education Study*. Washington, DC: United States Department of Education Office of Educational Research and Improvement.

Ballasy, Nicholas. 2012. "Jon Voight 'Feeding' Daughter Angelina Jolie Anti-Obama Information." http://dailycaller.com/2012/08/31/jon-voight-feeding-daughter-angelina-jolie-anti-obama-information-video/#ix825nsRhBAr. Accessed July 12, 2014.

Banks, Jeffrey S., and D. Roderick Kiewiet. 1998. "Explaining Patterns of Candidate Competition in Congressional Elections." *American Journal of Political Science* 33: 997–1015.

Barabas, Jason, Jennifer Jerit, William Pollock, and Carlisle Rainey. 2014. "The Question(s) of Political Knowledge." *American Political Science Review* 106: 840–855.

Bartels, Larry. 1996. "Uninformed Votes: Information Effects in Presidential Elections." *American Journal of Political Science* 40: 194–230.

Bartels, Larry. 2005. "Homer Gets a Tax Cut: Inequality and Public Policy in the American Mind." *Perspectives on Politics* 3: 15–31.

Bartels, Larry. 2008. *Unequal Democracy: The Political Economy of the New Gilded Age*. New York: Russell Sage Foundation and Princeton University Press.

Basu, Kaushik. 1999. "Child Labor: Cause, Consequence, and Cure, with Remarks on International Labor Standards. *Journal of Economic Literature* 37: 1083–1119.

Bechtel, Michael M., Jens Hainmueller, Dominik Hangartner, and Marc Heibling. 2014. "Reality Bites: The Limits of Framing Effects for Salient and Contested Policy Issues." *Political Science Research and Methods*. Available on CJO 2015 doi:10.1017/psrm.2014.39

Becker, James T., and Robert G. Morris. 1999. "Working Memory." *Brain and Cognition* 41: 1–8.

Bennett, Stephen. 1998. "'Know-Nothings' Revisited: The Meaning of Political Ignorance Today." *Social Science Quarterly* 69: 476–490.

Berent, Matthew K., Jon A. Krosnick, and Arthur Lupia. 2013. "Coding Open-Ended Answers to Office Recognition Questions From the 2008 ANES Time Series Interviews." *American National Election Studies Technical Report*. http://www.electionstudies.org/studypages/2008prepost/ANES2008TS_CodingProject.htm. Accessed August 1, 2013.

Berridge, Kent C. 2004. Motivation Concepts in Behavioral Neuroscience." *Psychological Behavior* 81: 179–209.

Billig, Michael, and Henri Tajfel. 1973. "Social Categorization and Similarity in Intergroup Behaviour." *European Journal of Social Psychology* 3: 27–52.

Bizer, George Y., Zakary L. Tormala, Derek D. Rucker, and Richard E. Petty. 2006. "Memory-based versus On-Line Processing: Implications for Attitude Strength." *Journal of Personality and Social Psychology* 42: 646–653.

Bjork, Robert A. 1999. "Assessing Our Own Competence: Heuristics and Illusions." In Daniel Gopher and Asher Koriat (eds.). *Attention and Performance XVII: Cognitive Regulation of Performance: Interaction of Theory and Application*. Cambridge, MA: MIT Press, 435–459.

Bobo, Lawrence, and Vincent L. Hutchings. 1996. "Perceptions of Racial Group Competition: Extending Blumer's Theory of Group Position to a Multiracial Social Context." *American Sociological Review* 61: 951–972.

Bohannon, John. 2011. "Searching for the Google Effect on People's Memory." *Science* 333: 277.

Boudreau, Cheryl. 2009. "Closing the Gap: When Do Cues Eliminate Differences Between Sophisticated and Unsophisticated Citizens?" *Journal of Politics* 71: 964–976.

Boudreau, Cheryl, and Arthur Lupia. 2011. "Political Knowledge." In James N. Druckman, James H. Kuklinski, Donald P. Green, and Arthur Lupia (eds.). *The Cambridge Handbook of Experimental Political Science*. New York: Cambridge University Press, 171–183.

Bovitz, Gregory L., James N. Druckman, and Arthur Lupia. 2002. "When Can a New Organization Lead Public Opinion." *Public Choice* 113: 127–155.

Bradley, Gifford W. 1978. "Self-Serving Biases in the Attribution Process: A Reexamination of the Fact or Fiction Question." *Journal of Personality and Social Psychology* 36: 56–71.

Brady, Henry E., and Paul M. Sniderman. 1985. "Attitude Attribution: A Group Basis for Political Reasoning." *American Political Science Review* 79: 1061–1078.

Brazile, Donna. 2012. "What Informed Voters Need to Know." *Chautauquan Daily*, July 3. http://chqdaily.com/2012/07/03/donna-brazile-what-informed-voters-need-to-know/on. Accessed August 18, 2012.

Brennan, Jason. 2009. "Polluting the Polls: When Citizens Should Not Vote." *Australasian Journal of Philosophy* 87: 535–549.

Brennan, Jason. 2012. "Most People Shouldn't Vote." http://press.princeton.edu/blog/2012/08/15/shame-on-you-voter-a-case-for-not-voting-from-jason-brennan/. Accessed August 19, 2012.

Briggs, Tracey Wong. 2007. "College Students Struggle on History Test." http://usatoday30.usatoday.com/news/education/2007-09-17-history-test_N.htm. Accessed July 1, 2013.

Brooks, David. 2007. "The Outsourced Brain." *New York Times*. http://www.nytimes.com/2007/10/26/opinion/26brooks.html. Accessed June 6, 2012.

Brown, John Seely, Allan Collins, and Paul Duguid. 1989. "Situated Cognition and the Culture of Learning." *Educational Researcher* 18: 32–42.

Brown, Rupert, and Miles Hewstone. 2005. "An Integrative Theory of Intergroup Contact." In Mark P. Zanna (ed.). *Advances in Experimental Social Psychology*. London: Elsevier Academic Press, 256–345.

Bruer, John T. 1999. *The Myth of the First Three Years: A New Understanding of Early Brain Development and Lifelong Learning*. New York: Free Press.

Bullock, John G. 2009. "Partisan Bias and the Bayesian Ideal in the Study of Public Opinion." *Journal of Politics* 79: 1101–1124.

Bullock, John G., Alan S. Gerber, Seth J. Hill, and Gregory A. Huber. 2013. "Partisan Bias in Factual Beliefs about Politics." *National Bureau of Economic Research Working Paper 19080*.

Burnett, Craig M., and Mathew D. McCubbins. 2010. "What Do You Know? Comparing Political and Consumer Knowledge." *Social Science Research Network*. http://papers.ssrn.com/sol3/papers.cfm?abstract_id=1493533.

Butler, David, and Austin Ranney. 1994. *Referendums Around the World: The Growing Use of Direct Democracy*. Washington, DC: American Enterprise Institute.

Butrovic, Zeljka, and Daniel B. Klein. 2010 "Economic Enlightenment in Relation to College-going, Ideology, and Other Variables: A Zogby Survey of Americans." *Economics Journal Watch* 7: 174–196.

Canham, Matt, and Mary Hegarty. 2010. "Effect of Knowledge and Display Design on Comprehension of Complex Graphics." *Learning and Instruction* 20: 155–166.

Caplan, Brian. 2007. *The Myth of the Rational Voter: Why Democracies Choose Bad Policies*. Princeton, NJ: Princeton University Press.

Carlson, Darren K. 2003. "Can Americans Name Key Foreign Leaders?" http://www.gallup.com/poll/7912/can-americans-name-key-foreign-leaders.aspx. Accessed July 23, 2014.

Carpenter, Daniel P. 2001. *The Forging of Bureaucratic Autonomy: Reputations, Networks, and Policy Innovation in Executive Agencies, 1862–1928*. Princeton, NJ: Princeton University Press.

Cheney, Richard. 2004. "Vice President's Remarks in Los Lunas, New Mexico." http://georgewbush-whitehouse.archives.gov/news/releases/2004/10/20041031-7.html. Accessed July 9, 2012.

Child, Dennis. 1973. *The Essentials of Factor Analysis*. London: Holt, Rinehart & Winston.

Chong, Dennis, and James N. Druckman. 2007. "Framing Theory." *Annual Review of Political Science* 10: 103–126.

Cialdini, Robert B., and Noah J. Goldstein. 2004. "Social Influence: Compliance and Conformity." *Annual Review of Psychology* 55: 591–621.

Cialdini, Robert B. 2009. *Influence: Science and Practice*, 5th ed. Boston: Pearson.

Claassen, Ryan L., and Benjamin Highton. 2006. "Does Policy Debate Reduce Information Effects in Public Opinion? Analyzing the Evolution of Public Opinion on Health Care." *Journal of Politics* 68: 410–420.

Clark, Andy. 1997. *Being There: Putting Brain, Body, and World Together Again*. Cambridge, MA: MIT Press.

Collins, Allan M., and Elizabeth F. Loftus. 1975. "A Spreading Activation Theory of Semantic Processing." *Psychological Review* 82: 407–428.

Cox, Gary W. 1997. *Making Votes Count: Strategic Coordination in the World's Electoral Systems*. New York: Cambridge University Press.

Cox, Gary W., and Mathew D. McCubbins. 2006. *Setting the Agenda: Responsible Party Government in the U.S. House of Representatives*. New York: Cambridge University Press.

Craik, Fergus I. M., and Robert S. Lockhart. 1972. "Levels of Processing: A Framework for Memory Research." *Journal of Verbal Learning and Verbal Behavior* 11: 671–684.

Crookes, Graham, and Richard W. Schmidt. 1991. "Motivation: Opening the Research Agenda." *Language Learning* 41: 469–512.

Dancey, Logan, and Geoffrey D. Sheagley. 2012. "Heuristics Behaving Badly: Party Cues and Voter Knowledge." *American Journal of Political Science* 57: 312–325.

Delli Carpini, Michael X., and Scott Keeter. 1996. *What Americans Know About Politics and Why It Matters*. New Haven, CT: Yale University Press.

Diermeier, Daniel. 1995. "Rational Choice and the Role of Theory in Political Science." *Critical Review* 9: 59–70.

Dietz, Thomas. 2013. "Bringing Values and Deliberation to Science Communication." *Proceedings of the National Academy of Science* 110: 14081–14087.

Doneson, Judith. 1999. "Is a Little Memory Better Than None?" In Peter Hayes (ed.). *Lessons and Legacies III: Memory, Memorialization, and Denial.* Evanston, IL: Northwestern University Press.

Downs, Anthony. 1957. *An Economic Theory of Democracy.* New York: Harper Collins.

Drennan, Jonathan. 2003. "Cognitive Interviewing: Verbal Data in the Design and Pretesting of Questionnaires." *Journal of Advanced Nursing* 42: 57–63.

Druckman, James N. 2001a. "On the Limits of Framing Effects: Who Can Frame?" *Journal of Politics* 63: 1041–1066.

Druckman, James N. 2001b. "Using Credible Advice to Overcome Framing Effects." *Journal of Law, Economics, and Politics* 17: 62–82.

Druckman, James N., and Toby Bolsen. 2011. "Framing, Motivated Reasoning, and Opinions about Emerging Technologies." *Journal of Communication* 61: 658–688.

Druckman, James N., and Arthur Lupia. 2000. "Preference Formation." *Annual Review of Political Science* 3: 1–24.

Druckman, James N., and Arthur Lupia. 2006. "Mind, Will, and Choice." In Charles Tilly and Robert E. Goodin (eds.). *The Oxford Handbook on Contextual Political Analysis.* Oxford, UK: Oxford University Press, 97–113.

Edsall, Thomas B. 2012. "What's Wrong with Pennsylvania?" *New York Times.* http://campaignstops.blogs.nytimes.com/2012/09/23/whats-wrong-with-pennsylvania/. Accessed June 5, 2013.

Egan, Timothy. 2014. "Bill O'Reilly's Gift for the Ages." *New York Times.* http://www.nytimes.com/2014/02/14/opinion/bill-oreillys-gift-for-the-ages.html?hp&rref=opinion&_r=0. Accessed February 14, 2014.

Elo, Kimmo, and Lauri Rapeli. 2010. "Determinants of Political Knowledge: The Effects of Media on Knowledge and Information." *Journal of Elections, Public Opinion, and Parties* 20: 133–146.

Embretson, Susan E., and Steven P. Reise. 2000. *Item Response Theory for Psychologists.* Mahwah, NJ: Lawrence Erlbaum Associates.

ERIC Development Team. 2001. *Civic Knowledge and Engagement at Age 14 in 28 Countries: Results from the IEA Civic Education Study.* www.eric.ed.gov.

Erickson, Lanae. 2011. "Commitment: The Answer to the Middle's Questions on Marriage for Gay Couples." http://www.thirdway.org/publications/463. Accessed July 18, 2013.

Evangelical Climate Initiative. 2006. "Climate Change: An Evangelical Call to Action." http://www.npr.org/documents/2006/feb/evangelical/calltoaction.pdf.

Fairleigh Dickinson University's Public Mind Poll. 2012. "What You Know Depends on What You Watch: Current Events Knowledge Across Popular News Sources." http://publicmind.fdu.edu/2012/confirmed/. Accessed July 25, 2013.

Falwell, Jerry. 2007. "The Myth of Global Warming." Reported in Nagle (2008: 78).

Fauconnier, Gilles, and Mark Turner. 2002. *The Way We Think: Conceptual Blending and the Mind's Hidden Complexities.* New York: Basic Books.

Fishbein, Martin, and Icek Ajzen. 1975. *Belief, Attitude, Intention, and Behavior: An Introduction to Theory and Research.* Reading, MA: Addison-Wesley.

Fortini-Campbell, Lisa. 2001. *Hitting the Sweet Spot: How Consumer Insights Can Inspire Better Marketing and Advertising*. Chicago: Copy Workshop.

Frank, Thomas. 2004. *What's the Matter with Kansas: How Conservatives Won the Heart of America*. New York: Henry Holt and Co.

Freedman, Andrew. 2012. "Senate Hearing Focuses on Threat of Sea Level Rise." http://sealevel.climatecentral.org/news/senate-climate-change-hearing-focuses-on-sea-level-rise/. Accessed May 16, 2013.

Frischen, Alexandra, Andrew P. Bayliss, and Steven P. Tipper. 2007. "Gaze Cueing of Attention: Visual Attention, Social Cognition, and Individual Difference." *Psychological Bulletin* 133: 694–724.

Gailmard, Sean, and Jeffery A. Jenkins. 2007. "Negative Agenda Control in the Senate and House: Fingerprints of Majority Party Power." *Journal of Politics* 69: 689–700.

Galston, William. 2001. "Political Knowledge, Political Engagement, and Civic Education." *Annual Review of Political Science* 4: 217–234.

Garfunkel, Sol, and David Mumford. 2011. "How to Fix Our Math Education." *New York Times*, August 24, A27.

Gerber, Elisabeth, Arthur Lupia, Mathew D. McCubbins, and D. Roderick Kiewiet. 2001. *Stealing the Initiative: How State Government Responds to Direct Democracy*. Upper Saddle River, NJ: Pearson Education.

Gibson, James L., and Gregory A. Caldeira. 2009. "Knowing the Supreme Court? A Reconsideration of Public Ignorance of the High Court." *Journal of Politics* 71: 429–441.

Gigerenzer, Gerd, Peter M. Todd, and the ABC Research Group. 1999. *Simple Heuristics that Make Us Smart*. New York: Oxford University Press.

Gilens, Martin. 2001. "Political Ignorance and Collective Policy Preferences." *American Political Science Review* 95: 379–396.

Gillis, Justin. 2012. "Rising Sea Levels Seen as Threat to Coastal U.S." *New York Times*. http://www.nytimes.com/2012/03/14/science/earth/study-rising-sea-levels-a-risk-to-coastal-states.html. Accessed May 16, 2013.

Glaser, Rashi, Joel H. Steckel, and Russell S Winer. 1992. "Locally Rational Decision Making: The Distracting Effect of Information on Managerial Performance." *Management Science* 38: 212–226.

Gopnik, Alison, Andrew N. Meltzoff, and Patricia K. Kuhl. 1999. *The Scientist in the Crib: Minds, Brains, and How Children Learn*. New York: William Morrow and Co.

Gould, Steven Jay. 1996. *The Mismeasure of Man*, revised ed. New York: W. W. Norton and Co.

Graber, Doris A. 1984. *Processing the News: How People Tame the Information Tide*. New York: Longman.

Graber, Doris A. 1994. "Why Voters Fail Information Tests: Can the Hurdles Be Overcome?" *Political Communication* 11: 337–346.

Graham, Bob, with Chris Hand. 2010. *America, The Owner's Manual: Making Government Work For You*. Washington, DC: Congressional Quarterly Press.

Granderson, L. Z. 2011. "Don't Let Ignorant People Vote." http://articles.cnn.com/2011-04-12/opinion/granderson.ignorant.vote_1_ignorant-voters-political-system-ignorant-people?_s=PM:OPINION. Accessed August 9, 2012.

Green, Melanie C., and Timothy C. Brock. 2000. "The Role of Transportation in the Persuasiveness of Public Narratives." *Journal of Personality and Social Psychology* 79: 701–721.

Guthrie, Robert V. 1998. *Even the Rat was White: A Historical View of Psychology*, 2nd ed. Needham Heights, MA: Allyn and Bacon.

Habermas, Jürgen. 1996. *Between Facts and Norms: Contributions to a Discourse Theory of Law and Democracy*. Translated by William Rehg. Cambridge, MA: MIT Press.

Hahn, Carole. 2003. "Democratic Values and Citizen Action: A View from U.S. Ninth Graders." *International Journal of Educational Research* 39: 633–642.

Haider-Markel, Donald P., and Mark R. Joslyn. 2001. "Gun Policy, Tragedy, and Blame Attribution: The Conditional Influence of Issue Frames." *Journal of Politics* 63: 520–543.

Hambleton, Ronald K., Hariharan Swaminathan, and H. Jane Rogers. 1991. *Fundamentals of Item Response Theory*. Newbury Park, CA: Sage Publications.

Harrison, Brian, and Melissa R. Michelson. 2013. "Listen, We Need to Talk: Opening Minds to Attitudinal Change Through In-group Identity Activation." http://papers.ssrn.com/sol3/papers.cfm?abstract_id=2301139. Accessed July 18, 2014.

Hastie, Reid, and Bernadette Park. 1986. "The Relationship Between Memory and Judgment Depends on Whether the Judgment Task is Memory-Based or On-Line." *Psychological Review* 93: 258–268.

Healy, Andrew, and Neil Malhotra. 2014. "Partisan Bias Among Interviewers." *Public Opinion Quarterly* 78: 485–499.

Hendley, Brian. 1989. "Hirsch and Dewey on Democracy and Education." *Interchange* 20: 53–60.

Hershey, Marjorie Randon. 1994. "The Meaning of a Mandate: Interpretations of 'Mandate' in 1984 Presidential Election Coverage." *Polity* 27: 225–254.

Hinkle, A. Barton. 2012. "The Wrong Side Absolutely Must Not Win." *Richmond-Times Dispatch*, August 20. http://www.timesdispatch.com/news/the-wrong-side-absolutely-must-not-win/article_820393d3-a906-5d6e-bbda-434f224167a9.html. Accessed May 15, 2014.

Hirsch, Eric D., Jr. 1987. *Cultural Literacy: What Every American Needs to Know*. New York: Houghton Mifflin.

Ho, Daniel E., Kosuke Imai, Gary King, Elizabeth A. Stuart. 2007. "Matching as Nonparametric Preprocessing for Reducing Model Dependence in Parametric Causal Inference." *Political Analysis* 15: 199–236.

Hochschild, Jennifer L. 2010. "If Democracies Need Informed Voters, How Can They Thrive While Expanding Enfranchisement." *Election Law Journal: Rules, Politics, and Policy* 9: 111–123.

Holbrook, Allyson L., Jon A. Krosnick, David Moore, and Roger Tourangeau. 2007. "Response Order Effects in Dichotomous Categorical Questions Presented Orally: The Impact of Question and Respondent Attributes." *Public Opinion Quarterly* 71: 325–348.

Hopkins, Daniel J. 2013 "The Exaggerated Life of Death Panels: The Limits of Framing Effects in the 2009-2013 Health Care Debate." http://papers.ssrn.com/sol3/papers.cfm?abstract_id=2163769. Accessed July 22, 2014.

Horst, Maja. 2011. "Taking Our Own Medicine: On an Experiment in Science Communication." *Science and Engineering Ethics* 17: 801–815.

Huffington Post Media. 2012. "Study Finds Fox News Viewers Least Informed of All Viewers." May 23. http://www.huffingtonpost.com/2012/05/23/fox-news-less-informed-new-study_n_1538914.html. Accessed July 11, 2013.

Huizenga, Leroy. 2012. "Opposing Gay Marriage is Rational, Not Religious." http://www.firstthings.com/onthesquare/2012/08/opposing-gay-marriage-is-rational-not-religious. Accessed August 10, 2012.

Hull, Kathleen E. 2001. "The Political Limits of the Rights Frame: The Case of Same-Sex Marriage in Hawaii." *Sociological Perspectives* 44: 207–232.

Hurst, Evan. 2012. "The Quality of Our Opponents' Arguments." May 8. http://www.truthwinsout.org/blog/2012/05/24966/. Accessed August 10, 2012.

Iacoboni, Marco. 2009. *Mirroring People: The Science of Empathy and How We Connect with Others*. New York: Picador Books.

Iyengar, Shanto. 1986. "Whither Political Information." Report to the American National Election Studies Board of Overseers, May 1986. http://www.electionstudies.org/resources/papers/documents/nes002253a.pdf. Accessed June 24, 2013.

Iyengar, Shanto, and Donald R. Kinder. 1989. *News That Matters: Television and American Opinion*. Chicago: University of Chicago Press.

Jackson, Matthew O., and Alison Watts. 2002. "The Evolution of Social and Economic Networks." *Journal of Economic Theory* 106: 265–295.

Jacoby, Susan. 2008. *The Age of American Unreason*. New York: Pantheon.

Jamieson, Kathleen Hall, and Michael Hennessy. 2007. "Public Understanding of and Support for the Courts: Survey Results." *Georgetown Law Journal* 95: 899–902.

Jastrow, Joseph. 1899. "The Mind's Eye." *Popular Science Monthly* 54: 312.

Jedwab, Jack. 2011. "Americans' Knowledge and Learning about Canada." http://www.acs-aec.ca/en/social-research/canada-us-international/. Accessed July 23, 2014.

Jerit, Jennifer. 2009. "Understanding the Knowledge Gap: the Role of Experts and Journalists." *Journal of Politics* 7: 442–56.

Jerit, Jennifer, and Jason Barabas. 2012. "Partisan Perceptual Bias and the Information Environment." *Journal of Politics* 74: 672–684.

Johnson, Dominic D. P., and James H. Fowler. 2011. "The Evolution of Overconfidence." *Nature* 477: 317–320.

Jussim, Lee. 2012. *Social Perception and Social Reality: Why Accuracy Dominates Bias and Self-Fulfilling Prophecy*. New York: Oxford University Press.

Kahan, Daniel M., and Donald Braman. 2006. "Cultural Cognition and Public Policy." *Yale Law and Policy Review* 24: 149–172.

Kahan, Daniel M., Hank Jenkins-Smith, and Donald Braman. 2010. "Cultural Cognition of Scientific Consensus." *Journal of Risk Research* 14: 147–174.

Kahan, Daniel M. 2015. "Climate Science Communication and the Measurement Problem." *Advances in Political Psychology* 36 (Supplement 1): 1–43.

Kahneman, Daniel. 2011. *Thinking Fast and Slow*. New York: Farrar, Straus, and Giroux.

Kam, Cindy D. 2007. "When Duty Calls, Do Citizens Answer?" *Journal of Politics* 69: 17–29.

Kandel, Eric, James H. Schwartz, and Thomas M. Jessell. 1995. *Essentials of Neural Science and Behavior* (chapter 36). Norwalk CT: Appleton and Lange.

Kane, Michael T. 2001. "Current Concerns in Validity Theory." *Journal of Educational Measurement* 38: 319–342.

Kelman, Mark. 2011. *The Heuristics Debate*. New York: Oxford University Press.

Keysar, Boaz, and Anne S. Henly. 2002. "Speakers' Overestimation of Their Effectiveness." *Psychological Science* 13: 207–212.

Kiewiet, D. Roderick, and Mathew D. McCubbins. 1991. *The Logic of Delegation. Congressional Parties and the Appropriations Process*. New York: Cambridge University Press.

Kifner, John. 1994. "Pollster Finds Error on Holocaust Doubts." *New York Times*, May 20. http://www.nytimes.com/1994/05/20/us/pollster-finds-error-on-holocaust-doubts. html. Accessed June 10, 2013.

Kinder, Donald R. 1998. "Communication and Opinion." *Annual Review of Political Science* 1: 167–197.

Kingdon, John W. 1989. *Congressmen's Voting Decisions*, 3rd ed. Ann Arbor, MI: University of Michigan Press.

Klein, Daniel B. 2011. "I Was Wrong and So Are You: A Libertarian Economist Retracts His Swipe at the Left—After Discovering that Our Political Leanings Leave Us More Biased Than We Think." *Atlantic*, October 26. http://www.theatlantic.com/magazine/ archive/2011/12/i-was-wrong-and-so-are-you/308713/. Accessed July 26, 2013.

Klein, Jeffrey T., Steven V. Shephard, and Michael L. Platt. 2009. "Social Attention and the Brain." *Current Biology* 19: R958–R962.

Kline, Paul. 1986. *A Handbook of Test Construction: Introduction to Psychometric Design.* London: Methuen & Co.

Koonin, Steven E. 2014. "Climate Science is Not Settled." *Wall Street Journal*, September 19. http://www.wsj.com/articles/climate-science-is-not-settled-1411143565. Accessed May 8, 2015.

Krasno, Jonathan S., and Donald Philip Green. 1988. "Preempting Quality Challengers in House Elections." *Journal of Politics* 50: 920–936.

Kreider, Tim. 2013. "I Know What You Think of Me." *New York Times*, June 16. http:// opinionator.blogs.nytimes.com/2013/06/15/i-know-what-you-think-of-me/?hp. Accessed June 17, 2013.

Kreps, David M., and Robert Wilson. 1982. "Reputation and Imperfect Information." *Journal of Economic Theory* 27: 253–279.

Krohne, Heinz W. 1993. "Vigilance and Cognitive Avoidance as Concepts in Coping Research." In Heinz W. Krohne (ed.). *Attention and Avoidance: Strategies in Coping with Aversiveness.* Ashland OH: Hogrefe and Huber, 19–50.

Krosnick, Jon A. 1991. "Response Strategies for Coping with the Cognitive Demands of Attitude Measures in Surveys." *Applied Cognitive Psychology* 5: 213–236.

Krosnick, Jon A., Arthur Lupia, Matthew DeBell, and Darrell Donakowski. 2008. "Problems with ANES Questions Measuring Political Knowledge." http://election-studies.org/announce/newsltr/20080324PoliticalKnowledgeMemo.pdf. Accessed August 1, 2013.

Krosnick, Jon A., and Stanley Presser. 2009. "Question and Questionnaire Design." In Peter V. Marsden and James D. Wright (eds.). *The Handbook of Survey Research.* Bingley, UK: Emerald Group Publishing, 263–314.

Krosnick, Jon A., Penny S. Visser, and Joshua Harder. 2010. "The Psychological Underpinnings of Political Behavior." In Susan T. Fiske, Daniel T. Gilbert, and Gardner Lindzey (eds.). *The Handbook of Social Psychology*, 5th ed. New York: John Wiley & Sons, 1288–1342.

Krugman, Paul. 2009. "The Coburn Amendment." *New York Times.* http://krugman. blogs.nytimes.com/2009/10/08/the-coburn-amendment/. Accessed August 1, 2013.

Kuklinski, James H., and Paul J. Quirk. 2001. "Conceptual Foundations of Civic Competence." *Political Behavior* 23: 285–311.

Ladd, Everett Carll. 1994. "The Holocaust Poll Error: A Modern Cautionary Tale." *Public Perspective*, July/August: 3–5.

Lakoff, George, and Mark Johnson. 1999. *Philosophy in the Flesh: The Embodied Mind and its Challenge to Western Thought.* New York: Basic Books.

Lakoff, George, and Elisabeth Wehling. 2012. *The Little Blue Book: The Essential Guide to Thinking and Talking Democratic.* New York: Simon and Schuster.

Langer, Gary. 2007. "If the Dunce Cap Fits, Wear It." http://abcnews.go.com/blogs/politics/2007/06/if-the-dunce-ca/. Accessed August 19, 2012.

Larkin, Jill H., John McDermott, Dorothea P. Simon, and Herbert A. Simon. 1980. "Expert and Novice Performance in Solving Physics Problems." *Science* 208: 1335–1342.

Lau, Richard R., and David P. Redlawsk. 2006. *How Voters Decide: Information Processing in Election Campaigns.* New York: Cambridge University Press.

Lau, Richard R., and Mark Schlesinger. 2005. "Policy Frames, Metaphorical Reasoning, and Support for Public Policies." *Political Psychology* 26: 77–114.

LeDoux, Joseph E. 2003. *Synaptic Self: How Our Brains Become Who We Are.* New York: Penguin Books.

Levendusky, Matthew S., and Simon D. Jackman. 2008. "Heterogeneity in the NES Interviewer Rating." Paper prepared for the Annual Meeting of the Midwest Political Science Association, Chicago.

Levendusky, Matthew S. 2011. "Rethinking the Role of Political Information." *Public Opinion Quarterly* 75: 42–64.

Lloyd, John, and John Mitchinson. 2006. *The Book of General Ignorance: Everything You Think You Know Is Wrong.* New York: Harmony Books.

Lodge, Milton, Kathleen M. McGraw, and Patrick Stroh. 1989. "An Impression Driven Model of Candidate Evaluation." *American Political Science Review* 83: 399–419.

Lodge, Milton, Patrick Stroh, and John Wahlke. 1990. "Black-Box Models of Candidate Evaluation." *Political Behavior* 12:5–18

Lord, Frederic M. 1980. *Applications of Item Response Theory to Practical Testing Problems.* Mahwah, NJ: Lawrence Erlbaum Associates.

Luntz, Frank. 2007. *Words That Work: It's Not What You Say, It's What People Hear.* New York: Hyperion.

Lupia, Arthur. 1992. "Busy Voters, Agenda Control, and the Power of Information." *American Political Science Review* 86: 390–403.

Lupia, Arthur. 1994a. "Shortcuts versus Encyclopedias: Information and Voting Behavior in California Insurance Reform Elections." *American Political Science Review* 88: 63–76.

Lupia, Arthur. 1994b. "The Effect of Information on Voting Behavior and Electoral Outcomes: An Experimental Study of Direct Legislation." *Public Choice* 78: 65–86.

Lupia, Arthur, and Mathew D. McCubbins. 1994. "Who Controls? Information and the Structure of Legislative Decision Making." *Legislative Studies Quarterly* 19: 361–384.

Lupia, Arthur, and Mathew D. McCubbins. 1998. *The Democratic Dilemma: Can Citizens Learn What They Need to Know?* New York: Cambridge University Press.

Lupia, Arthur. 2000. "Evaluating Political Science Research: Information for Buyers and Sellers." *PS: Political Science and Politics* 33: 7–13.

Lupia, Arthur. 2001a. "Dumber than Chimps? An Assessment of Direct Democracy Voters." In Larry J. Sabato, Bruce Larson, and Howard Ernst (eds.). *Dangerous Democracy: The Battle Over Ballot Initiatives in America.* Lanham, MD: Rowman and Littlefield, 66–70.

Lupia, Arthur. 2001b. "Delegation of Power: Agency Theory." In Neil J. Smelser and Paul B. Baltes (eds.). *International Encyclopedia of the Social and Behavioral Sciences 5.* Oxford, UK: Elsevier Science Limited, 3375–3377.

Lupia, Arthur. 2002. "Who Can Persuade Whom? Implications from the Nexus of Psychology and Rational Choice Theory." In James H. Kuklinski (ed.). *Thinking about Political Psychology*. New York: Cambridge University Press, 51–88.

Lupia, Arthur. 2006. "How Elitism Undermines the Study of Voter Competence." *Critical Review* 18: 217–232.

Lupia, Arthur, Adam Seth Levine, Jesse O. Menning, and Gisela Sin. 2007. "Were Bush Tax Cut Supporters 'Simply Ignorant'? A Second Look at Conservatives and Liberals in 'Homer Gets a Tax Cut.'" *Perspectives on Politics* 5: 761–772.

Lupia, Arthur. 2008. "Procedural Transparency and the Credibility of Election Surveys." *Electoral Studies* 27: 732–739.

Lupia, Arthur, Yanna Krupnikov, Adam Seth Levine, Spencer Piston, and Alexander Von Hagen-Jamar. 2010. "Why State Constitutions Differ in their Treatment of Same-Sex Marriage." *Journal of Politics* 72: 1222–1235.

Lupia, Arthur. 2011. "How Do Scholars Know What Voters Want? An Essay on Theory and Measurement." In Benjamin Highton and Paul M. Sniderman (eds.). *Facing the Challenge of Democracy: Explorations in the Analysis of Public Opinion and Political Participation*. Princeton, NJ: Princeton University Press.

Lupia, Arthur. 2013. "Communicating Science in Politicized Environments." *Proceedings of the National Academy of Sciences* 110: 14048–14054.

Lupia, Arthur, Yanna Krupnikov, and Adam Seth Levine. 2013. "Beyond Facts and Norms: How Psychological Transparency Threatens and Restores Deliberation's Legitimating Potential." *Southern California Law Review* 86: 459–493.

Luskin, Robert. 2002. "From Denial to Extenuation (and Finally Beyond): Political Sophistication and Citizen Performance." In James Kuklinski (ed.). *Thinking about Political Psychology*. New York: Cambridge University Press.

Luskin, Robert C., and John G. Bullock. 2011. "'Don't Know' Means 'Don't Know': DK Responses and the Public's Level of Political Knowledge." *Journal of Politics* 73: 547–557.

Maddox, John. 1993. "Willful Public Misunderstanding of Genetics." *Nature* 364: 281.

Madison, James. 1787. "The Federalist No. 10: The Utility of the Union as a Safeguard Against Domestic Faction and Insurrection (continued)." *New York Daily Advertiser*, November 2.

Matthews, Gerald, and Adrian Wells. 1999. "The Cognitive Science of Attention and Emotion." In Tim Dalgleish and Mick J. Power (eds.). *Handbook of Cognition and Emotion*. West Sussex, UK: John Wiley & Sons, 171–192.

McCarty, Nolan, Keith T. Poole, and Howard Rosenthal. 2001. "The Hunt for Party Discipline in Congress." *American Political Science Review* 95: 673–687.

McKelvey, Richard D., and Peter C. Ordeshook. 1985. "Elections with Limited Information: A Fulfilled Expectations Model Using Contemporaneous Poll and Endorsement Data as Information Sources." *Journal of Economic Theory* 36: 55–85.

McKelvey, Richard D., and Peter C. Ordeshook. 1990. "A Decade of Experimental Research on Spatial Models of Elections and Committees." In Melvin J. Hinich and James Enelow (eds.). *Government, Democracy, and Social Choice*, 99–144.

Mendelson, Nina. 2012. "Should Mass Comments Count?" *Michigan Journal of Environment and Administration* 2: 173–183.

Michels, Robert. 1915. *Political Parties: A Sociological Study of the Oligarchical Tendencies of Modern Democracy*. Translated by Eden and Cedar Paul. Glencoe, IL: Free Press.

Milgrom, Paul, and John Roberts. 1986. "Relying on the Information of Interested Parties." *RAND Journal of Economics* 17: 18–32.

Miller, Dale T., and Michael Ross. 1975. "Self-Serving Biases in the Attribution of Causality: Fact or Fiction?" *Psychological Bulletin* 82: 213–225.

Miller, Earl K., and Timothy J. Buschman. 2015. "Working Memory Capacity: Limits on the Bandwidth of Cognition." *Daedalus: Journal of the American Academy of Arts and Sciences* 144: 112–122.

Miller, George A. 1956. "The Magical Number Seven, Plus or Minus Two: Some Limits on Our Capacity for Processing Information." *Psychological Review* 63: 81–97.

Miller, Melissa, and Shannon K. Orr. 2008. "Experimenting with a 'Third Way' in Political Knowledge Estimation." *Public Opinion Quarterly* 72: 768–780.

Miller, Ted. 2011. *Mortal Gods: Science, Politics, and the Humanist Ambitions of Thomas Hobbes*. University Park, PA: University of Pennsylvania Press.

Mondak, Jeffery J. 1999. "Reconsidering the Measurement of Political Knowledge." *Political Analysis* 8: 57–82.

Montinola, Gabriella R., and Robert W. Jackman. 2002. "Sources of Corruption: A Cross-Country Study." *British Journal of Political Science* 32: 147–170.

Moon, Robert. 2012. "Democrats Use Biased 'Study' to Smear Fox News." http://www.examiner.com/article/leftists-use-fake-biased-study-to-smear-fox-news. Accessed July 25, 2013.

Moore, Michael. 2010. Interview on "The Joy Behar Show," March 11. http://www.youtube.com/watch?v=ZQ2_N9RdBF8.

Nagle, John Copeland. 2008. "The Evangelical Debate over Climate Change." *University of St. Thomas Law Journal* 5: 53–86.

National Scientific Council on the Developing Child. 2010. "Early Experiences Can Alter Gene Expression and Affect Long-Term Development." Working Paper 10, Harvard University Center on the Developing Child.

National Vaccine Advisory Committee. 2014. *Reducing Patient and Provider Barriers to Maternal Immunizations*. Washington, DC: United States Department of Health and Human Service.

Neff, Roni A., and Lynn R. Goldman. 2005. "Regulatory Parallels to *Daubert*: Stakeholder Influence, 'Sound Science,' and the Delayed Adoption of Health-protective Standards." *American Journal of Public Health* 95: S81–S91.

Neuman, W. Russell. 1986. *The Paradox of Mass Politics: Knowledge and Opinion in the American Electorate*. Cambridge, MA: Harvard University Press.

Nyhan, Brendan, and Jason Reifler. 2010. "When Corrections Fail: The Persistence of Political Misperceptions." *Political Behavior* 32: 303–330.

Nyhan, Brendan, and Jason Riefler. 2015. "Does Correcting Myths about the Flu Vaccine Work? An Experimental Evaluation of the Effects of Corrective Information." *Vaccine* 33: 459–464.

O'Keefe, Daniel J. 2002. *Persuasion: Theory and Practice*, 2nd ed. Thousand Oaks, CA: Sage Publications.

Ohman, Arne, Anders Flykt, and Francisco Esteves. 2001. "Emotion Drives Attention: Detecting the Snake in the Grass." *Journal of Experimental Psychology: General* 130: 466–478.

Oreskes, Naomi, and Erik M. Conway. 2008. *Merchants of Doubt: How a Handful of Scientists Obscured the Truth on Issues from Tobacco Smoke to Global Warming*. New York: Bloomsbury Press.

Ostrom, Elinor. 1990. *Governing the Commons: The Evolution of Institutions for Collective Action*. New York: Cambridge University Press.

Oye, Kenneth A. 1985. "Explaining Cooperation under Anarchy." *World Politics* 38: 1–24.

Page, Scott E. 2010. *Complexity and Diversity*. Princeton, NJ: Princeton University Press.

Palfrey, Thomas R. 2007. "Laboratory Experiments." In Barry R. Weingast and Donald Wittman (eds.). *The Oxford Handbook of Political Economy*, 915–936.

Palmer, Carl L., and Rolfe D. Peterson. 2013. "Beauty and the Pollster: The Impact of Halo Effects on Perceptions of Political Knowledge and Sophistication." http://cas.illinoisstate.edu/clpalme/research/documents/Beauty_and_the_Pollster_revision.pdf. Accessed January 7, 2014. Revised version of paper presented at the Annual Meeting of the Midwest Political Science Association.

Patty, John W., and Elizabeth Maggie Penn. 2014. *Social Choice and Legitimacy: The Possibilities of Impossibility*. New York: Cambridge University Press.

Peart, Neil. 1980. "Freewill." *Rush: Permanent Waves*. Mercury CD.

Pellegrino, James W., Naomi Chudowsky, and Robert Glaser (eds.). 2001. *Knowing What Students Know: The Science and Design of Educational Assessment*. Washington, DC: National Academies Press.

Pessoa, Luiz, Sabine Kastner, and Leslie G. Ungerleider. 2002. "Attentional Control of the Processing of Neural and Emotional Stimuli." *Cognitive Brain Research* 15: 31–45.

Petersen, Steven E., and Michael I. Posner. 2012. "The Attention System of the Human Brain: 20 Years After." *Annual Review of Neuroscience* 35: 73–89.

Pew Research Center for the People and the Press in collaboration with the American Association for the Advancement of Science. 2009. *Scientific Achievements Less Prominent Than a Decade Ago: Public Praises Science; Scientists Fault Public, Media*. http://www.people-press.org/files/legacy-pdf/528.pdf. Accessed October 7, 2012.

Pew Research Center for the People and the Press. 2012. *What The Public Knows About the Political Parties*. http://www.people-press.org/files/legacy-pdf/04-11-12%20Knowledge%20Release.pdf. Accessed July 26, 2013.

Pew Research Center for the People and the Press. 2014. *Beyond Red versus Blue: The Political Typology*. http://www.people-press.org/files/2014/06/6-26-14-Political-Typology-release1.pdf. Accessed July 23, 2014.

Pfeffer, W. Tad, Joel T. Harper, and Shad O'Neel. 2008. "Kinematic Constraints on Glacier Distributions to 21st-Century Sea-Level Rise." *Science* 321: 1340–1343.

Pierrehumbert, Raymond T. 2014. "Climate Science Is Settled *Enough:* The *Wall Street Journal*'s Fresh Face of Climate Inaction." http://www.slate.com/articles/health_and_science/science/2014/10/the_wall_street_journal_and_steve_koonin_the_new_face_of_climate_change.html. Accessed May 8, 2016.

Pietryka, Matthew T., and Randall C. MacIntosh. 2013. "An Analysis of ANES Items and Their Use in the Construction of Political Knowledge Scales." *Political Analysis* 21: 407–429.

Pious, Richard. 2004. "What's Wrong with Rational Choice." *Frameworks E-Zine*. http://www.frameworksinstitute.org/ezine28.html. Accessed December 16, 2012.

Poole, Keith T., and Howard Rosenthal. 2000. *Congress: A Political-Economic History of Roll Call Voting*. New York: Oxford University Press.

Popkin, Samuel L. 1991. *The Reasoning Voter: Communication and Persuasion in Presidential Campaigns*. Chicago: University of Chicago Press.

Pornpitakpan, Chanthika. 2004. "The Persuasiveness of Source Credibility: A Critical Review of Five Decades Evidence." *Journal of Applied Social Psychology* 34: 243–281.

Posner, Michael I., and Mary K. Rothbart. 2002. "Attention, Self-Regulation, and Consciousness." In John T. Cacioppo, Gary G. Berntson, Ralph Adolphs, C. Sue Carter, Richard J. Davidson, Martha K. McClintock, Bruce S. McEwen, Michael J. Meaney, Daniel L. Schacter, Esther M. Sternberg, Steve S. Suomi, and Shelley E. Taylor (eds.). *Foundations of Social Neuroscience.* Cambridge MA: MIT Press, 215–234.

Potter, Rachel. 2012. "Conditional Agency Autonomy in Administrative Rulemaking." Manuscript, University of Michigan Interdisciplinary Workshop on American Politics, December 14.

Prior, Markus. 2014. "Visual Political Knowledge: A Different Road to Competence?" *Journal of Politics* 76: 41–57. http://dx.doi.org/10.1017/S0022381613001096.

Prior, Markus, and Arthur Lupia. 2008. "Money, Time, and Political Knowledge: Distinguishing Quick Recall from Political Learning Skills." *American Journal of Political Science* 52: 168–182.

Prior, Markus, Gaurav Sood, and Kabir Khanna. 2013. "You Cannot Be Serious: Do Partisans Believe What they Say?" Manuscript, Princeton University, April 25.

Pronin, Emily, Thomas Gilovich, and Lee Ross. 2004. "Objectivity in the Eye of the Beholder: Divergent Perceptions of Bias in Self versus Others." *Psychological Review* 111: 781–799.

Rahmstorf, Stefan. 2007. "A Semi-Empirical Approach to Projecting Future Sea-Level Rise." *Science* 315: 368–370.

Rapeli, Lauri. 2014. "Comparing Local, National and EU Knowledge: The Ignorant Public Reassessed." *Scandinavian Political Studies* 37: 428–446.

Roeder, Amy. 2015. "Measles Outbreaks Worrying, but 'On-Time' Childhood Vaccination Remains Norm in U.S." Harvard T. H. Chan School of Public Health. http://www.hsph.harvard.edu/news/features/measles-outbreaks-worrying-but-on-time-childhood-vaccination-remains-norm-in-u-s/. Accessed March 12, 2015.

Roper Public Affairs. 2011. "National Geographic-Roper Public Affairs 2006 Geographic Literacy Study." http://www.nationalgeographic.com/roper2006/pdf/FINALReport2006GeogLitsurvey.pdf. Accessed July 23, 2014.

Rosenbaum, Dennis P., and Gordon S. Hanson. 1998. "Assessing the Effects of School-based Drug Education: A Six-year Multilevel Analysis of Project DARE." *Journal of Research in Crime and Delinquency* 35: 381–412.

Ruiz, Erica. 2012. "University Study Determines Fox News Has Least-Informed National Audience Based on These Questions." http://www.theblaze.com/stories/2012/05/23/university-study-determines-fox-news-has-least-informed-national-audience-based-on-these-questions/. Accessed July 11, 2013.

Ryan, Timothy J. 2014. "No Compromise: The Politics of Moral Conviction." Doctoral dissertation, University of Michigan.

Schaeffer, Nora Cate, and Jennifer Dykema. 2011. "Questions for Surveys: Current Trends and Future Directions." *Public Opinion Quarterly* 75: 909–961.

Schattschneider, Elmer E. 1960. *The Semisovereign People: A Realist's View of Democracy in America.* New York: Holt, Rinehart, and Winston.

Schulz, Wolfram, and Heiko Sibberns (eds.) 2004. *IEA Civic Education Study Technical Report.* Amsterdam: International Association for the Evaluation of Educational Achievement.

Schwartz, Shalom H., and Wolfgang Bilsky. 1987. "Toward a Universal Psychological Structure of Human Values." *Journal of Personality and Social Psychology* 53: 550–562.

Schwartz, Shalom H., and Klaus Boehnke. 2004. "Evaluating the Structure of Human Values with Confirmatory Factor Analysis." *Journal of Research in Personality* 38: 230–255.

Sekhon, Jasjeet. 2005. "The Varying Role of Information across Democratic Societies." Manuscript, University of California, Berkeley.

Sen, Amartya. 1998. "The Possibility of Social Choice. Nobel Lecture, December 8, 1998." *American Economic Review* 89: 349–378.

Shaker, Lee. 2012. "Local Political Knowledge and Assessments of Citizen Competence." *Public Opinion Quarterly* 76: 525–537.

Shanks, David R. 2010. "Learning: From Association to Cognition." *Annual Review of Psychology* 61:273–301.

Sharot, Tali. 2011. *The Optimism Bias: A Tour of the Irrationally Positive Brain*. New York: Pantheon.

Shenkman, Rick. 2008a. "The Dumbing Down of Voters." *Boston Globe*, June 15. http://www.boston.com/bostonglobe/editorial_opinion/oped/articles/2008/06/15/the_dumbing_down_of_voters/. Accessed December 12, 2012.

Shenkman, Rick. 2008b. *How Stupid Are We? Facing the Truth about the American Voter*. New York: Basic Books.

Simmons, Joseph P., Leif D. Nelson, and Uri Simonsohn. 2011. "False-positive Psychology: Undisclosed Flexibility in Data Collection and Analysis Allows Presenting Anything as Significant." *Psychological Science* 22: 1359–1366.

Simmons, Joseph P., Leif D. Nelson, and Uri Simonsohn. 2014. "P-Curve and Effect Size: Correcting for Publication Bias Using Only Significant Results." *Perspectives on Psychological Science* 9: 666–681.

Sin, Gisela, and Arthur Lupia. 2013. "How the Senate and the President Affect the Timing of Power-sharing Rule Changes in the U.S. House." *Journal of Law, Economics, and Organization* 29: 1184–1216.

Sinclair, Lisa, and Ziva Kunda. 1999. "Reactions to a Black Professional: Motivated Inhibition and Activation of Conflicting Stereotypes." *Journal of Personality and Social Psychology* 77: 885–904.

Singer, Eleanor, Robert M. Groves, and Amy D. Corning. 1999. "Differential Incentives: Beliefs about Practices, Perceptions of Equity, and Effects of Survey Participation." *Public Opinion Quarterly* 63: 251–260.

Skitka, Linda J. 2010. "The Psychology of Moral Conviction." *Social and Personality Psychology Compass* 4: 267–281.

Sniderman, Paul M., Richard A. Brody, and Philip E. Tetlock. 1991. *Reasoning and Choice: Explorations in Political Psychology*. New York: Cambridge University Press.

Sniderman, Paul M. 2000. "Taking Sides: A Fixed Choice Theory of Political Reasoning." In Arthur Lupia, Mathew D. McCubbins, and Samuel L. Popkin (eds.). *Elements of Reason: Cognition, Choice and the Bounds of Rationality*. New York: Cambridge University Press.

Sniderman, Paul M., and John Bullock. 2004. "A Consistency Theory of Public Opinion and Political Choice: The Hypothesis of Menu Dependence." In Willem E. Saris and Paul M. Sniderman (eds.). *Studies in Public Opinion: Attitudes, Non-Attitudes, Measurement Error, and Change*. Princeton, NJ: Princeton University Press, 133–165.

Sniderman, Paul M., and Sean Theriault. 2004. "The Structure of Political Argument and the Logic of Issue Framing." In Willem E. Saris and Paul M. Sniderman (eds.).

Studies in Public Opinion: Attitudes, Non-Attitudes, Measurement Error, and Change. Princeton, NJ: Princeton University Press, 133–165.

Sniderman, Paul M., and Edward H. Stiglitz. 2012. *The Reputational Premium: A Theory of Party Identification and Policy Reasoning.* Princeton, NJ: Princeton University Press.

Sobel, Joel. 2009. "Signaling Games." In Robert A. Meyers (ed.). *Encyclopedia of Complexity and System Science.* New York: Springer-Verlag, 8125–8139.

Somin, Ilya. 1999. "Voter Ignorance and the Democratic Ideal." *Critical Review* 12: 413–458.

Somin, Ilya. 2004. "When Ignorance Isn't Bliss: How Political Ignorance Threatens Democracy." CATO Institute Policy Analysis No. 525. September 22, 2004. http://www.cato.org/sites/cato.org/files/pubs/pdf/pa525.pdf. Accessed August 21, 2013.

Somin, Ilya. 2013. *Democracy and Political Ignorance: Why Smaller Government is Smarter.* Stanford, CA: Stanford University Press.

Spence, Alexa, and Nick Pidgeon. 2010. "Framing and Communicating Climate Change: The Effects of Distance and Outcome Frame Impressions." *Global Environmental Change* 20: 656–667.

Squire, Larry R., and John T. Wixted. 2015. "Remembering." *Daedalus: Journal of the American Academy of Arts and Sciences* 144: 53–66.

Steele, Claude M., and Joshua Aronson. 1996. "Stereotype Threat and the Intellectual Test Performance of African Americans." *Journal of Personality and Social Psychology* 69: 797–811.

Stein, Arthur A. 1982. "Coordination and Collaboration: Regimes in an Anarchic World." *International Organization* 36: 299–324.

Stern, Chadly, Tessa V. West, and Peter G. Schmitt. 2014. "The Liberal Illusion of Uniqueness." *Psychological Science* 25: 137–144.

Stone, Jeff, and Chad McWhinnie. 2008. "Evidence that Blatant Versus Subtle Stereotype Threat Cues Impact Performance Through Dual Processes." *Journal of Experimental Social Psychology* 44: 445–452

Strom, Kaare. 2000. "Delegation and Accountability in Parliamentary Democracies." *European Journal of Political Research* 37: 261–289.

Strom, Kaare, Wolfgang C. Müller, and Daniel Markham Smith. 2010. "Parliamentary Control of Coalition Governments." *Annual Review of Political Science* 13: 517–535.

Sudman, Seymour, Norman M. Bradburn, and Norbert Schwarz. 1996. *Thinking about Answers: The Application of Cognitive Processes to Survey Methodology.* San Francisco: Jossey-Bass.

Taber, Charles S., and Milton Lodge. 2006. "Motivated Skepticism in the Evaluation of Political Beliefs." *American Journal of Political Science* 50: 755–769.

Tauberer, Josh. 2011. "Kill Bill: How Many Bills Are There? How Many Are Enacted?" http://www.govtrack.us/blog/2011/08/04/kill-bill-how-many-bills-are-th ere-how-many-are-enacted/on. Accessed December 18, 2012.

Tebaldi, Claudia, Benjamin H. Strauss, and Chris E. Zervas. 2012. "Modeling Sea Level Rise Impacts on Storm Surges Along U.S. Coasts." *Environmental Research Letters* 7: 014032 doi:10.1088/1748-9326/7/1/014032.

Terhune, Kate. 2013. "Retired Justice Sandra Day O'Connor, in Boise, Laments 'Alarming Degree of Public Ignorance.'" *Idaho Statesman*, September 5. http://www.isc.idaho.gov/links/Newsclippings-09-06-13.pdf. Accessed July 11, 2014.

Tilly, Charles. 2006. *Why? What Happens When People Give Reasons ... and Why.* Princeton, NJ: Princeton University Press.

Torney-Purta, Judith, Rainer Lehmann, Hans Oswald, and Wolfram Schulz. 2001. *Citizenship and Education in Twenty-Eight Countries: Civic Knowledge and Engagement at Age Fourteen.* Amsterdam: International Association for the Evaluation of Educational Achievement.

Tourangeau, Roger, Lance J. Rips, and Kenneth Rasinski. 2000. *The Psychology of Survey Response.* New York: Cambridge University Press.

Tversky, Amos, and Daniel Kahneman. 1981. "The Framing of Decisions and the Psychology of Choice." *Science* 211: 453–458.

Tversky, Amos, and Daniel Kahneman. 1986. "Rational Choice and the Framing of Decisions." *Journal of Business* 59: S251–S278.

Tyrangiel, Joel. 2012. "A Congressional Exit Interview." *Bloomberg Businessweek,* June 21. http://www.businessweek.com/articles/2012-06-21/a-congressional-exit-interview#p1. Accessed June 22, 2012.

van Boven, Leaf, Justin Kruger, Kenneth Savitsky, and Thomas Gilovich. 2000. "When Social Worlds Collide: Overconfidence in the Multiple Audience Problem." *Personality and Social Psychology Bulletin* 26: 619–628.

Ward, Bob. 2011. "Scientists Frustrated in Climate Change Debate." *Financial Times.* http://www.ft.com/intl/cms/s/0/82eac5ca-1a96-11e1-ae14-00144feabdco.html#ax828ZaBH7Dh. Accessed October 6, 2012.

Warner, Bethany. 2001. "Study of Young Teens Finds Civics Ranks Low; 28-nation Study Bodes Ill for Citizenship." *Washington Times,* March 16, A9.

Wedeen, Lisa. 2010. "Reflections on Ethnographic Work in Political Science." *Annual Review of Political Science* 13: 255–272.

Westen, Drew, Pavel S. Blagov, Keith Harenski, Clint Kilts, and Stephan Hamann. 2006. "Neural Bases of Motivated Reasoning: An fMRI Study of Emotional Constraints on Partisan Political Judgment in the 2004 U.S. Presidential Election." *Journal of Cognitive Neuroscience* 18: 1947–1958.

Whitaker, Eric A., and John M. Fulwider. 2012. "Perceptions of Similarity and Agreement in Partisan Groups." In John H. Aldrich and Kathleen McGraw (eds.). *Improving Public Opinion Surveys: Interdisciplinary Innovation and the American National Election Studies.* Princeton, NJ: Princeton University Press, 195–219.

White, Halbert. 1996. *Estimation, Inference, and Specification Analysis.* New York: Cambridge University Press.

Wittgenstein, Ludwig. 1953. *Philosophical Investigations.* New York: MacMillan Co.

World Health Organization and UNICEF. "United States of America: WHO and UNICEF Estimates of Immunization Coverage: 2013 Revision." http://www.who.int/immunization/monitoring_surveillance/data/usa.pdf. Accessed March 12, 2015.

Wurtz, Robert H. 2015. "Brain Mechanisms for Active Vision." *Daedalus: Journal of the American Academy of Arts and Sciences* 144: 10–21.

Wyer, Robert S., Hao Shen, and Alison Jing Xu. 2013. "The Role of Procedural Knowledge in the Generalization of Social Behavior." In Donal E. Carlston (ed.). *Oxford Handbook of Social Cognition.* New York: Oxford University Press, 257–281.

Wynne, Brian E. 2006. "Public Engagement as a Means of Restoring Public Trust in Science—Hitting the Notes, but Missing the Music." *Public Health Genomics* 9: 211–220.

Zaller, John. 1986a. "Analysis of Information Items in the 1985 NES Pilot Study." American National Election Studies Pilot Study Report, No. nes002261. http://www.

electionstudies.org/resources/papers/documents/nes002261.pdf. Accessed August 21, 2013.

Zaller, John. 1986b. "Pre-Testing Information Items in the 1986 NES Pilot Study." Memo to the American National Election Studies Board of Overseers.

Zaller, John. 1992. *The Nature and Origins of Mass Opinion*. New York: Cambridge University Press.

Zaller, John, and Stanley Feldman. 1992. "A Simple Theory of the Survey Response: Answering Questions Versus Revealing Preferences." *American Journal of Political Science* 36: 579–616

Zernike, Kate. 2001. "DARE Program Revamping its Curriculum." *New York Times* News Service, February 15. http://articles.chicagotribune.com/2001-02-15/news/0102150201_1_drug-abuse-resistance-education-dare-president-and-founding-director on. Accessed December 18, 2012.

Index